A Sense of Place

A Sense of Place

Montgomery's Architectural Heritage

JEFFREY C. BENTON

Photography by Jim Goodwyn

Foreword by Robert C. Gamble

RIVER CITY PUBLISHING
Montgomery, Alabama

River City Publishing
P.O. Box 551
Montgomery, AL 36101

A Sense of Place: Montgomery's Architectural Heritage

© 2001 by Jeffrey C. Benton
Photographs © 2001 by Jim Goodwyn
All Rights Reserved under International and Pan-American Copyright
conventions. Published in the United States by River City Publishing, LLC,
P.O. Box 551, Montgomery, Alabama, 36101.

Manufactured by Vaughan Printing in the United States of America.
This book was written, edited, photographed, and designed
in Montgomery, Alabama.

Library of Congress Cataloging-in-Publication Data:

Benton, Jeffrey C., 1945–
A sense of place : Montgomery's architectural heritage / by Jeffrey C.
Benton ; photography by Jim Goodwyn ; foreword by Robert C. Gamble.
p. cm.
Includes index.
ISBN 1-881320-55-3
1. Architecture--Alabama--Montgomery. 2. Historic
buildings--Alabama--Montgomery. 3. Montgomery (Alabama)--Buildings,
structures, etc. 4. Montgomery (Alabama)--History. I. Title.
NA735.M668 B46 2000
720'.9761'47--dc21
00-010379

This book is
dedicated to
those who
cherish
their heritage—
to all those who,
by their
stewardship of
our architectural
legacy, give
testimony that
ours is not a
throw-away
society.

Contents

Preface
9

Acknowledgments
11

Listing of Structures
14

Introduction
16

The Structures
21

Index
267

Preface

I vividly recall my first real impression of Montgomery's architecture. It was more than thirty years ago—early spring—and I had joined several hundred other Alabama teenagers for the annual youth legislature held at the State Capitol. One afternoon a friend and I decided to explore the city. Starting from downtown, we drove slowly out Court Street and over to Perry, and then meandered along wisteria-hung side streets until we finally ended up in Old Cloverdale. I was enchanted. "What a beautiful place!" I thought.

In those days, two interstate highways had not yet gouged their way through town, and Montgomery still preserved a wonderful visual coherence that is now all but impossible to imagine. The business district along Dexter Avenue merged gently into venerable if already slightly down-at-the-heels residential neighborhoods. And the main thoroughfares running south from downtown—Court, Perry, Hull—presented a nearly unbroken procession of dignified old houses beneath great spreading trees.

Now, more than three decades later, Montgomery is a much different city, both physically and socially. It is less parochial, less the drowsy, if charming, Deep Southern city it once was. It is also physically more fragmented. In fact, Montgomery, at the beginning of the millennium, seems to be in the process of architecturally reinventing itself—although whether by accident or design is often hard to tell.

East of town, where just a few years ago there was only rolling farmland, a "new" city is growing up, with a cultural park, shopping malls, and posh subdivisions that could be anywhere in America. Unfortunately, ugly strip development also claims its share of this pell-mell surge. In the "old" city, gleaming new office buildings break the traditional downtown skyline, although their positioning displays little regard for preexisting scale and streetscape, nor any particular long-range civic vision. On the perimeter of the old downtown, early residential neighborhoods have either disappeared entirely or find themselves in flux: some show signs of modest revitalization; others waver between stagnation and decline.

Thanks to the untiring efforts of the Landmarks Foundation, several notable individual specimens of Montgomery's early architecture have been rescued from destruction by moving them to Old Alabama Town, the city's official enclave of historic buildings. Still, unlike many other American cities that have elected to rehabilitate historic business and residential neighborhoods as an adjunct to new development, official Montgomery appears to have adopted a largely laissez-faire attitude toward most of its older landmark neighborhoods. The result is that much of the beguiling nineteenth- and early-twentieth-century architecture that once gave a distinct flavor to Montgomery has disappeared—including one of the South's finest assemblages of Greek Revival and Italianate-style domestic architecture.

Yet despite all this, and as the following pages confirm, many very good buildings remain—certainly enough to signpost the architectural evolution of the city since its founding 180 years ago as a raw, ambitious outpost on the plantation frontier. Painstakingly, Jeff Benton has ferreted these places out and pieced together their sometimes contradictory and confusing stories. History and architectural description are interwoven to establish each structure within the context of Montgomery's past.

To be sure, a city only nine generations old is quite young by most standards. But a community's "sense of place," its own special personality, derives not so much from sheer longevity as from the simple process of cumulative experience. The buildings and neighborhoods it produces through successive cycles of prosperity and decline, growth and stagnation, become tangible embodiments of that character. Collectively, the buildings discussed here define Montgomery as a unique place with its own special history expressed in a pleasing and instructive variety of architecture.

When Gottfried Boehm accepted the Pritzker Prize for architectural design in 1986, he observed that "the future of architecture does not lie so much in continuing to fill up the landscape as in bringing back life and order to our cities and towns." If Boehm is right, then the restoration of order in today's all too chaotic architectural landscape must begin in each community with architectural self-awareness: an appreciation of those older buildings and building groups that define and symbolize the city's experience through time. It is no coincidence that cities with the keenest sense of their architectural past—Charleston and Boston for instance—have also produced some of the most sensitive and forward-looking schemes for the urban habitat of tomorrow, through the graceful interplay of old and new.

Jeff Benton's celebration of Montgomery's architectural heritage affirms that Alabama's capital city has the same potential. It is a challenge to Montgomery's citizens and officials to fulfill the promise of a city that can imaginatively safeguard its past while looking to the future.

Robert C. Gamble
Senior Architectural Historian
Alabama Historical Commission

▼

Acknowledgments

Preparation of this book has been a community project. It could not have been done any other way—at least by me. William Brown and Elizabeth Via Brown of the *Montgomery Advertiser* were willing to risk an untried author. From January 1994 through July 1995, in celebration of the city's 175th anniversary, they published the weekly articles that form the basis of this book.

The articles elicited letters and many telephone calls. To me these have been testimonials to the love that Montgomerians and former Montgomerians have for their city and its heritage. They also corrected my errors and provided research leads. Few authors have the luxury of having a running critique before their books are published. Staff members at city churches, Oakwood Cemetery, the Alabama Department of Archives and History, the main branch of the Montgomery Library, the Franklin S. Moseley Depository at Huntingdon College, the special collection of the library of Auburn University at Montgomery, and the Office of the Historian of Air University have provided invaluable support. So too have John and Cameron Napier. Of critical importance were the records of National Registry nominations to which Carolyn Henson of the Alabama Historical Commission gave me free access. Eva Mae and Reuben Scott also freely gave of their collection of Montgomery memorabilia.

Many have also provided professional advice: James Loeb, chairman emeritus of Landmarks Foundation; Carole King, curator of Landmarks Foundation; Edward Patillo, former museum curator at the Alabama Supreme Court; and Richard Bailey, author of *Neither Carpetbaggers Nor Scalawags: Black Officeholders During the Reconstruction of Alabama, 1867–1878* and *They Too Call Alabama Home: African American Profiles, 1800–1999*. Vinson McKenzie allowed me to read his manuscript of *Pioneering African American Architects*. Mary Ann Neeley, executive director of Landmarks Foundation, and Robert Gamble, senior architectural historian at the Alabama Historical Commission, were absolutely indispensable. Both repeatedly and graciously gave information, advice, and guidance. Their knowledge is prodigious, and their love of our heritage is contagious.

The book would also have been impossible without the approval and cooperation of the owners of the buildings included. They responded to a knock on the door or a telephone call by setting aside their work, rearranging their schedules, and sharing their knowledge of and affection for their homes and places of work. Southern hospitality is still alive.

The publishing company even convinced Jim Goodwyn to do the photography work for the book. Its quality speaks for itself.

Finally I would like to acknowledge my wife and two daughters for their understanding. Karen encouraged and advised me from the inception of the idea for the articles and the book. Perhaps now that the project is complete we will be able to enjoy the city's architectural heritage together.

—Jeff Benton

The Structures

Edgewood	21
First White House of the Confederacy	24
Winter Building	27
Figh-Pickett House	30
Falconer House	34
Chappell House and Confederate Powder Magazine	36
First Presbyterian Church	40
Lomax House	43
Knox Hall	46
Teague House	49
Alabama State Capitol	52
Murphy House	56
House of the Mayors	60
Jackson House	63
McBryde-Screws-Tyson House	66
Governor Shorter House	69
St. Peter's Roman Catholic Church	72
St. John's Episcopal Church	75
Smith-Joseph-Stratton House	79
Gerald-Dowdell House	82
Central Bank of Alabama Building	85
Brittan House	88
Winter Place	91
Montgomery Theatre Building	95
Kahl Montgomery Synagogue (Catoma Street Church of Christ)	98
Dowe House	101
"The Four Sisters"	104
St. John's African Methodist Episcopal Church	107
Dexter Avenue King Memorial Baptist Church	109
City Water Works	112
Church of the Holy Comforter	115
Pepperman-Ludlow House	118
Mills House	120
Tyson-Maner House	123
Scott Street Firehouse	127
Sayre Street School	130
Steiner-Lobman and Teague Buildings	132

Governor Jones House 135
Dexter Avenue United Methodist Church 138
Stay House 141
Cassimus House 145
Kennedy-Sims House 148
Union Station 151
Great Western Railway of Alabama Freight Depot
    (Riverfront Center) 156
Gay House 159
Davenport-Harrison Shotgun 162
Carnegie Building 166
Highland Avenue School 169
Sabel-Cantey House 171
Moses-Haardt House 174
First Baptist Church 177
Tulane Building and Tulane-Simmons House 180
Governor's Mansion 183
Bell Building 186
Belser House 189
John Jefferson Flowers Memorial Hall 193
Day Street Baptist Church 196
Church of the Ascension 198
St. Andrew the Apostle Roman Catholic Church 202
First Baptist Church, Colored 205
Dexter Avenue King Memorial Baptist Church Parsonage 208
Lewis House 211
Old Ship African Methodist Episcopal Zion Church 214
Whitfield House 217
Agudath Israel Synagogue (The Ephod Church) 220
Sidney Lanier High School 223
Kress Building 226
Davis Theatre for the Performing Arts 230
Tower House 233
Austin Hall 236
Quisenberry-Bryan House 239
Frank M. Johnson Jr. Federal Building 242
First United Methodist Church 245
Senior Officers' Quarters 249
Fort Dixie (Armory Learning Arts Center) 252
St. Jude's Roman Catholic Church 255
Archives and History Building 258
Grove Court Apartments 261
Garrett Coliseum 265

Montgomery's Architectural Heritage   15

Introduction

In late 1993, I began to look at Montgomery's architectural heritage in a systematic way. My belief was that by examining what Montgomery had built, and how the city has maintained its built environment, I might come to better understand the city.

I learned that antebellum Montgomery, although the home of William Lowndes Yancey (a *fire-eater*, as several of the leading secessionists were called) was not overwhelmed by sentiments for immediate secession. In fact, Jefferson Davis questioned selection of the city for the capital of the Confederacy because of its strong Unionist sympathies. There were few distinctions between those who made their fortunes as planters and those who were in commerce; many of the most prominent citizens were engaged in various business enterprises and in planting. Furthermore, the city was rather tolerant. There do not seem to have been significant barriers between Protestant and Roman Catholic, Jew and gentile. Society was fluid; wealth seems to have been the great discriminator. Distinctions between blacks and whites were important, of course, but so too were distinctions within the black community itself. Not until late in the nineteenth century or perhaps early in the twentieth century were socioeconomic walls erected.

Montgomery was founded and came to maturity during the period of greatest relative change that the nation has ever experienced. Between 1820 and 1860, the total American population tripled, while Alabama's increased ninefold. The number of states increased from twenty-three to thirty-three, almost doubling the country's land area. Population per square mile doubled. The percentage of urban population almost tripled. Immigration increased twentyfold. The federal budget more than tripled. The United States became the world's second industrial power. This unprecedented physical change was accompanied by a corresponding change in values.

The old American ideals of household, community, commonwealth, and stewardship were replaced by the nuclear family, individualism, self-sufficiency, and exploitation of resources. That this value shift occurred is an historic fact; why it occurred is a subject of scholarly debate. Some maintain that the inclination for the new values had always been present in the American character; others attribute it to the psychological upheavals associated with westward expansion; even others attribute westward expansion itself to the values placed on individual acquisition of wealth.

In any case, early Montgomery's values conformed not to the old values, but to the new. While on the surface, Montgomery and its Black Belt hinterland seemed to be an extension of the coastal South, at another level it was akin to the frontier West (what is today called the Old Southwest and Old Northwest). Montgomery was then a frontier town, with the values of the frontier. The steamboat and railroad made mobility possible; the American population of the first half of the nineteenth century was a people on the move. A mobile, transient society is by its nature individualistic; there is little impetus to invest in community. There was, therefore, little genuine interest in public institutions or education, much less the arts and sciences, or even religion. Although the term is relative new, the Bible Belt was not in the Old South, but in the Northeast. In fact, sincere religious belief was viewed as somewhat subversive of Southern institutions. Consequently, the Southern version of Christianity tended not to move much beyond the individual and his personal relationship with God. Because this version of Christianity did not concern itself with what a personal relationship with God meant about relationships with others, Southern Christianity was not particularly interested in establishing a community of love based on Christ's example of inclusive love.

These comments may seem quite remote from an examination of Montgomery's architectural legacy. But, of all the arts, architecture exerts the greatest impact on us; we can never escape our built environment. Perhaps, and only perhaps, television has changed this fact. So what Montgomerians built, and are building, and what Montgomerians have done, and are doing, can tell us something of Montgomerians' values.

Commerce has formed cities as they are known today—although government and the military, as well as religious, charitable, and educational institutions have helped shape the development of individual cities. Montgomery has been dominated by commerce; even the large military presence here does not seem to have had any real impact on the character and values of the city. How has this commercial value system been played out?

The nature of Montgomery's commerce and its antebellum economy are important. Montgomery was founded by land speculators and populated by those who came here to get rich, and get rich quick. In fact, a visiting German aristocrat noted that there would be no other reason to come to Montgomery other than to get rich. Although a significant portion of Montgomery's antebellum population was very rich, even the rich were not particularly genteel and refined. Of course, there were exceptions, but the city as a whole was not dedicated to education, religion, the arts or sciences, or even politics in the sense of fashioning a more perfect society.

Almost from the very beginning, Montgomerians built expensive houses and public buildings in the latest fashion; Montgomerians even used leading national architects to design their more important buildings. There is not, however, any evidence of interest in architectural style or philosophy, such as held by Thomas Jefferson and some of the other founding fathers. Considering what Montgomerians have done with their built environment, there is also little evidence that there was a real appreciation for aesthetics either. Both the written evidence and the evidence of deeds indicate that the interest was in fashion and in the socioeconomic statements that buildings might make. Only this can explain why, from very early on, Montgomerians have built fine buildings, only to demolish them and rebuild in the latest fashion.

The loss has been tremendous. In the mid-nineteenth century, one visitor called Montgomery the most handsome inland Southern city. The loss was not due to the Civil War or to adverse consequences of Reconstruction. Quite the contrary, there was little physical damage to the city during the war. Even its economy was not damaged for long. Rather, Montgomery's treatment of its environment is closely connected with alternating periods of boom and bust. Although known for demolition and rebuilding, the city still had a sizeable legacy of nineteenth-century buildings, including major antebellum ones, as late as the 1950s.

Perhaps more important than the loss of individual buildings has been the loss of streetscape. With only a few exceptions, the city's legacy has been reduced to individual buildings. By the destruction of the integrity of Montgomery's streetscapes, we have been reduced to appreciating buildings of architectural significance isolated from their surroundings. Although our loss has been tremendous, a great deal of importance remains. We cannot recover what has been lost, but we can preserve what we have inherited. The nature of the built environment is that we can alter it—for better or worse. We can enhance our inheritance, or we can squander it.

In my examination of Montgomery's architectural legacy, I have discovered that a great many people—and not just those who own, live, and work in the city's older buildings—deeply appreciate their architectural legacy. I have asked many of them why we have treated our legacy as we have. Two responses recur. Construction of two interstate highways through the city caused great physical and psychological damage to the city. And the city looks neither to the past nor the future; it is present-oriented. There has been no vision of what a city can and ought to be. This value system is not unique to Montgomery; in the early nineteenth century, it became the dominant value system of the United States. However, many cities are now trying to emphasize human as well as commercial values. And many cities have realized, and even capitalized on, the connection between historic preservation and a thriving economy.

Montgomery's architectural legacy is much greater than I realized at the beginning of my study. I could not see the city's treasures because I was distracted by vacant lots, parking lots, ugly or mediocre in-fill, and gross differences in scale. Poor siting and landscaping, and the lack of signage and utility-line restrictions, made it even more difficult to appreciate what has survived.

Although the order of the buildings in this book is roughly chronological, the length of my comments on individual buildings is not indicative of their relative importance. And there are, as I have discovered, many more buildings worthy of recognition than I have been able to include. The buildings of Old Alabama Town are of great significance. To keep this book to a manageable length, but more importantly because Old Alabama Town has professional interpretation, I have omitted those buildings. The one exception is the Brittan House, which was acquired by Old Alabama Town after I had completed the entry on it.

Montgomerians will, I hope, seek out and maintain our legacy. It is of value, not because it is old, but because it is relevant to our understanding of who we are and who we can become; it is relevant because its preservation is necessary if we are to establish a community based on continuity and permanence.

—Jeff Benton

LOCAL TRADITION maintains that Edgewood may have been built for Zachariah T. Watkins in 1821, only a few years after the first white settlers entered what is now Montgomery County. Montgomery was incorporated as a town on December 3, 1819, from two even smaller towns—Andrew Dexter's New Philadelphia and General John Scott's East Alabama. In February 1821, Montgomery was a frontier town of a few hundred inhabitants. There were forty-nine frame buildings and thirty-eight log buildings. Although the town had no school or church buildings, there were ten stores and three taverns.

Edgewood, however, was not built in the new town of Montgomery, but on a plantation several miles to the southeast. The nucleus of the house is believed to have been moved to a 346-acre plantation at its current location as early as 1831. Subsequently, the house underwent major changes.

In 1855, the plantation was acquired by Peachy Ridgeway Gilmer. His brother George had been governor of Georgia, and his sister, Sophie Bibb, became a leader in memorializing the Confederate cause. Peachy Gilmer and his second wife, Caroline Thomas, widow of Colonel Jett Thomas, had two daughters and two sons. Gilmer died in the winter of 1861, leaving his widow to manage the plantation during the Civil War. She managed, even enduring a visit by Wilson's Raiders in April 1865. The house was ransacked and, as family tradition has it, a Union officer rode his horse into

▼

Edgewood

3175 Thomas Avenue

Montgomery's Architectural Heritage

the entrance hall, where he slashed the portrait of Peachy Gilmer.

After the war, Caroline Thomas Gilmer married John Gregory Thomas. She was both his great-aunt and step-grandmother. The plantation prospered under their stewardship. The Gilmer/Thomas family, which lived in Edgewood for 132 years, subdivided the plantation in 1916. (In 1907, fifty-eight acres became the campus of what is now Huntingdon College.) It was almost a century after being moved to its current location that Edgewood was incorporated into Montgomery proper.

This frontier plantation house is probably Montgomery's most important house surviving from the Federal period. It is not pure Federal, however, having been built at the time that the Federal style was giving way to the Greek Revival style. Moreover, Edgewood was also built in a vernacular, or folk, tradition that developed during the preceding century on the Atlantic Seaboard and eventually spread to most of the eastern part of the United States. In the South, this tradition is defined by chimneys external to the gables and walls, by being raised on piers, and by windows placed symmetrically around a central door on a long side of the house. This symmetrical plan produced an order, balance, and harmony that came to be viewed as aesthetically pleasing, and which possibly still dominates popular taste in the United States. Even young children today are likely to draw such a structure when asked to draw a house.

Although built as a plantation house on the frontier, Edgewood's Federal and Greek Revival stylistic elements go well beyond the vernacular tradition. The sophisticated stylistic elements include the simple, attached two-tiered portico topped by a pediment. The tapered, squared columns are larger on the first level than on the second. Structural evidence uncovered by the major restoration done by Jim and Jane Barganier in the late 1980s indicates that the portico, as well as the heart-pine modillion blocks under the eaves, are original, not added to the house at a later date. The portico's square columns and balusters are also original; the handrails are replacements. The window lights above and to either side of the main door are associated with both the Federal and Greek Revival styles, as is the double-beaded flush siding on the portico. Flush siding was also used on an L-shaped rear porch that no longer exists.

Edgewood's appearance after its restoration approximates the house's mid-nineteenth century appearance. The kitchen house to the south of the main house is a replica of the original kitchen that, at some time, was moved to the rear of the house. However, Edgewood's original kitchen survives. It has been moved to the rear of the property and adapted for alternative use. The replica now rests on the exact location of the original kitchen. Although a brick underpinning has been substituted for the original cypress blocks on which the house sat, the elevation approximates the origi-

Doorway with transom, sidelights, and double four-panel doors.

nal. Old cedar shakes, found in the attic, were replicated for the fashionable low-pitched hipped roof. For safety considerations, the chimneys were taken down and then rebuilt using the same brick. The shutters, which are reproductions but which use the original hardware, have fixed top louvers and movable bottom ones. Many of the windows are original. In the customary Federal style, large double-hung windows have thin muntins, or glazing bars, and nine lights in each sash, rather than the Greek Revival practice of six lights in each sash. The entire house, interior and exterior, was originally painted white. The heart-pine floors are bleached, as they probably were originally. The main staircase, which is divided into three flights, and the floorboards throughout the house, with the exception of the entrance hall, are original.

The west and south sides look as they did when Edgewood was first built. The north and east sides have been significantly altered. The house was originally L-shaped, with three rooms over three rooms, and a central stair hall. Most of the rooms are twenty feet square. The first alteration was the one-story addition of a room that was joined to the house's northwest room, making a double parlor. The construction techniques, milled lumber, and nails indicate that this addition may have been made in the 1850s. At that time, mantels and woodwork of the main rooms were modernized. Over time, this U-shaped house was added to, until it acquired today's two-story, approximately square shape.

Documentation has not established an architect or builder for the house. It could have been modeled on a builder's guide such as Asher Benjamin's 1806 *American Builder's Companion*. Details, including the updated mantels, were probably copied from Benjamin's 1830 *Practical House Carpenter*. Edgewood is the home of Herbert and Esther Scheuer.

First White House of the Confederacy

644 Washington Avenue

EVENTS WERE happening quickly in Montgomery in February 1861. On the 4th, the nation known as the Confederate States of America was organized by seven secessionist states. On the 8th, a provisional constitutional congress met in Alabama's Capitol to elect a president, and, on the 9th, Jefferson Davis was elected. On the 18th, he was inaugurated as provisional president, just two days after arriving in Montgomery from Brierfield Plantation, his home near Vicksburg. A year later, in Richmond, he was inaugurated as permanent president, after having been elected in November for a six-year term.

On February 21, the provisional congress authorized leasing a furnished and staffed mansion. Apparently unable to find a mansion, what Mrs. Davis was to call a "gentleman's residence" was leased from Colonel Edmond Harrison for the exorbitant sum of five thousand dollars a year. The house had just been refurbished.

Mrs. Davis arrived by riverboat on March 4. She went straight to the executive mansion at the corner of Bibb and Lee streets. The Davises stayed at the nearby Exchange Hotel on the corner of Montgomery and Commerce streets until the executive mansion was ready for occupancy.

Varina Anne Howell (Davis) of Natchez, granddaughter of a governor of New Jersey and cousin of Aaron Burr, knew that Montgomery, a town of eight thousand and the state capital only since 1847, would not be like the Washington she had known as wife of Jefferson Davis. He had served as a U.S. congressman, President Pierce's secretary of war, and a U.S. senator. She knew to go to New Orleans to hire a French cook and order an executive carriage before coming to Montgomery. She then returned to Brierfield to get their three children and supplemental furnishings for the executive mansion.

Hardships aside, she presided over elegant teas, receptions, dinners, and salons. Mary Boykin Chestnut, who seems to have been everywhere from Washington to Charleston to Montgomery to Richmond, was suitably impressed with the performance of the thirty-five-year-old Mrs. Davis.

Mrs. Davis maintained the mansion until the end of May, when the Confederate government moved to Richmond. The house on the corner of Bibb and Lee streets that served as the executive mansion for that period of less than three months was basically the same as the house today. Several dependencies, including stables and a kitchen connected to the main house by a lattice passage, no longer exist. The lot was larger, but the same iron fence is used at the house today. Considerable effort has been made to return the house to its 1861 appearance and to furnish it with Davis pieces or with appropriate period pieces.

The house is believed to have been built between 1832 and 1835 for William Sayre, one of the city's earliest merchants and one of the founders of the First Presbyterian Church. After Sayre left Montgomery for Mobile, the house was owned by a succession of prominent Montgomerians: George Whitman, William Knox, George Mathews, Fleming Freeman, and Joseph Winter. Colonel Winter, who remodeled the house in 1855, sold it to Colonel Edmond Harrison just before the war.

The original house was a simple, symmetrical structure five bays wide. Identical rooms were placed opposite one another across a central stair hall. This is the prototypical American house that developed on the Atlantic Seaboard from English antecedents. In the early nineteenth century, Georgian decorative details gave way to Federal ones. These, in turn, gave way to Greek Revival and Italianate details. Victorian gingerbread and sawwork followed. Today this type of house is commonly called "Colonial."

As William Sayre's house was a fine one, it was two rooms deep; therefore there were four rooms on each floor rather than two, which a less imposing house would have had. The architectural details were in the Federal style.

Two external brick chimneys were on each side, serving the four rooms on either side of the house. The Federal-style double-hung windows had nine lights in each sash. The door has side lights and a transom, also in the Federal style. Exterior louvered shutters protected the house from the sun. Following the Southern building tradition, the house was raised off the ground on brick piers. The openings between the piers, now bricked in, were once covered with lattice.

The interior is almost as simple as the original exterior. The four rooms

Federal-style double-hung window with nine lights in each sash.

Pendant brackets and ventilator covers.

of the first floor and the stair hall, including the staircase itself, have raised-panel wainscoting. The second-floor rooms have a simple chair rail rather than wainscoting. Door and window framing is very simple. The six-panel doors are in the so-called cross and Bible pattern. The Federal mantels are identical throughout the original part of the house. The walls and ceilings are smooth plastered; there is no cornice.

During the 1850s, Italianate decorative elements were added to many houses in Montgomery, including this one. The original stoop was replaced by a porch three bays wide. Its fluted columnettes are connected by a balustrade. The porch roof is decorated with cast-iron acanthus leaves, acorns, and oak leaves. Under the porch's raised-seam metal roof, the wall is wood, cut to simulate stone blocks. The Federal front door has been replaced by an Italianate one.

A heavy cornice with pendant brackets was also added. Underneath the cornice are unusual cast-iron ventilator covers. Each one is ornamented with a Phrygian, or liberty, cap encircled by a laurel wreath. During the American and French revolutions, the Phrygian cap was used as a symbol of liberty. Believing themselves to be the true heirs of the American Revolution, the Confederates also used this symbol.

During modernization in 1855, a dining room, study, rear hall, several service rooms, and porches (now enclosed) were added to the rear of the original house. Extremely simple Greek Revival woodwork is used in the rooms of this one-story addition. The doors, for example, are four-panel. The double-hung windows, however, use nine-over-nine lights in the Federal style, rather than the customary six-over-six lights of Greek Revival windows. During this remodeling, sliding double doors were constructed between the parlors, making a double parlor. The woodwork of these doors is Greek Revival.

After the war, the house was owned by Willis Calloway and by William Crawford Bibb, before becoming the townhouse of Archibald Tyson of Lowndesboro. On his death in 1873, it was rented out, eventually becoming a boarding house.

In 1900, a ladies' organization was formed to save the house. A lot was bought from the Kohn family and, after great difficulty, the house was moved to its present location, adjacent to the Archives and History Building. On June 3, 1921, the restored house was dedicated in a great ceremony on the 113th anniversary of Jefferson Davis's birth.

The First White House of the Confederacy is owned by the State of Alabama. The White House Association of Alabama, the fourth-oldest historic preservation organization in the country dedicated solely to the preservation of a house museum, owns the furnishings and manages the house. Both the state and the association are dedicated to maintaining the house as it was in the spring of 1861. The house is open to the public.

O N APRIL 10 AND 11, 1861, General Leroy Pope Walker, secretary of War for the Confederate States of America, telegraphed General P. T. G. Beauregard, Confederate commander in Charleston, directing him to try to convince Major Robert Anderson, the Union commander, to evacuate Fort Sumter. If negotiations failed to achieve the Confederate objective without bloodshed, General Beauregard was given the authority to attack the Union fort. Major Anderson attempted to hold out until April 15, at which time he would evacuate the fort unless he had further instructions from Washington. These terms were unacceptable. Several hours later, Confederate batteries fired on Fort Sumter.

The telegram that resulted in the firing on Fort Sumter was sent from the Southern Telegraph Company on the second floor of what is today the Winter Building. (The broken, white-marble monolithic column that commemorated this event now stands in the entrance court of the main city-county library on High Street.)

On February 18, 1861, the building was a silent witness to Jefferson Davis as he left the Exchange Hotel to go to the Capitol to be sworn in as the provisional president of the Confederacy. Thirty-two years later, it witnessed Davis's funeral procession.

On March 12, 1965, the building witnessed thousands of voting rights demonstrators, who, having marched from Selma, passed the Jefferson Davis Hotel and paraded through Court Square on their way to the Capitol.

Winter Building

2 Dexter Avenue

Indeed, the Winter Building has always been a silent observer of most of Montgomery's momentous events, because it is located at the very heart of the city. It was here that the street grids of Andrew Dexter's New Philadephia and General John Scott's East Alabama met to form the new town of Montgomery. It was here at Court Square that the first courthouse was built.

About 1841, John Gindrat—a native of Charleston and a merchant, cotton broker, and banker—erected a building to house the Montgomery branch of the Bank of St. Mary's (Georgia). Mary Elizabeth Gindrat Winter inherited the building on her father's death in 1854. Her husband, Joseph Samuel Prince Winter, was a bank official and the owner of an iron works.

The Winters lived in one of the finest houses ever built in Montgomery: the Italianate villa designed about 1851 by Samuel Sloan of Philadelphia, one of the nation's leading architects. That house (the Winter–Freeman), razed in 1919, was on the northwest corner of Madison Avenue and North Perry Street.

For antebellum Southern houses, the Italianate style was as popular as Greek Revival and more popular than Gothic Revival. Montgomery was once nationally known for its numerous examples of Italianate buildings. In 1861, a visiting newspaper correspondent noted that Montgomery's houses were predominantly Italianate. Today, only a handful survive, and none of these are in high-style Italianate.

The three-story, stucco-over-brick Winter Building is a fine example of an early Italianate-style commercial building. However, it did not begin as an Italianate building. In fact, it began as two buildings. The old shake-covered roofs of these buildings still exist—behind the cornice and under the low, hipped roof of the modernized Italianate building.

With the exception of exterior shutters and, possibly, small balconies, the second and third floors have been restored to the restraint and simplicity of the building's early Italianate appearance. The projecting cornice is supported by pendant brackets over a course of dentils. The windows have flat lintels, with the exception of the center windows on Dexter Avenue, which have pediments supported by pilasters.

Covered galleries on the upper floors, perhaps added in 1855, were not reconstructed. The ground floor facades, which probably had attached sheds or covered walkways, have not been restored to their nineteenth-century post-and-lintel commercial appearance. The exterior staircase has also not been restored.

The interior of the building has been considerably altered. Nineteenth-century features do survive, however. The most notable are the Greek, or battered, window surrounds on the second and third floors. The windows on the second floor are floor-to-ceiling. Some old glass survives in the six-over-six, double-hung sash windows. Some of the heart-pine flooring also survives. During restoration, pre-1850 brick arches, with later brick in-fill, were discovered. These have been left exposed. On the second floor, several cast-iron supporting pillars with simple acanthus leaf capitals survive. The western half of the building has a full basement. Six-over-six windows, once lit from wells or pits opening at street level, remain in the basement.

The Winter Building was restored by the law firm of Smith, Bowman, Thagard, Crook, and Culpepper, now associated with the Birmingham law firm of Balch and Bingham, L.L.P. The firm has not only restored the Winter Building, but also numbers 14 and 18 Dexter Avenue. Old interior features have been retained, and these buildings are now connected to the Winter Building.

Number 14 Dexter Avenue, constructed in 1837 by John Poston Figh, originally had a rather plain facade. Today's facade is a restoration of the 1890s late-Victorian appearance, with a Moorish horseshoe arch and other exuberant decorative motifs. The facade, above the sympathetically reconstructed first floor, is made of pressed metal and cast-iron. Number 18 Dexter Avenue, also constructed in 1837, has had all three floors of its facade restored to its 1893 appearance. The balustraded canopy is supported by three iron pillars with bolsters on the capitals.

The firm has also restored the facade of 68 Dexter Avenue to its 1870s appearance. The building itself was built in the 1830s or 1840s.

The firm of Balch and Bingham has played a leading role in the preservation and restoration of downtown Montgomery's architectural heritage and, perhaps more significantly, in preservation and restoration of the integrity of the city's streetscape. It is streetscape, rather than individual buildings, that distinguishes one city from another.

▼

Figh-Pickett House

512 South Court Street

THE RADICALLY changing nature of a downtown neighborhood is evident in the varied uses of what was once an extremely handsome house at 14 Clayton Street. It was built about 1837 as the private residence of Montgomery's principal building contractor. It then became the home of the widow of Alabama's first historian, before becoming one of Montgomery's major private schools. It has also been used as an automobile repair shop, a paint store (at which time the red brick walls were painted), and a convenience store. In June 1996, the massively built structure was moved so its lot could be used for an expansion of the adjacent Federal Building.

Before coming to Montgomery, John Poston Figh, a native of Virginia and son of an Irish immigrant, built the University of Alabama at Tuscaloosa. His son George rebuilt the university after Union troops destroyed most of the school buildings in 1865.

Between 1830 and 1860, John Figh built some of Montgomery's finest brick structures: the 1835 and 1854 courthouses (both demolished), the 1847 and 1850 Capitols (the first burned; the second stands today as the central block of the Capitol), the 1845 First Presbyterian Church, the ca. 1845 Lomax House, and the 1854 First Baptist Church (demolished).

In 1836, John Figh bought the lot at the corner of Clayton and Molton streets for five hundred dollars. He built a fine red-brick house for his wife, Jane McCain, and what would be a family of nine children.

As a contractor, Figh followed the designs of architects or the plans in builders' guides, but he may have exhibited his creativity when he built his own house. The main block of the house is rectangular, five bays wide and four bays deep. The Clayton Street elevation* is two stories high, and the other three elevations are three stories high.

The two-foot-thick walls are made of brick from Figh's own brickyard. The four chimneys, now removed, were internal. The low hipped roof, with wide eaves supported by Italianate brackets, is surmounted by a large skylight.

The double-hung windows on the main floor had nine lights in each sash. This is an indication that the house may have been transitional between the Federal and the Italianate styles. The shorter windows on the top floor had the usual Italianate-style six lights in each sash. All windows had exterior shutters with movable louvers.

The main and top floors had central doors with sidelights and transoms, which are Greek Revival or Italianate-style features. The house originally may have had a two-story Federal portico, rather than the one-story Italianate porch that survived until at least the 1940s. The porch, three bays wide, rested on piers filled with brick lattice. The porch had chamfered columnettes and saw-work brackets and balustrade.

Attached to the northwest corner of the house was a long, two-story service wing. Its brick ground floor had two doors and four windows facing east and a number of windows facing west. On the east side was an overhanging second story of latticework separated into six bays by wooden Tuscan pilasters. In the center of each bay was a large oval with wooden spokes, behind which may have been interior shutters. The kitchen (which was paved with square bricks), the smoke house, and the carriage house were in the fenced or walled yard.

John Figh, a remarkable man, was self-made and self-educated. He was Masonic Grand Master of Alabama. He regularly attended services at the Baptist Church, but never became a member. Although he strongly opposed secession, he supported the Confederacy once it was declared. His 1833 will indicates his character: he requested that his wife send each of their sons, when he reached his sixteenth or seventeenth year, to a free state to learn a mechanical trade of his choice. Realizing the potential for dissipation in the privileged sons of a slave society, he wanted his sons to learn to work. He also wanted them to be honest and keep good company. When Figh died on Christmas Day, 1865, he left an estate of almost $137,000. His children were grown; one of his sons was a Baptist minister.

In 1858, the Fighs sold their house to Albert James Pickett for $10,500. Pickett was the privileged son of a prominent land-holding family. He had been educated in Connecticut and in Virginia, before reading law under his brother. His interests, however, were elsewhere. He wrote on political, economic, and historical subjects for local newspapers. During the Creek War of 1836, he served as Governor Clement C. Clay's aide-de-camp, receiving the title of colonel.

With his marriage to Sarah Smith Harris, he added a large fortune to

*The house is here described as it was sited before the 1996 move.

The house at the time of the federal Historic American Buildings Survey in the 1930s.

his own assets, uniting Cedar Grove near Autaugaville with his wife's Forest Farm at Picketts' Springs, now Chisholm. The Picketts had twelve children, nine of whom survived to adulthood.

Pickett, an ardent Jacksonian Democrat, was Alabama's first historian. His 1851 *History of Alabama* was highly regarded.

On first coming to Montgomery from Cedar Grove in 1837, Pickett lived on Commerce Street. He died two weeks after buying the Figh house on Clayton Street. He never lived in the house, but his widow lived there until her death in 1894.

A description of the house during Mrs. Pickett's residence notes that the main floor had a central hall, library, and double parlors, separated by folding doors. Pickett's library may have been one of the best private libraries in the South.

The floor of the large, rectangular dining room in the basement was paved with marble squares taken from the 1847 Capitol after it burned in 1849. There were also three bedrooms in the basement. The top floor had additional bedrooms, and a picture gallery under the large skylight. One of the paintings was of Andrew Jackson, a gift from the president to his friend Colonel Pickett in 1837.

Prominent guests were entertained in the house: Jefferson Davis, Robert Toombs, Robert B. Vance, Leroy Pope Walker, J. B. Hood, and Braxton Bragg.

At the end of the Civil War, when Montgomery was in danger of falling to Union forces, Mrs. Pickett and her son-in-law Samuel Smith Harris, who later became Episcopal Bishop of Michigan, hid the family silver in the house's skylight. (Some of the silver had been used at a ball to honor the Marquis de Lafayette when he visited Montgomery in 1825.) As a ruse, a large trunk, weighted with bricks, was sent to Forest Farm. The plantation was subsequently raided, but the silver remained safe in town—and just *over* the Union officers' noses, as the Pickett House was commandeered by Union troops.

After the war, Mrs. Pickett was forced to open her home as a genteel boarding house—with the help of her loyal servants, Bird, Joe Curtis, and Sallie Lewis. Jerre, a coachman who loved horses and children, seems to have gone. Before the war, there was no vegetable garden, because vegetables were brought from the family plantations. Presumably, after the war, a vegetable garden replaced the extensive flower gardens.

In 1906, Elly Rufus Barnes bought the house, and Hugger Brothers remodeled the interior for a school. It opened on Robert E. Lee's birthday in 1907.

The first Barnes school, founded by Justus McDuffie Barnes in 1856, was Strata Academy. After moving in 1881, it became Highland Home College. In 1898, father and son came to Montgomery and opened a school on Mobile Street. J. M. Barnes was primarily occupied with promoting electric-power generation and railroads, and in preaching (he was the founder of Montgomery's Church of Christ that, after 1902, occupied the Catoma Street synagogue built by George M. Figh). Consequently, running the school fell on the son's shoulders. Barnes School for Boys, stressing character, scholarship, and moderate athletics, prepared young men for college and for business until 1942.

The main floor had two large study rooms, cloak rooms, an office, and the restroom for the six male teachers. On the top floor were four classrooms and the library. In the basement were the playroom (with a concrete floor over the marble squares), a bicycle room, boiler room, and the restroom for the 125 boys. Advertisements emphasized sanitary conditions, light, and ventilation.

Both the exterior and interior of this, one of Montgomery's oldest surviving brick buildings, have been drastically altered. All that remains of the interior is the staircase, which was probably added in 1906. The Figh-Pickett House was acquired by the Montgomery County Historical Society for its headquarters, and was moved to 512 South Court Street, from its original site at the northwest corner of Clayton and Molton streets, to allow for expansion of the Federal Building. Excellent photographic documentation has allowed for fine restoration of the building's exterior.

The view above, from the left rear, shows the unusual decorative lattice on the attached service wing. Below, a detail from the same side.

Montgomery's Architectural Heritage

Falconer House

428 South Lawrence Street

JOHN FALCONER, who had prospered as a merchant in South Carolina, came to Alabama in the fall of 1817. He provided the funds to pay for the section of land that was to be New Philadelphia—land that Andrew Dexter "bought" that August. Consequently, the patent of 1821 was in Falconer's name, and all deeds of property in New Philadelphia emanated from him. In 1832, Falconer sold a lot for $150 to Asa Hoxey who sold it to Seth Robinson in 1837. This is Falconer's only known connection with the Falconer House.

The cottage is believed to have been built by Seth Robinson between 1842 and 1845. It is not mentioned in a document until 1845, when Robinson willed it to his wife, Mary Jane. The cottage was originally located at the northwest corner of South Perry and Alabama streets. To save it from demolition, the Young Women's Christian Organization moved it to its present location in 1967. Only the porch, front parlors, and center hall were moved. The rear wing was in such bad condition that it could not be saved.

The modest frame cottage, five bays wide and one bay deep, has Greek Revival, Italianate, and later-Victorian features. The double-hung windows, with exterior louvered shutters, have two lights in each sash. These are late-nineteenth-century replacements for the antebellum six-over-six windows.

The architraves over the windows are probably early. The four-panel, raised-molding door is flanked by leaded sidelights. The transom has three lights. There are rectangular ventilator covers between the paired brackets. The hipped roof has a very low pitch.

The attached porch, with stairs to the south side only, is three bays wide. The balustrade is saw-work, but between the chamfered columnettes is lattice in an arched configuration. The frame cottage was originally built on a half-sunk full basement of masonry. The appearance of the exterior was reproduced, including the setback from the street and the three small round-headed arched openings under the porch. These provided ventilation for the servants' room and kitchen that were in the basement. The basement was paved with brick, and its dome-shaped bake oven was made of small bricks. Both standard and small size bricks were handmade. Some of the bricks had imprints of animal paws and human thumbs and feet. The basement did not have an internal staircase to the main floor of the cottage.

The entrance hall gives access to the rear of the cottage and to a parlor on each side. The tall, double parlor doors have three raised panels each. Just within the jambs of each of these doorways are freestanding, turned columnettes that support delicate saw-work architraves. Door and window framing is very simple. Except for the parlors' double doors, the remaining doors are six-panel in the so-called cross and Bible pattern. The panels are raised on one side and flat on the other. The floor boards of the three original rooms are quarter-sawn pine and run from wall to wall. The parlor ceilings are very high, but the entrance hall ceiling is approximately three feet higher—a feature made possible by the pitch of the hipped roof. The parlors are identical except for the mantels. One is a fanciful Victorian mantel with metal firebox surround that is decorated with grapes, leaves, and birds. The other mantel, of painted and incised slate in the Eastlake style, has a central mantelshelf flanked by two lower shelves.

The original dining room, which was in the rear wing, had a 12-inch-square, 32-foot-long, hand-hewn beam with metal rings to support the large swinging fan, or "shoo-fly." The new addition to the rear of the cottage uses doors from the original structure.

The YWCO used the cottage for craft lessons and a consignment shop. Subsequently, the Junior League leased the cottage. It is now owned and occupied by Turner, Wilson, and Sawyer, attorneys at law.

Chappell House

1020 Bell Street

Confederate Powder Magazine

northern end of Eugene Street

THE WEST MONTGOMERY site now occupied by Riverside Heights, the Housing Authority of the City of Montgomery, and Powder Magazine Park was preceded by a variety of structures that highlight local history.

The oldest known man-made structures on the site were two Indian mounds. The larger was about ninety feet square and twenty-five feet high. In 1833, the clay in the two mounds was used to make brick for the Planters' Hotel on Montgomery Street. During excavation, human remains were found interred in the mounds. According to Abram Mordecai, who came to what is now Montgomery County in 1789 as a trader, and later as operator of the first cotton gin in Alabama (for cotton raised by the Creek Indians), an Alabama Indian town existed on the site as late as the American Revolution. Colonel Benjamin Hawkins, United States Indian agent from 1796 until 1816, located the Indian town of Ecunchate (red earth) on the site.

In 1818, the site became the town of Alabama, a speculative venture of the Alabama Company, which was founded by Georgia Militia General John Scott, Thomas Bibb, and Dr. Manning. A resident of New Philadelphia, a mile to the east, once remarked that there was not a merchant or trader among the settlers of Alabama town. Its inhabitants made their livings as public officials or by farming in the nearby Big Bend area of the Alabama River. Although the county's first jail and first session of circuit court were held in Alabama town, the settlement did not thrive. This may have been because there were no merchants. There may have been no merchants because access to the river was difficult, or because settlements to the east were siphoning off settlers as they came down the Federal Road

A Sense of Place

that ran to the southeast of New Philadelphia. In the year of Alabama town's founding, the Alabama Company regrouped and founded East Alabama on the southern bank of the Big Bend of the Alabama River. When East Alabama and New Philadelphia were merged to form Montgomery in 1819, the county seat was moved. Alabama town soon vanished.

Some of the land was acquired by James Chappell, who built a plantation house there in 1845. That building now serves as Montgomery's Housing Authority. In the 1840s, a cottage-sized brick house was unusual. However, the builder was not only a planter, but also a brickmaker. The clay to make the brick was dug from a ravine to the west, near what is now Maxwell Air Force Base. The front and back of the house are of an orange-red brick with thin mortar pointing; the east side is of brown brick with crude pointing. The west side is no longer visible because, in the late 1950s, an addition was made to the house. The brick is laid in common bond with seven courses of stretchers separated by a single course of headers.

The one-story hipped-roofed house is raised off the ground, following Southern building practices. The house is five bays wide and four bays deep. The windows have flat, or jack, arches of rubbed brick. Although there are no longer exterior shutters, hinge mounts are still on the window frames. The 1950s addition replicated the wide, plain cornice and watertable that encircled the original house, but could not duplicate the original brick.

Besides the fine brickwork, little now distinguishes the house other than the small Greek Revival front porch. The porch features four crudely proportioned, tapered, and fluted Doric columns of masonry that support a small entablature. The delicate, finely made original porch railing was removed in the late 1990s. The four-panel front door is flanked by sidelights and topped with a wide transom in the Greek Revival style.

At the back of the wide central hall is a similar, but slightly narrower, doorway. Presumably, there were originally two rooms on both sides of the central hall, but extensive remodeling that changed the interior configuration has either obscured or obliterated evidence of the original plan. No interior features are evident; however, the double-hung windows, which are not original, follow the Greek Revival practice of having six lights in each sash.

Originally, there seems to have been a back porch extending from the central door to the northeast corner of the house. The addition to the almost-square house resulted in an L-shaped building. The original back porch was rebuilt into a gallery, but with a railing that duplicated that of the front porch, and with simple masonry columns that may be similar to those of the original back porch.

James Chappell's plantation did not encompass the whole of the Alabama town site. The Ashleys retained land there; in March 1861, William Ashley sold a one-acre site to the state of Alabama for the construction of a powder magazine. Powder was stored outside town for safety reasons. The magazine was built in 1862 and used throughout the war to store powder.

The Confederate magazine is a 37-by-28-foot one-story building. The slate hipped roof is original; the common bond brick walls are two feet thick. To help keep the powder dry, there is a ventilation space between inner and outer walls. Although there are no windows, there are small ventilation holes. The sturdy double door, on the eastern wall, has an iron sill and a brick jack arch lintel with iron bars in the transom above. The only exterior decoration is a projecting patterned-brick frieze. The magazine's one room has a brick floor. Four piers and four engaged columns support the roof's three brick barrel vaults. Iron tie rods reinforce the arches. This powder magazine is one of two remaining Confederate powder magazines in Alabama. The other is in Eufaula.

More recently, the area of Montgomery west of where Interstate 65 now crosses the Alabama River was called the West End. It was a rough, poor, predominantly white neighborhood. Most of its residents worked in the numerous mills in the Bell Street–Birmingham Highway area. In addition to lumber yards and furniture factories, there were cotton cloth and yarn mills, the last of which closed in the late 1940s.

At the turn of the century, conditions were appalling in the textile mills, especially for the quarter of the workers who were under sixteen years old.

The Montgomery Ministerial Association, led by the Reverend Edgar Gardner Murphy, rector of St. John's Episcopal Church, worked for child labor laws. A strong law was not enacted in Alabama until 1907.

From 1929 to 1937, Benjamin Travis Miers and his family occupied the Chappell House and ran a used-car and parts business on the adjoining land, which was previously cotton fields. Later the house was used as the office for a cotton mill located on the site of Riverside Heights community center. This mill, which maintained houses for its workers, was used as a military barracks during World War II.

In the late 1940s, the Chappell House became the office for Riverside Heights. Between 1936 and 1938, the Federal Housing Administration had constructed 100 one-story units for whites. This project followed the building of 160 Paterson Court units for blacks (Paterson Court was the second federal housing project built in the South).

Subsequently, two-story units were built. At the beginning of World War II, Algernon Blair of Montgomery built 400 one-story units in 200 days. At the peak, his company employed more than 6,000 workers. These housing units were used by federal civilian employees during the war and by military personnel until the 1960s.

Architecturally, the units of interest are those built between 1936 and 1938. These one-story, multifamily units had slate hipped roofs, which were recently replaced with modern shingles, and galleries down both sides of the buildings. The columns supporting the front gallery roofs are similiar to, but smaller than, those on the rear gallery of the Chappell House. These units were designed by Harry Jones and Walter Ausfeld, son of Frederick Ausfeld, one of Montgomery's most prominent turn-of-the-century architects.

The architectural legacy of this west Montgomery site illustrates the diversity of Montgomery's rich historical heritage.

First Presbyterian Church

52 Adams Street

Example of a blind ogee arch framing a Gothic arch.

MONTGOMERY'S Presbyterians were the first denomination to erect a church building of their own. The building is the oldest church in the city, constructed between 1845 and 1847. It was preceded by the 1827 Union Church, located on the corner of Court and Church streets where the Federal Building is today. The Union Church, which was shared by Baptists, Methodists, and Presbyterians, was subsequently demolished.

Three years after their organization in 1829, the Presbyterians built a one-story, one-room frame church on land donated by Andrew Dexter of Boston, one of the founders of Montgomery and of Montgomery's First Presbyterian Church. Today's brick church building stands on the site of the original wooden building, which was rolled back to make way for construction of a new building in 1845. The new brick building was dedicated in February 1847. Alexander McKenzie, a member of the church, was the "architect," probably adapting the building's design from one of the builders' guides that were so commonly used at the time. The contractor was John Poston Figh, builder of many antebellum brick buildings. Construction cost the congregation of about a hundred members $16,000.

The exterior of the building has changed very little from its 1847 appearance. The brickwork has been somewhat damaged by sandblasting to remove the white paint that was applied in 1940 in an attempt to control moisture, a problem that may have resulted from ivy planted in 1887 as part of the church's anniversary celebrations.

The building's style is Gothic Revival, fashionable in part because of the popularity of Sir Walter Scott's romantic novels, but also because some denominations then considered the style appropriate for "Christian" buildings. This was in opposition to the "pagan" Greek Revival, the other fashionable style of the time. Gothic Revival, at the beginning of the movement, bears little resemblance to actual Gothic buildings in Europe; architecturally accurate Gothic-style buildings were not constructed until late in the nineteenth century.

First Presbyterian's building is basically a traditional American meeting house to which Gothic decorative elements have been applied. These include crenellated parapets on the tower's bell chamber, arch windows with wooden tracery, and arches imposed on the four rectangular leaves of the main door, that is itself surmounted by decorative crenellations. The windows along the sides are surmounted by blind Gothic arches, and the windows on the facade are surmounted by blind ogee arches. The unusual marble keystones in the window arches are not Gothic elements.

Unlike the exterior, the interior has been changed considerably. Originally the sanctuary was a rectangular room with an apse behind the small podium on which there was a tub pulpit. An arched window, identical to those along the side walls, was on each side of the apse, a large semicircular niche originally used to project the voice. Nineteenth-century stenciling has survived in the apse, and is now hidden behind the organ. Several rows of pews flanked the pulpit and were perpendicular to the pews in the main body of the sanctuary. The pews in the body of the sanctuary were box pews. A U-shaped balcony opposite the pulpit wall extended two-thirds of the way along the side walls, terminating with squared-off ends. This balcony was for black members of the congregation. (Except for financial support, the separation of black and white members of the congregation, which began as early as 1883, was complete in 1890.)

The original ceiling was somewhat higher than today's ceiling. Photographs indicate that the ceiling and cornice had trompe l'oeil decorations. These painted decorations would have given the illusion of fine detail and depth on what was actually a flat surface. To this neoclassical interior were added Gothic elements: arched panels on rectangular doors (set in Greek Revival–style door frames) and the Gothic, arched windows. These windows, many of which were partially obscured by the balcony, had clear glass.

The sanctuary underwent several configurations before acquiring its current appearance. For example, the original U-shaped balcony was replaced by a gracefully curved one that extended halfway down the side walls. That balcony was replaced, in a major renovation in 1897, by the existing large balcony that extends across the back of the sanctuary and over

Montgomery's Architectural Heritage

the vaulted entrance vestibule. Two free-standing, curving staircases, dating from the antebellum period, flank the vestibule.

After the initial controversy had subsided over whether congregational singing should be accompanied by instrumental music, an organ was installed in the balcony opposite the pulpit. That organ's replacement was located on the floor of the sanctuary against the east wall, to the left of the pulpit. While the organ was in that location, Sidney Lanier, Confederate soldier and poet, was church organist. (While living in Montgomery from 1866 until 1867, Lanier wrote poetry and *Tiger-Lilies*, a novel based on his war experiences, and supported himself teaching school at Prattville Academy and clerking at the Exchange Hotel, which his grandfather had acquired in the 1850s.) In 1897, the organ was moved to its present location behind a large choir and rostrum.

The pulpit has always been in a central location, in keeping with the church's focus on proclaiming the Gospel and teaching the faith. The 1906 pulpit has fine brass decorative elements in the Gothic style. Below the rostrum, on the floor of the sanctuary, is an oak communion table and a marble baptismal font, perhaps the oldest furnishing of the church. The walls, scored to resemble stone, were slate gray before being painted off-white.

The most significant alteration of 1897, however, was the lowering of the ceiling and the installation of wooden beams with drop pendants. This alteration, and the addition of five memorial stained-glass windows, gave the sanctuary a completely different appearance from the essentially neo-classical appearance of the original sanctuary. The handsome oak wainscot paneling and oak pews also date from the beginning of the twentieth century.

The history of First Presbyterian Church has, in many respects, been the history of Montgomery itself. Early members included Andrew Dexter, William Sayre, and William Graham. Arguably the church's most famous member was William Lowndes Yancey, a fire-eater, as several of the leading secessionists were called. An unusually interesting member of First Presbyterian Church was Dr. J. Marion Sims, a pioneering gynecologist who left Montgomery in 1853. Four years later, he founded the charity Woman's Hospital of the State of New York. Because of his divided loyalties, he went to Europe during the Civil War. He was knighted by the King of the Belgians and, after treating Empress Eugenie of France, received the Legion of Honor. He was finally recognized in Montgomery in a triumphal visit in 1877.

First Presbyterian Church also illustrates an unfortunate phenomenon in today's Montgomery: a stampede to the east. In 2000, First Presbyterian, by an extremely slim majority, voted to desert its historic building and the city, and move east.

JOHN POSTON FIGH may have started construction of the Greek Revival mansion at 221 South Court Street as early as 1845. That the brickwork is very fine is not surprising, because he was himself a contractor and brickyard owner. Although Figh intended to live in the house himself, he sold it in about 1846 for $5800 to James J. Gilmer, brother of Governor George Gilmer of Georgia. James Gilmer was also not destined to occupy the house, as his wife died before they moved in. Consequently, in 1849, he sold it to Reuben Clark Shorter, Jr., brother of John Gill Shorter, governor of Alabama from 1861 to 1863. Reuben Shorter died at twenty-eight in 1853 after five years of marriage. It was his twenty-three-year-old widow, Caroline Billingslea, who would live in the house until her death in 1907—but as Mrs. Tennent Lomax.

In 1857, the widow Shorter married Tennent Lomax, who was ten years her senior. Lomax, a descendant of the prominent Middleton family of South Carolina, had served with distinction as a captain in the Mexican War. In 1857, after graduating from Randolph-Macon College, he came to Alabama as a planter. Colonel Lomax, commander of the Third Alabama Infantry Regiment, was killed in June 1862 at the Battle of Seven Pines, Virginia. His commission as a brigadier general was found in his pocket, unopened.

The Lomaxes' daughter, Carrie Lizzie, died at the age of two. Tennent Lomax, Jr., born in 1858, lived in the house with his mother until his death

Lomax House

221 South Court Street

Montgomery's Architectural Heritage

in 1902. He had shown great promise as a lawyer, county solicitor, and politician. In his memory, his mother gave an annex to the Court Street Methodist Church. Over the years, she had grown quite stout, so the annex was called "Mrs. Lomax's bustle." Notwithstanding the tragedy and early deaths associated with the house, it was a center of Montgomery's social and political life for sixty years.

On Mrs. Lomax's death, the Lomax House became a school for boys. In 1932, the Preferred Life Assurance Society, later the Preferred Life Insurance Company, bought the house. It served as the company's home office until 1993.

The Lomax house is not as grand as Knox Hall (1848), the Teague House (1848), or the Murphy House (1851)—the other surviving Greek Revival brick mansions of the period of Montgomery's first economic boom. It is, however, a very handsome building, made all the more appealing by the warmth of its brickwork. (The Teague House, now painted, and the sides of the Murphy House, also now painted, were originally red brick.)

The facade, with its four Doric pilasters, is dominated by the projecting portico of four unfluted Doric columns that support a pedimented gable. Each of the other three surviving Greek Revival mansions has six columns that extend across the entire facade and support plain entablatures. The Lomax House's gabled portico, the unpainted brick laid in common bond, and especially the gabled ends with a parapet linking the double end chimneys, are evocative of an earlier style on the Atlantic Seaboard. This house's design may be derived directly from Chester Hills's 1834 *Builder's Guide* or, indirectly, by way of the Governor Thomas Bibb House in Huntsville. The latter, although designed by George Steele, seems to have combined elements of Hills's "Doric house" and "Ionic house."

The marble-paved portico is reached by broad marble steps, once flanked by the marble recumbent lions that now grace the entrance to Knox Hall. The slightly recessed, masonry center facade is painted. The heavy door frames are battered; that is, they are wider at the bottom than at the top. The doorway has sidelights and a transom. A similar doorway opens onto the cast-iron balcony directly above the main door.

The original part of the house has the conventional center hall plan with two rooms on either side. The most striking features of the wide hall are the elaborate plaster cornice and, at the rear of the hall, a beautiful staircase that rises in a continuous curve to the two rooms in the attic. The newel post and the balusters are turned. Opening on the south side are double parlors that were originally connected by double doors. Although the simple battered framing survives, the doors are gone. The Greek Revival mantels are also gone. The southwest parlor has a heavy plaster cornice decorated with floral motifs and an elaborate, circular ceiling medallion. The northwest room on the main floor has a simple, circular ceiling medallion. There are raised panels under the windows on both floors.

The room arrangement on the second floor is identical to that on the main floor, including a wide, interconnecting doorway between the two rooms on the south of the central hall.

Throughout the house, the original floors have been covered or replaced with narrow oak. The original interior and exterior doors have been modified or replaced by doors featuring leaded glass. Some of the house's fixed-louver shutters have survived. The one-over-one window sashes, however, are not original.

The two-story wing that was added to the rear of the house in 1939 is compatible with the original block; its six-over-six window sashes conform to the Greek Revival style. This addition contains extremely handsome rooms with heavy, raised-panel mahogany wainscoting, exceptionally wide cornices, solid-brass box locks, and brass lighting fixtures. The former office of the president of Preferred Life is extremely fine, with floor-to-ceiling mahogany paneling in the Georgian style. The floor in the office is of pegged quarter-sawn oak.

Lomax House is now owned and occupied by the law offices of Edward B. Parker II.

Knox Hall

419 South Perry Street

IT IS NOT SURPRISING that Knox Hall is the finest Greek Revival mansion in the city. It was designed about 1848 by Stephen Decatur Button, a native of Connecticut who began his career as an architect in New York and eventually settled in Philadelphia. While working in Georgia, he was selected as the architect of the first (1847) Capitol in Montgomery.

The house was built for William Knox, a native of Ireland, who prospered in real estate and banking after arriving in Alabama in the 1830s. He was one of the building commissioners for the Capitol. As president of the Central Bank of Alabama, he also engaged Button to design a bank building in the Italianate style (now 1 Dexter Avenue). Knox, who was financially ruined by the collapse of the Confederate government, lived in the house until his death in 1869, and Mrs. Knox lived there until her death in 1890.

The Sigmund Roman family lived in the house for about a decade, selling to the Beauvoir Club in 1902. When the club moved to the twelfth floor of the Bell Building in 1907, the mansion was in danger of demolition. However, it was reprieved to become a genteel boarding house, and then, in the 1920s, an apartment house. Conversion into an apartment house entailed removal of the columns and partitioning the large rooms into apartments. A four-story addition to the front of the old mansion came almost to the sidewalk.

In the early 1970s, this addition was demolished, and demolition was begun on the former mansion itself. It was soon discovered that the historic mansion still retained significant evidence of its former grandeur, chiefly above ceilings that had been lowered and behind the partitions that divided the once large rooms into smaller rooms.

At one time, Montgomery boasted half a dozen mansions of the quality of Knox Hall. This one has survived because of the tireless efforts of those citizens who aided Landmarks Foundation in raising the thousands of dollars needed to restore it. Restoration of the exterior and the main floor was also made possible because of photographic evidence and because sufficient physical evidence survived of the original.

Stephen Button probably relied on Minard Lafever's 1835 *Beauties of Modern Architecture*, one of the leading Greek Revival pattern books of the period. In the 1820s, Greece, which was struggling for its independence from the Ottoman Empire, caught the American fancy. Recognized as the source of Western democracy, Greece was seen to be fighting a dissipated Eastern empire. Although Thomas Jefferson and others advocated building in the Classical style because they deemed it an architecture fit for a democracy, the Greek Revival style began to dominate public and private building, not for philosophical reasons, but because of the relentless quest for fashion. Even today, Classical Revival styles are still popularly thought of as the appropriate styles for American government buildings.

Knox Hall is thoroughly Greek Revival. It was the first of the Greek Revival mansions of central Alabama to have a huge hexastyle, or six-column, portico. The building is imposing because of its monumental scale, its siting well back from the street, the six huge

Fluted columns with Tower of the Winds Corinthian capitals.

Greek Revival–style doorway with transom and sidelights.

Montgomery's Architectural Heritage 47

Stuccoed wall scored and painted to resemble stone.

Greek Revival–style double-hung window with six lights in each sash.

Solid interior shutters and exterior shutters with movable louvers.

columns and plain entablature of the facade, and even the large wooden cupola, a reconstruction, that crowns the nearly flat roof. But Knox Hall's beauty is also based on the quality of its detail. This includes the marble steps, terrace, and window and door lintels, and the gray walls of finely scored and painted lines that give the illusion that the solid brick, stuccoed house is built of stone. Fine detail is evident also in the Tower of the Winds Corinthian capitals, the applied-zinc wreaths over each column, and even the stone caps on each chimney top. All of these have been restored based on photographic or surviving physical evidence. Exterior louvered shutters soften the somewhat austere north and south sides.

Balance, proportion, symmetry, and scale are even more imposing in the interior. The entrance hall is enhanced by two freestanding Corinthian columns that divide the central hall. The black and white marble floor, installed during the recent restoration to replace multicolored tiles that were probably added by the Roman family, corresponds to the flooring of the portico. The doors are capped by elaborate, carved-wood decorations in the Greek style. The ceiling has fine plasterwork. Beyond the staircase, at the rear of the house, is a small circle of fluted columns that support the stair landing. A small glass skylight dome can be seen by looking up through these columns and through a circular hole in the stair landing. Although this is not an original feature, it enhances the beauty of the house.

The most impressive interior features are the triple parlors that extend the full six-bay depth of the house on the north side. These identical rooms are grand in scale—thirty by twenty-seven feet with eighteen-foot ceilings. The plasterwork of the ceilings and cornices is elaborate and bold. On the north wall there are three simple black marble mantels, copies of those original to the house. The windows and the extremely wide doors that connect the three rooms are decorated with rich, Greek-style decorations. The double-hung windows, in the customary Greek Revival style, have six lights in each sash. As the windows have interior solid shutters, draperies are unnecessary and the full splendor of the architecture is revealed.

The two couchant, or recumbent, lions that flank the front steps were purchased in Italy for James Powell in the 1850s. After gracing several Montgomery houses, they were brought to Knox Hall in the early 1890s. They were removed when the house was sold to the Beauvoir Club, stored, used at a house on Thomas Avenue, and finally returned to Knox Hall in 1983, a gift of Mrs. Roman Weil.

Knox Hall is occupied by Reid-O'Donahue Advertising, an advertising and public relations firm.

MANY CONSIDER the Teague House to be the quintessential Southern mansion. It certainly is a very fine Greek Revival building. But it does not fit the romantic view of an antebellum mansion, having been built not as a plantation house but as the townhouse of Berry Owen, a prosperous livery stable operator.

In 1852, four years after he built the house, he sold it and his business and left Montgomery. On April 12, 1865, three days after Robert E. Lee had surrendered at Appomattox, the house was occupied by Union troops under General James Wilson, before they moved east to Tuskegee and then to Columbus, Georgia.

After having been owned by the prominent Ware and Graham families, the mansion was acquired by William Martin Teague and his wife, Eugenia Isabelle Jackson, in 1889. Teague, a Confederate veteran who had been captured at Gettysburg, farmed and ran a mercantile business in Greenville after the war. He came to Montgomery in 1883 and founded a hardware business. Later, he served as a city alderman and mayor and, with his son-in-law, John Gay, built the Gay-Teague Hotel on the southwest corner of Commerce and Bibb streets. The house remained in the Teague family until 1955, when it was bought by the Alabama State Chamber of Commerce (after 1985, the Business Council of Alabama).

▼

Teague House

468 South Perry Street

Montgomery's Architectural Heritage

The square, solid-brick Greek Revival mansion has a handsome portico attached to the facade. This portico is the dominant feature of the house. Its simple entablature was embellished early in the twentieth century with a cornice, dentils, and classical brackets under the eaves. The entablature is supported by six unfluted columns. These plastered brick columns rest on masonry bases and have wood and masonry Ionic capitals. Above the portico's black and white marble terrace is a balcony with a wooden floor and cast-iron balustrade. The front steps are white marble, and the walk is of both white and black marble, matching the portico's floor. The large double-hung windows with white lintels and sills are in the usual Greek Revival style with six lights in each sash. The windows have exterior louvered shutters.

The mansion, with the exception of two small additions, consists of four large square rooms, on both floors, that open onto central halls. The entrance hall is divided by two freestanding fluted columns with Tower of the Winds Corinthian capitals. The staircase, with heavy newel post and heavy turned balusters, rises with half turns and two landings. On either side of the central hall are double parlors separated by wide, sliding pocket doors. The doors on the main floor are the so-called Egyptian or Greek key doors. The framing over the doors is a shouldered or eared architrave, and the side jambs are battered, being wider at the bottom than at the top. The windows, with wooden panels at the bottom, have identical Egyptian or Greek key framing. There are unusual square and rectangular ceiling medallions, as well as one common circular medallion. Chandeliers on the main floor are of the period. With the exception of the northwest parlor, which has a Colonial Revival–style mantel, the fireplace surrounds are simple Greek Revival ones.

The second floor has a similar floor plan to that of the main floor. The woodwork is very plain, except for the Greek Revival door opening from the central hall onto the portico's balcony. The mansion's original front door was probably similar in design, with sidelights and a transom, but more elaborate in detail.

The Teague House has been little changed over the years. Two small brick wings were added, one to the north side and one to the rear. These housed bathrooms. The low pitched, standing-seam tin roof has been altered, and Victorian terra-cotta chimney pots have been added, as have the two metal lions flanking the front steps. Early in this century, the front door with its elaborate surround in the Colonial Revival style replaced the original Greek Revival–style doorway. The door's original Greek Revival framing remains in the entrance hall. The house's original red brick has been painted.

The brick carriage house and the kitchen, connected to the house by a lattice-enclosed passage, were built between 1850 and 1880 to replace the original servants' quarters and other dependencies, or outbuildings, that were further west on the lot. Survival of the carriage house and kitchen is significant, because so few dependencies have survived in Montgomery. These two dependencies illustrate that much of the work of a nineteenth-century household was done, not in the big house, but in the yard. In addition to a carriage house and a kitchen (generally consisting of a room to prepare the food and one in which to clean up), a typical large house would have had servants' quarters. There would have been a washhouse for laundry, a well, chicken coops, and outhouses. There could have also been stabling for a cow and a horse or two. All this would have been enclosed by a wall or fence. The high brick wall that enclosed the back of the Teague House was removed in the 1980s.

It is appropriate that one of the city's finest remaining Greek Revival-style mansions is the home, since 1993, of the Alabama Historical Commission, whose purpose is to safeguard the state's historical buildings and sites. It is all the more fitting because the Teague House has retained the integrity of its siting. The front of the house is surrounded by a period iron fence, two dependencies are intact at the back of the house, and there are some fine old trees.

Alabama State Capitol

Bainbridge Street
at 600 Dexter Avenue

ALABAMA has had several capital cities: St. Stephens, Huntsville, Cahawba, Tuscaloosa, and Montgomery. Andrew Dexter, founder of New Philadelphia, one of the two towns that united to form Montgomery in 1819, was so convinced that the capital would eventually locate here that, in 1817, he reserved the commanding hill at the head of Market Street (now Dexter Avenue) for the state's capitol building. Dexter did not live to see his conviction borne out, because the capital did not move to Montgomery until 1846–47. The move was necessary because the state's political and economic center had shifted south and east, especially after the annexation of Creek Indian territory in 1832.

One of the drawing cards was that the city of Montgomery would finance a capitol building. This was very important because the Capitol at Tuscaloosa was considered to be so extravagantly grand that the architect was forced to resign and the legislators refused to complete the building; apparently, some thought that such lavish public buildings could lead to despotism.

The first Capitol at Montgomery was designed by Stephen Decatur Button, who began his professional career in New York. He was working in Georgia when he was selected as architect for the new state house. Button eventually went to Philadelphia, where he became a nationally prominent architect. The design was not particularly original; it was merely a variation on a theme that had been used repeatedly, especially since the 1830s. Many state capitols are built as variants of this style.

In the first half of the nineteenth century, this national style of neoclassicism grew out of the discussion about the proper kind of architecture for a republic. Not only were republican civic virtues linked to the architecture of classical Greece and Rome, but the neoclassical architecture was believed to be able to promote these virtues in the general public. Government architecture is a form of propaganda, and neoclassical architecture was being used in the young United States to convey an aspiration for power, tradition, and greatness. (Ironically, authoritarian and totalitarian governments have also used neoclassical architecture as propaganda: Napoleonic France, Imperial Great Britain, Nazi Germany, and the Stalinist Soviet Union.)

Button's Capitol was built in 1847. All of the master craftsmen, except the bricklayers, were imported from the North. The building burned in 1849. Although its details were taken from Minard Lafever's 1835 *Beauties of Modern Architecture*, the building appears to have had finer aesthetic design, building materials, and interior furnishings than its 1850–51 replacement. Daniel Pratt, an early Alabama industrialist and builder, prepared a bizarre design for the new building. It was rejected in favor of a modification of Button's design done by Barachias Holt of Maine.

The 1847 Capitol had a raised two-story hexastyle portico supporting a pedimented gable, whereas the 1850–51 building has a three-story portico with a plain entablature and an amateurish, awkward clock replacing the pedimented gable. The City of Montgomery, although unable to finance a second capitol building, did provide the clock. The portico's Corinthian capitals, used on both buildings, were also derived from Lafever, who had based his designs on the capitals of Athens's Tower of the Winds (circa 40 B.C.). The capitals were cast at Janney's Foundry in Montgomery.

Button's dome, although not as low as a classical Roman dome, was lower and more hemispherical than the current elongated dome that rests on a lighted drum encircled with twelve Corinthian columns. The 1850–51 dome is in the Renaissance Revival style. The elongated dome may have been based on the ca. 1700 dome for London's St. Paul's Cathedral. (Sir Christopher Wren's dome at St. Paul's was the inspiration for Thomas Ustic Walter's great cast-iron dome that was added to the national Capitol during the Civil War.) The dome is crowned with a lantern that lights the inner dome of stained glass that was added to the rotunda in 1906.

Today's Capitol is considerably different from that of the nineteenth century. The original building, including the projecting portico, was only eleven bays wide. The first addition was the 1885 east wing, which housed the Supreme Court library and the offices of the justices and their staffs. By the turn of the century, the building was inadequate. Consequently, south and north wings were built, in 1906–07 and 1911–12 respectively. Frank

Lockwood, who was to become one of Montgomery's most prominent architects of the first third of the twentieth century, did the designs; Charles Follen McKim of New York, one of the most famous national architects of the time, served as a consultant for the design of the south wing. Although the wings are technically in the Beaux Arts style (McKim being one of that style's first American advocates), it is so restrained that the wings complement the 1850–51 neoclassical structure.

In conjunction with the recent restoration, a formal facade was added to the east wing. This design by Nicholas H. Holmes of Mobile conforms to the original building and to Lockwood's additions. The four cardinal elevations now have imposing porticos.

The restoration that was completed in 1992 has returned various interior spaces to specific periods. Highlights include the three-story curved staircase, probably the work of Horace King, a native of South Carolina, who was brought to Alabama in 1832. He was trained in a school for slave artisans. Because of his service to Phenix City, Alabama, and Columbus, Georgia, as a bridge and house builder, he was manumitted in 1846. He subsequently became a slaveowner himself. King was one of the first blacks to serve in the Alabama legislature, from 1870 until 1873. He is noted, however, for his bridge building, especially for the 614-foot Chattahoochee River bridge of 1873.

The old Senate chamber has been restored to its 1861 appearance. It was in this room that delegates from the seceding states organized the Confederacy. The original House chamber, Supreme Court chamber, Governor's suite, and Secretary of State's suite have been restored to their appearances in the 1870s–1880s. Several of these rooms feature period and reproduction furnishings.

The restored rooms have yellow pine and poplar doors grained to imitate mahogany. The walls in these rooms are painted using trompe l'oeil techniques. This illusionary painting, incorrectly called fresco at the time, fools the eye by making flat surfaces appear to be paneled or decorated with moldings or raised ornaments. The trompe l'oeil effect, achieved by manipulation of light, shadow, and color, was the work of Prussian-trained Peter Schmidt and Irish-American Frank O'Brien, who met Schmidt in Philadelphia. They arrived in Montgomery just before the Civil War and worked decorating churches and homes. Their antebellum work also included the Montgomery Theatre at 39 North Perry Street. Their work on the Capitol dates from 1869–79. O'Brien eventually went to Birmingham, became rich, and was elected mayor. Schmidt's and O'Brien's work was soon out of fashion and was papered or painted over. Fragments of their work were discovered in the early 1980s. The trompe l'oeil work was restored in 1991–92.

In 1906, the trompe l'oeil decorations in the rotunda were covered with white plaster and neoclassical decorations. Between 1927 and 1930, Roderick

Mackenzie, a Scottish-born artist working in Mobile, painted eight large romanticized, historical scenes on canvas for the rotunda. They have been restored, as has his brown, red, tan, and gold color scheme.

In the restoration, the Capitol was painted cream. This color is not only historically accurate, it is aesthetically pleasing, because it allows the architectural details of the building to be seen—glare from pure white buildings makes them appear flat and sterile.

Significant events of the state and nation have occurred at the Capitol, including the February 1861 inauguration of Jefferson Davis as provisional president of the Confederacy and the termination in March 1965 of the Selma-to-Montgomery civil rights march led by Dr. Martin Luther King, Jr.

The Alabama State Capitol is open to the public, and has literature to amplify architectural, decorative, and historical features of the building.

Murphy House

22 Bibb Street

JOHN H. MURPHY had been in Montgomery a mere seven years when, in 1851, he built one of the city's finest Greek Revival mansions. But in that time, as a warehouse owner and cotton commission merchant, he had become one of the city's richest citizens.

Murphy, born in Scotland in 1806, immigrated to Westmoreland County, Virginia, during the middle or late 1820s. Perhaps he and Susan, his second wife, moved west to Alabama because, at the time, there were great socioeconomic opportunities for men of talent, drive, and luck. Murphy was such a man and, like others of his kind, amassed a fortune in a short time. The year before he built his mansion, his real estate holdings were valued at $75,000, a large amount at the time. He also owned twenty-three slaves, making him one of the city's largest slave owners.

The Murphys built their house as other fine houses and public buildings were being built in the same neighborhood. These buildings, some of which were designed by nationally prominent architects, were in the fashionable styles of the days of prosperity and cotton fortunes that preceded the Civil War. Among these were two of the most significant houses ever built in Montgomery. Just a block to the east on Madison Avenue was the Italianate villa of Joseph Samuel Prince Winter and Mary Elizabeth Gindrat Winter. Their mansion was designed about 1851 by Samuel Sloan of Philadelphia, one of the nation's leading architects. The house was razed in

1919. Also in the neighborhood, at the northwest corner of Jefferson and Lawrence streets, was the Greek Revival mansion of Colonel Charles Pollard and Emily Virginia Scott Pollard. Stephen Decatur Button of Philadelphia, architect of the 1847 Capitol and, a year later, of Knox Hall, the first of Montgomery's Greek Revival mansions, probably designed the Pollards' mansion. It was very similar to the Murphy House, but was finer in decorative detail. It was demolished about 1938. The Winters, Gindrats, Pollards, Scotts, and Knoxes, all of whose fortunes were based on business, were also all communicants of St. John's Episcopal Church, a block east of the Murphy House. St. John's, built in the mid-1850s, was designed by Frank Wills of New York, a nationally noted architect of the Gothic Revival. Immediately across Bibb Street from the Murphy House was the Baptist Church (1854). (It was designed in the Renaissance Revival style by Thomas Ustic Walter of Philadelphia, whose work includes the 1851–65 dome on the national Capitol.) This handsome building ceased serving as the Baptist Church in 1908 and was eventually demolished.

Corinthian capital and fluted column.

In 1851, the Murphy household was large: John, age forty-four; Susan, age twenty-six; their three children, ages seven, five, and one; as well as Thomas, age twenty-two, and Eurely, age fourteen, probably children of John's first marriage. (Three Murphy children, all born in Westmoreland County, Virginia, had died within one week in the winter of 1850, before the Murphys moved into the Bibb Street mansion. They were buried side by side in Oakwood Cemetery.) Probably also living in the house were house servants, three of Murphy's clerks, and a thirty-six-year-old Irishwoman, Mary Gorren, probably the governess.

The Murphy family fortunes declined; John Murphy, who died in 1859, was not there to resurrect them. The family had to rent out rooms in their home. For a short time in 1861, the Reverend Basil Manly, committed secessionist and minister of the Baptist Church from 1861 to 1863, boarded with the Murphys, while his wife, Sarah, stayed on their Tuscaloosa plantation.

Yet the Murphy House was the scene of social activity during the war. Notable Confederate visitors included Jefferson Davis, in the winter and early spring of 1861, and William Lowndes Yancey, who, Abraham Lincoln supposedly said, single-handedly started the war. The heady days did not last. In April 1865, the mansion was requisitioned as the headquarters of the Federal provost marshal.

The mansion is in the Greek Revival style, with a characteristic full-height hexastyle portico attached to the front of the house. The six fluted, masonry columns (originally white) with Corinthian capitals (originally painted dark) rest on a white-marble raised terrace and support a simple entablature, whose block dentils, egg-and-dart molding, and acanthus-leaf brackets date from the first decade of the twentieth century. At the portico's second-floor level, a cast-iron balcony is accessed by a single door with

Montgomery's Architectural Heritage

sidelights and a transom. The portico facade of the two-story house is stuccoed, scored, and painted several colors to imitate stone. The side walls, now painted, were originally unpainted red brick.

The low-rise hipped roof is hidden behind the parapet that encircles the house. Some of the cast-iron ventilators around the base of the house are originals; others were cast using original patterns from the Janney's Foundry collection.

Windows on the side of the house and on the second floor of the facade are unusual in that each of the sashes has four lights, rather than six in the usual Greek Revival fashion. Windows opening on the portico's terrace are full-length double-hung sashes with four-over-six lights. They give access to the terrace from the front parlors. The windows have exterior movable-louvered shutters and are capped by cast-iron hoods decorated with a classical motif. There are also interior solid shutters that fold into the deep window casings.

The main entrance is recessed in an alcove behind two small, engaged Corinthian columns identical to the full-height ones supporting the entablature. The double doors, with panels below and glass above, are flanked by sidelights and surmounted by a transom.

The main entrance opens into a wide center hall lined with pilasters whose Corinthian capitals are gilded. The coffered ceiling is decorated with gilded classical motifs. Originally the staircase rose in a semicircle from the back of the central hall. The configuration of the staircase today dates from 1930. The floor, of black marble and white marble, was added in the early 1970s.

Double parlors to the left of the center hall extend the full four bays of the original main block of the house. They are unusual in that they are not separated by an arch or sliding doors. The wide plaster cornice is decorated with gilded classical motifs. The two original Rococo Revival brass gasoliers (now converted to electricity) hang from simple circular medallions. Along the long side wall are two coal-burning fireplaces. The low Italian-marble mantels are similar, but not identical.

This room, the only one in the house to have been restored to its antebellum appearance, is furnished with period pieces. Between the two floor-to-ceiling windows on the front of the house is a tall French pier mirror in an ornate, Rococo Revival gilt frame; the mirror is original to the house. The large, circular conference table was reputedly used in the Alabama Capitol by the Confederate cabinet in the winter and early spring of 1861. Most of the furnishings belong to the Water Works Board, which now occupies the building, but some items are on loan, such as the portrait of Mrs. Murphy and child.

Originally, the main two-story block had an attached one-story transverse wing at the back. This wing extended one bay on either side of the five-bay main block. This wing housed servants' quarters, a kitchen, and two baths. Each bathtub was made of a solid block of marble. Behind this one-story wing were the gardens, stables, and other dependencies.

In 1930, the Elks Lodge, which had used the house as early as 1894 and bought it in 1902, replaced the one-story wing with the current two-story addition. The elaborate ceiling of the Lodge's ballroom is preserved above the lowered ceiling in the rear addition.

The building may have been damaged by shock waves that were sustained when dynamite was exploded to help contain the fierce fire of 1927 that swept through the area now occupied by the Civic Center parking lot. This was the second time the house was threatened by a major fire. The first was in April 1865, when Confederate troops burned warehouses—including Murphy and Company's warehouse—containing 85,000 bales of cotton. The resulting fire would have been even more destructive had it not been for the loyal service of the city's "volunteer" black fire company. The retreating Confederates did not want the cotton to fall into the hands of Wilson's Raiders. They not only burned the cotton that had been piling up in Montgomery because the port of Mobile had been blockaded by the Union navy, but they also destroyed 60,000 bushels of corn, and large stores of liquor and molasses—by pouring them into the streets. The city was a mess when Wilson's Raiders arrived.

Of all the fine antebellum buildings of the neighborhood, only St. John's Church, the Montgomery Theatre building, and the Murphy House have survived. In 1969, the Murphy House was saved from destruction by Landmarks Foundation and, especially, by the board of directors of the Water Works and Sanitary Sewer Board of Montgomery, which responded to the need to move from city hall by acquiring and restoring a significant element of Montgomery's historical legacy. Restoration of the double parlors and exterior was as accurate to the house's antebellum appearance as possible. Even the types of shrubbery in front of the house are known to have been grown in antebellum Montgomery.

Since 1970, the Murphy House has served as the home of the Water Works and Sanitary Sewer Board—perhaps a fitting use, because, in 1854, John Murphy was one of the incorporators of the city's first water works company.

House of the Mayors

532 South Perry Street

BETWEEN 1849 AND 1853, an Italianate mansion was built on South Perry Street for Jack Thorington, who had been the second mayor (1839–40) after the city's incorporation in 1837. Thorington, a native of Ireland who arrived in Montgomery as a young man, rose to prominence as a merchant and as a lawyer. He became director of the Montgomery branch of the State Bank and president of the Montgomery-Wetumpka plank road company. During the Civil War, he served as a colonel, commanding Hillard's Legion, which he and his law partner, Henry W. Hillard, had raised. Thorington and his second wife, Mary Lord Parker, had four sons born between 1844 and 1848.

In 1868, Mordecai Lyon Moses bought the house for ten thousand dollars, probably from John Whiting, who appears to have traded houses with Jack Thorington in 1854. The mansion was located on South Perry Street, which had been nicknamed, as early as 1860, as Montgomery's Fifth Avenue. In the 1870s, Moses had the Italianate house renovated in the popular Queen Anne style.

In 1861, a year after being graduated from the College of Charleston, Mordecai Moses came to Montgomery to join his brother Alfred. Although he had read law, he worked in his brother's hardware store. He enlisted in the Confederate army, 46th Alabama, but then served as an agent for the Confederacy in Canada and the West Indies.

After the war, the Moses brothers, by then supplemented by the entire Moses family, established a banking, insurance, and real estate firm. The firm prospered and, in 1888, built Montgomery's first skyscraper, a six-story High Victorian building with a central tower, on the northern side of Court Square. The building, which had the city's second elevator, was replaced in 1907 by the First National Bank building that is today hiding behind a modernized exterior at 8 Commerce Street.

Mordecai Moses, who served as president of several companies, was also the city's first Democratic mayor after Reconstruction ended. In 1875, he found the city government pillaged; when he left office after serving three two-year terms, the city's finances were on a sound footing. He then served as president of the Montgomery Gas and Electric Company, the State Fair Association, and the North Alabama Land and Immigration Company. The finances of Moses Brothers, however, did not fare well; they were ruined in 1891. Mordecai, who never married, accompanied his brother Alfred and his family to St. Louis. He sold the house to Joseph Norwood in 1893.

Joseph Norwood, a native of South Carolina, moved to Lowndes County before the Civil War. After attending the Agricultural and Mechanical College at Auburn, he returned to Fort Deposit, where he farmed and ran a mercantile business. From 1885 to 1887, he served as the mayor of that town. He later came to Montgomery and served as the vice-president of the Exchange Bank. His daughter Virginia married E. S. Watts, Sr., son of Thomas Hill Watts, a wartime governor of Alabama. E. S. Watts was an early preservationist who tried to save the 1854/1894 county courthouse; it was demolished in 1958. (Jack Thorington was one of the three commissioners for the 1854 courthouse.)

The House of the Mayors was divided into apartments in 1940; Virginia Watts lived in a second-floor apartment until her death in 1975.

This brick mansion reflects several styles of architecture and decoration. Few visible reminders of the antebellum Italianate mansion have survived. The asymmetrical layout of the house, with the exception of the large bay that was added later, is original. A pair of columns in the entrance hall, and doors and windows with eared architraves and battered jambs (wider at the bottom than at the top) have also been retained.

Gray paint covers the original red brick. Stacked cast-iron porches have replaced the Queen Anne gingerbread porch that was added after the Civil War and removed in 1940. The original treatment of the facade is unknown.

Even the old, decorative metal roof is not original. In the late nineteenth century, the house had a gable over the southeast wing, as well as several dormers on the front elevation. This treatment was Queen Anne, not Italianate. The house's original double-hung windows, probably with six lights in each sash, have been replaced with late-nineteenth-century windows with one light in each sash. The corbelled chimneys are also the result of late-nineteenth-century modernization.

The main entrance, reached by steps, has double doors surmounted by a leaded-glass transom. They open into a small vestibule with a multicolored tile floor and paneled wainscoting. A second pair of doors, with leaded and colored glass, is set in the battered door surround, which is original. The hall has a cove ceiling and quarter-sawn oak flooring bordered with mahogany. It has white and cream door surrounds and wainscoting, pale pink walls, a very wide teal-blue cove cornice, and even some dark purple molding on the mustard ceiling. These colors were taken from the large stained-glass window displayed in the entrance hall.

When the house was converted into apartments in 1940, the High Victorian stair-landing window was removed and left in the back yard. The window was found damaged when the house was restored in 1978. Landmarks Foundation headed a drive to raise the funds necessary to restore the window, which has fine ripple glass of subtle tones, and an unusually large number of faceted "jewels." This glass and the other leaded stained-glass, enhanced with the faceted "jewels," were installed by Mordecai Moses about 1890.

The entrance hall is divided from the stair hall by two free-standing fluted columns with Tower of the Winds Corinthian capitals, similar to those on the porticos of the Capitol and Knox Hall. These columns are survivors from the original Italianate house. The gently rising staircase is a Queen Anne modification to the house. The balustrade, with a very heavy handrail, and the wainscoting that also follows the rise of the staircase, are oak. The house originally had a parlor, living room, dining room, and bedroom on the main floor, and four main rooms on the second floor. Outbuildings, including the original brick kitchen, were demolished in 1940 when a two-story wing was added to the back of the house.

The house features several very fine brass chandeliers, some of which once accommodated both gas and electricity. Although none of these are original to the house, they are from around 1900.

In 1975, the house was destined for demolition by developers when Landmarks Foundation intervened and acquired it. Subsequently, a group of businessmen bought the house in 1978 with the purpose of restoring it. Money for restoration was raised by private contributions of civic-minded citizens, including members of the Thorington, Moses/Loeb, and Norwood/Watts families. After restoration, it was rented to the state and used by the Alabama Bureau of Publicity and Information.

In 1992, the house was acquired from the state for the Montgomery Area United Way as its headquarters. No United Way campaign contributions were used to acquire, remodel, or furnish the house. United Way considers itself a steward of this Montgomery landmark.

IN 1853, JEFFERSON FRANKLIN JACKSON built a simple, but stylish, house befitting his station. He was not only a prominent Whig lawyer, but also the U.S. attorney for Alabama's Middle and Northern Districts, posts assigned to him by presidents Zachary Taylor and Millard Fillmore. Jackson, born in what is now Barbour County in 1821, was graduated from Yale College in 1846. He attended Boston's Cambridge School of Law from 1846 to 1847. A year later, he married Eleanor Clark Noyes, the daughter of a prominent Boston family. In 1860, Eleanor Jackson's mother, Mary Noyes, was living in the Jackson household. Also living in the house was William Wallace Screws, a twenty-one-year-old lawyer, who, after the Civil War, became editor and then publisher of the *Montgomery Advertiser*.

Jackson was a philanthropist who, in 1860, donated land for the Orphan Asylum. Like most Alabama Whigs, he did not favor immediate secession, but hotter heads prevailed. Jackson died in 1862. His widow, who seems to have been an unreconstructed secessionist, was reprimanded by Federal occupation officials for continuing to play "defiant, obnoxious rebel tunes." Thirteen years after her husband's death, she married his former law partner, Thomas Hill Watts, who had been an antisecessionist, but who had nevertheless served as a member of the Confederate cabinet and as Alabama's second wartime governor.

Jackson House

409 South Union Street

Montgomery's Architectural Heritage

The Jackson House is essentially a traditional, or vernacular, house with overlaid Greek Revival and Italianate-style details. Its imposing nature and subtle dignity are the results of its scale and mass and, especially, its siting on terraces made into the rising slope of the hill. Because of the slope, the front of the house is set on high brick piers that have now been filled in with cinder block.

The original house was a rectangular two-story clapboard structure with a low hipped roof and very little decoration. There are small brackets under the eaves. A porch with a standing-seam metal roof extends across the west (front) and north sides. The porch's saw-work balustrade has two differing patterns indicating that there have been alterations. The porch also has slender chamfered columnettes and simple brackets. The four-panel front door has sidelights, a transom, and a pedimented Greek architrave. French doors with transoms and fixed-louver shutters also open onto the porch.

The chimney configurations are unusual. Each of the two chimneys on the south side is decorated with a diamond pattern made of blue headers. These two chimneys follow the usual Southern custom of being external to the walls of the structure. On the north side, however, there is only a single chimney serving back-to-back fireplaces in the four rooms.

Before 1900, the two-story rear porch was enclosed, and other changes and additions were made to the rear of the house. Other than an outbuilding connected to the house in the late nineteenth century, only one outbuilding survives. This shotgun house, probably for servants, predates 1900. A masonry smokehouse, converted into a dwelling house, was demolished in the 1980s because of structural problems.

The original house consisted of two main rooms on either side of a central stair hall. On the main floor, the two rooms on the south side are double parlors, connected by sliding pocket doors. Fireplaces in these rooms are on the exterior walls. The two rooms on the north side are connected by doors on either side of back-to-back fireplaces. French doors with transoms open onto the porch along the west and north sides of the house. The simple door and window surrounds are battered (wider at the bottom than the top) in the Greek Revival style. The high baseboards have a beaded molding. There are identical, simple molded-plaster cornices in each of the main floor rooms. Modest ceiling medallions are in the center of each room. The chandeliers have not survived. French doors with sidelights connect the two front rooms with the front entrance hall; structural evidence suggests that these were once sliding pocket doors similar to those connecting the south parlors.

The front and back entrance halls are separated by a plaster arch, decorated in the classical style, that springs from brackets. The Greek Revival–style doorways at both ends of the hall have sidelights and transoms. The back door has been altered somewhat, because the rear porch has been enclosed. Underneath the straight-run staircase, which rises from the back hall, is a large plastered niche facing the front door.

The four rooms on the second floor are identical in configuration to those on the main floor, but without the sliding pocket doors. The doors are four-panel, with simple surrounds, not in the battered fashion used on the main floor. Heart pine, six-inch floorboards are original. The double-hung windows are in the usual Greek Revival style with six lights in each sash. This window configuration is also used on the main floor, except in the French windows opening onto the porch.

Since 1943, when Jackson's descendants sold the house, it has been owned by the City Federation of Women and Youth Clubs. This federation was organized in 1939 by five black women's clubs, the oldest of which was The Ten Times One is Ten Club, founded in 1888 at the 1872 Congregational Church on High Street (burned 1995). The federation bought the Jackson House to provide a place for black youth activities. When blacks were not allowed to use the Carnegie Library, the city's only public library, one was provided at the Jackson, or Community, House. The library, a branch of the city public library, operated from 1948 until 1962, three years before the city's public library was desegregated. Over the years, the Community House has provided facilities for Girl and Boy Scouts, a kindergarten, Head Start, and teenage school dropouts, as well as for the meetings, seminars, and social events of the federated clubs.

McBryde-Screws-Tyson House

433 Mildred Street

IN JUNE 1853, a month after her husband, Dr. Andrew McBryde, died, Ann Allen McBryde bought a two-acre lot on Mildred Street at the head of South Goldthwaite Street. At the time, it was just beyond the built-up area of town, in what was to become one of Montgomery's most exclusive residential neighborhoods.

Mrs. McBryde was the daughter of Wade Allen, who had come to Alabama from South Carolina in 1817. He had prospered as the first contractor to carry the mail between Montgomery and Mobile, operator of a stagecoach line between Montgomery and Mobile, and a partner in a steamboat line.

Slightly more than a year after her first husband's death, Mrs. McBryde married Benjamin Thiess, a druggist. The house at 433 Mildred Street was built just before or after they were married. They lived there with three McBryde children and three Thiess children. Thiess died in 1862, and his widow lived in the house until 1885, when she sold it to William Wallace Screws for seven thousand dollars.

Screws, a native of Barbour County, came to Montgomery before the Civil War and prepared himself for a career in law. However, his battlefield letters to the *Montgomery Advertiser* were so popular that, on his return, he was given a position with the newspaper and an interest in its ownership. From 1865 until his death in 1913, as editor and later as publisher, he wrote witty, urbane, and conservative editorials on city, state, and regional affairs. He also served as Alabama's secretary of state from 1878 to 1882, as Montgomery's postmaster in 1895, and in the United States Library of Congress during the first Cleveland administration (1884–88).

In 1890, Screws sold the house to John Caius Tyson, a Lowndesboro planter who came to Montgomery that year. Tyson, who was in real estate and the brokerage business, also took an active part in politics, serving several terms as alderman and on the city commission from 1914 to 1918. He was in charge of city finances and administration of the water works. On his death, the house was inherited by his son and daughter, the latter the wife of Thomas W. Martin, president of Alabama Power Company.

The house occupies a commanding location on a terrace at the head of South Goldthwaite Street. Even today the dignified house, the old trees on its grounds, and the two neighboring antebellum mansions at Winter Place help recall the lost beauty of the neighborhood.

This is the most modest of the five remaining Greek Revival–style mansions in the city. It is the only one of frame construction with clapboard siding. In some ways, the house is more akin to country houses in the Carolinas than to a Greek Revival mansion of the Deep South.

The front of the house is dominated by a projecting entrance pavilion three bays wide. The pavilion's portico has four boxed, wooden Doric columns that support a wide entablature with dentils and a paneled parapet. Corners are decorated with pilasters. At the second-floor level is a wooden balcony with turned balusters that extends across the entire three bays.

The door to the balcony and the front door are similar. Both are framed by squared Doric pilasters, entablature with dentils, sidelights, and transoms. Fixed louvers shield the doors, sidelights, and transoms. (In normal use, the sidelights and transoms were probably removed for the summer.) The textured glass in the first-floor sidelights and transom is not original, although some of the original ruby glass survives on the second floor.

The house has retained its four exterior brick chimneys and its Greek Revival–style double-hung windows with six lights in each sash. All windows have external louvered shutters. The house is raised on piers that are filled with brick or brick lattice. The one-story open porch on the east side, which may have been added in the 1890s, has chamfered columnettes and saw-work trim and balustrade.

Whereas the exterior has retained its Greek Revival appearance, the interior was Victorianized in 1890. Most of this was stripped in the 1980s.

The hall is shaped like an upside-down T, with the entrance in the

Montgomery's Architectural Heritage

center of the crossbar, flanked by two floor-to-ceiling windows. This very unusual arrangement results in a foyer spanning the three bays of the pavilion. The staircase, with Greek Revival newel post and turned balusters, is along the stem of the T. The staircase rises to a landing where it divides; one part rises to the second-story front hall and front bedrooms, and the other to a landing and the back bedrooms.

On either side of the central hall are double parlors connected by sliding pocket doors. The double parlors on the east have doors accessing the side porch. The double parlors on the west were originally one great hall, separated by four tapered hexagonal columns, which are now partially concealed in the wall between the two rooms. In 1890, the rear parlor was altered with the installation of raised-panel wainscoting, a raised-panel frieze, and a ceiling of molded box beams and diagonal beadboard paneling. A similar ceiling is in one of the second-floor bedrooms.

There are four bedrooms on the second floor. Like the rooms below, they are also connected, two by sliding pocket doors and two by a double folding door. The bedroom windows are unusual in that they extend almost to the floor, but are considerably short of the ceiling. This is because of the width of the exterior entablature. Two of the bedrooms have original, simple Greek Revival mantels. Each of the two front bedrooms has an adjoining small room with a floor-to-ceiling window; these rooms are directly over the unusual foyer.

Parquet floors, installed in 1890, cover the original pine on the first floor. Original, high molded baseboards survive. The original Greek Revival four-paneled doors and wide, heavy door and window surrounds also survived the 1890 modernization.

The kitchen is in a wing off the southwest corner of the house. There are other attachments to the back of the house, including bathrooms on the east side of the rear porch.

The house was unoccupied from the early 1940s until the late 1990s.

FROM 1854 TO 1856, John Dickerson built a fine house in the Italianate style. This and the Greek Revival style were the two popular antebellum styles in Montgomery. Jacob Greil, a former Confederate officer who became a leading businessman and civic leader, acquired the house in 1878. It remained in the Greil family until 1920. The house was known as the Greil House for more than a century.

Today, the house is known as the 1861–62 residence of Governor John Gill Shorter and his wife, Mary Jane Battle of Eufaula. A native of Georgia, Shorter came to Alabama in 1837 after having been graduated from Franklin College (University of Georgia). He worked as an attorney. An ardent secessionist, he defeated Thomas Hill Watts for governor in 1861. In the early years of the war, Union troops invaded north Alabama and inflicted savage destruction. Consequently, Confederate patriotism degenerated into reluctant support and eventually into obstructionism. The "peace society" almost rose in armed rebellion in north Alabama.

In 1863, Watts defeated Governor Shorter by a four-to-one margin. Watts, who had been a Whig and a strong antisecessionist, became a seces-

Governor Shorter House

305 South Lawrence Street

Montgomery's Architectural Heritage

sionist after Abraham Lincoln's election. He raised his own regiment and later served as attorney general in the Confederate cabinet. His governorship was extremely difficult. Alabama also elected six pacifists to the Confederate Congress, a sign of widespread defeatism and opposition to Jefferson Davis.

With Governor Shorter's defeat, the mansion on South Lawrence Street stopped serving as the governor's mansion. As there was no official residence for the governor, Governor Watts lived in his own high-style Italianate villa at the southeast corner of Adams and Ripley streets.

John Dickerson's two-story, red-brick Italianate house has undergone several major remodelings. The main block's six-over-six window lights and cast-iron window hoods have survived. The full, sunken basement with large, round-headed arched openings, shouldered window jambs, and fireplaces also seems little changed.

In the remodeling of the 1890s, the interior was Victorianized. The double front door surmounted by a single-light transom probably dates from this time. Also from this period is the surviving interior woodwork, such as mitered window and door surrounds, four-panel doors, raised-panel wainscoting, and unusual High Victorian surrounds with a heavy, hooded entablature of the three staircase windows.

The most dramatic remodeling was in 1910. At that time, if not earlier, the house was covered with cement and scored to resemble stone, exterior louvered shutters were removed, and the wooden porch with saw-work balustrade and standing-seam metal roof was removed. Marble steps and a marble-floored portico with six fluted Tuscan columns were added to the front of the house. A small wrought-iron balcony was added over the front door. During the period of Montgomery's second cotton fortunes, numerous older houses were updated in the so-called Colonial Revival style.

In the 1910 remodeling, a new dining room was constructed. It was once considered to be one of the most magnificent rooms in Alabama. The five-foot solid-mahogany raised paneling, topped with a running Greek key band, is separated into bays by sixteen mahogany, Roman Doric fluted pilasters. Above the paneling and between the pilasters are rectangular inset plaster panels. The room has a full Roman Doric frieze and a broad projecting cornice, both of mahogany. The fireplace, flanked by free-standing Roman Doric fluted columns, has a simple mantel; the firebox is surrounded by three white marble slabs. The modified cove ceiling features box beams and a skylight. Opposite the built-in mahogany sideboard backed with a horizontal mirror is an unusual triple window.

Though there have been interior alterations since 1920, some of the simple antebellum mantels survive, as does evidence of the sliding doors connecting the double parlors on the north side of the house, and of the sliding doors connecting these two rooms to the central hall.

After the house passed out of the Greil family, it was occupied by the

University Club (1920), State Board of Education (1929), and Junior League (1968). In November 1973, while the house was occupied by the Junior League, Alabama Historical Commission, and Dixie Boys Club, there was an extremely destructive fire after a late-night party. Not only was the house extensively damaged and the magnificent staircase completely lost, but historical records were lost. These included six thousand photographs, hundreds of slides, and three hundred books. After the fire, Landmarks Foundation became the caretaker and oversaw the subsequent restoration.

The house is currently owned by Montgomery County and is occupied by Haskell, Slaughter, Young, and Gallion, L.L.C.

St. Peter's Roman Catholic Church

219 Adams Avenue

THE FIRST ROMAN CATHOLIC mass celebrated in what is now Montgomery County may have been said by Spanish priests accompanying Hernando de Soto's 1539–42 expedition. Montgomery's first public Roman Catholic mass was celebrated at the Masonic Hall in 1831. In April 1834, a Roman Catholic church was consecrated by Bishop Michael Portier of Mobile. The small frame building was located at the corner of Adams Avenue and South Lawrence Street, on land given by Edward Hanrick. The first priest was Father Gabriel Chalon, a cousin of Bishop Portier.

The parish grew slowly in what was essentially a Protestant town. But the parish was not isolated from the wider Roman Catholic world. In February of 1850, Father Theobold Matthews, Ireland's "Apostle of Temperance," preached in Montgomery. He administered the pledge to hundreds of citizens. (How successful these citizens were in maintaining their pledges is not known. Public drunkenness and rowdiness remained a serious problem in the city until well after the street fairs were ended and the state fair was moved to Birmingham in 1888.)

In 1854, twenty years after the consecration of the first church building, the core of the present St. Peter's Church was consecrated by Bishop Timon of Louisiana, assisted by Bishop Portier. The building cost seven thousand dollars, which was paid in gold.

The Spanish Colonial style of today's building, with its stuccoed walls and red-tile roof, may seem strange for antebellum Alabama, especially in what was essentially an Irish parish. But the building's original appearance was quite different, having been built in the Romanesque Revival style. Today, St. Peter's is the oldest Romanesque Revival building in Alabama.

The building's Spanish Colonial–style exterior has been attributed to the source of the building's financing. Father Anthony Dominic Pellicer, the parish's priest from 1850 to 1864, first got financial support in Mexico. When he was returning to the United States, however, bandits held up his stagecoach on the road to Vera Cruz. He then went to Cuba to get financial support for construction. Father Pellicer was later made the first bishop of San Antonio, Texas.

The asymmetrical facade with two towers, the most Spanish Colonial aspect of the building, was not completed until 1882, when twenty-five feet was added to the front of the 1854 building. The taller of the two towers projects from the southwest corner of the building. Both this square tower, with its belfry, and the smaller, circular tower projecting from the northwest corner of the facade, are capped by small red domes surmounted by crosses. Both combine Spanish Colonial and classical decorative elements.

The building's interior is Romanesque Revival, not Spanish Colonial. Except for the old baptistry in the base of the smaller tower, and the entrance and staircase to the organ and choir loft in the larger tower, the interior follows the rectangular basilica plan that has been used for church buildings since the fourth century. The nave, with its high vaulted ceiling, is separated from the flanking aisles by a row of cluster columns with floriated Romanesque capitals, from which spring arches that extend the entire length of the nave. The aisle ceilings are flat and not as high as the nave's vaulted ceiling. In 2000, a polychrome coffered ceiling, modeled on Bramante's ceiling of the Altar of the Chair in St. Peter's Basilica in Rome, was added to the nave's vault.

The building follows the ancient practice of being oriented to the east; that is, worshipers face the altar on the east wall. The three wooden altars in the Victorian Romanesque style rise almost to ceiling height. The altars,

Montgomery's Architectural Heritage

which are painted cream and trimmed in gold, incorporate tabernacles and niches for polychrome, full-round statuary. The high altar has a statue of Christ flanked by two angels; the altar to the left, the Blessed Virgin; and the altar to the right, St. Joseph and the Holy Child. These altars replaced less elaborate ones that were in place before the 1890s. Above the original high altar was an apse with wall paintings.

The large, round-headed aisle windows are filled with stained and painted glass in the Victorian style—realistic, large-scale figures. The windows on the north side are associated with the evangelists and the life of Christ. With the exception of the baptism of Jesus, the windows on the south side are associated with the Old Testament. Two windows at the back are memorials to those who served in the army and navy during World War I. The parish priest himself had served as a chaplain in France. These fourteen richly colored windows, made by Emil Frei Art Glass Company of St. Louis and Munich, date from 1922. When these windows were installed, the side balconies were removed. Between the windows are exceptionally fine, polychrome plaster stations of the cross in full round.

After almost thirty years of silence, the restored 1891 Kilgen tracker organ pipes and new pipe organ were dedicated in 1992. The pipes are decorated with their original stenciling in gray, blue, olive, and brown; although new, the gold and silver leaf is identical to the original design. This organ is the largest functioning pipe organ in the city.

The 1969 rectory, offices, and parish hall complement the Spanish Colonial style of the church building to the north. Originally, there was a two-story Victorian rectory on this site.

Montgomery's Roman Catholic educational institutions date from 1873. The 1951 St. Mary's of Loretto High School replaced two earlier schools, one for boys and one for girls, both of which were housed in antebellum Greek Revival mansions: the Jourdan mansion at the corner of Adams Avenue and South McDonough Street, and the Gerald-Bethea mansion at the corner of Adams Avenue and South Lawrence Street. St. Peter's parish was also responsible for establishing St. Margaret's Hospital (1902–88).

Although relatively small in number compared with the Protestant majority, Roman Catholics were prominent in the city. Indicative of the city's religious tolerance was the election of Mordecai Moses, a Charleston Jew, as mayor (1875–81) and Thomas Carr, an Irish-born, Northern-reared Roman Catholic, as mayor (1903–05). The latter's election was also an example of socioeconomic mobility that had characterized the city from its founding. Thomas Carr was an active layman at St. Peter's.

St. Peter's is the site of the annual Red Mass at the beginning of the judicial year. This celebration is named after the red vestments of the celebrants; red symbolizes the tongues of fire at Pentecost and, hence, the Holy Spirit. Although an ancient ceremony, it was begun in Montgomery in 1973 at the request of Alabama Supreme Court Chief Justice Howell Heflin, who had previously observed the ceremony in New Orleans.

MONTGOMERY'S first Episcopal parish was organized in 1834. Its parishioners met in the Baptist and Universalist church buildings until the parish built a small church at the southeast corner of North Perry and Jefferson streets, the first brick church in Montgomery. This modest building, with only forty-eight pews, served the Episcopal parish until 1855, when the present building was constructed. The old building was given to the black communicants; consequently, the new building did not have the customary slave balcony, although it did have an organ and choir loft at the rear of the nave.

The new building was designed by Frank Wills, an Englishman working in New York. Although he did not have the reputation of Richard Upjohn or James Renwick, Wills and his partner Henry Dudley were major architects in what can be called the Episcopal school of architecture, or the "ecclesiological movement." This movement was based on the Cambridge, England, Camden Society's bimonthly publication, *The Ecclesiologist*, which promoted fine Gothic design.

This turn away from the Georgian and Greek Revival styles was influenced by the fashion for the picturesque (perhaps begun by the Romantic Movement) and the association of classical styles with pagan antiquity, and of medieval styles with the Christian Age of Faith. In the Anglican/Episcopal Church, Gothic Revival was also influenced by the return to spirituality and a more medieval liturgy promoted by the Oxford Movement.

The horizontal, symmetrical, and static emphasis of classical architecture gave way to the vertical, irregular, and dynamic Gothic Revival style or to the horizontal, symmetrical, and rhythmical Romanesque Revival style. Episcopalians, Roman Catholics, and Presbyterians tended to build in the spiritual Gothic Revival style, whereas Baptists, Congregationalists, and Methodists tended to build in the more severe Romanesque Revival style. (This generality did not hold in Montgomery, where, perhaps, the logic behind the styles may not have been understood, and where taste alone may have led to choice of building styles.)

St. John's 115-foot tower and spire, attached to the southwest corner of the rectangular building, is the most distinguishing feature of the exterior. It rises from a two-story square base supported by stepped corner buttresses to the belfry with louvered lancet openings. The belfry transitions to an octagonal, crenellated parapet. The octagonal parapet spire, which has Gothic, louvered spire-light openings, is topped with a six-foot bronze cross.

Attached stepped buttresses separate the nave's seven bays, each of which has an arched window. The nave and tower have a heavy, molded drip-course. Originally, the stuccoed exterior was scored to resemble stone; waterproofing, painting, and repairing the stucco have obscured the scoring. The steeply pitched roof is covered with metal shingles, painted red.

The facade, also supported by buttresses, is decorated by a large central stained glass window with geometric tracery in the style of the four-

St. John's Episcopal Church

113 Madison Avenue

76

A Sense of Place

teenth century. There are two entrances to the nave, one in the base of the tower and the other in the center of the gabled facade, the latter flanked by two Gothic windows with bar tracery. Both the doors and windows have hood molding.

The arch-braced roof is supported by huge curved timbers springing from stone corbel brackets between the windows. There are iron tiebars at the top of the nave walls; perhaps the weight of the roof cannot be supported by the buttresses alone. The nave's crenellated cornice is said to be "symbolic of the warfare to be waged against the world, the flesh, and the devil."

The long, wide nave with center and side aisles originally had a plastered ceiling divided by ribs into sections. The ceiling was intended to have polychromatic decorations. This was not completed, perhaps because the building cost twenty-seven thousand dollars rather than the sixteen thousand dollars that had been estimated. In 1869, the original plaster ceiling, which was intended to resemble stone vaulting, was replaced by wood, painted midnight blue, and stenciled with forty large gold medallions.

The chancel was built in 1869–70 from the salvaged brick of the 1837 church building. It was doubled in size in 1906. The chancel is not as wide as the nave, and its roof is not as high. When the 1837 building was demolished, the organ and choir stalls were moved to the new chancel to make room for the black communicants in the former organ and choir loft. The organ and choir were returned to the loft in 1961, long after the Church of the Good Shepherd was founded in 1900 for the parish's black communicants. (St. John's is noted for the superior quality of its sacred music. The forty-two-rank Wicks organ, modeled on Baroque organs, is one of the finest in the Southeast.)

It is not surprising that the church whose rolls have included many of the city's most prominent citizens would be richly decorated. All the memorial windows are stained or painted glass; they illustrate the changing fashions in stained glass over the years. Furnishings and decorations reflect Victorian sentimentalities and taste. Memorials include Gothic-arched brass doors at the front of the nave, a thirteenth-century-style marble baptismal font, a fifteenth-century-style brass eagle lectern that represents St. John the Evangelist covering the world with the Gospel, an intricate brass raised pulpit, two large brass angels flanking the chancel steps, two large marble angels supporting a seven-branch candelabra flanking the altar, a brass-framed reredos, and four large brass plaques on which are engraved the Ten Commandments, the Lord's Prayer, and the Apostles' Creed.

A church so old and with strong connections to the life of the city and the region, such as having been instrumental in the founding of the University of the South at Sewanee, cannot but have an interesting history.

At the end of the Civil War, when the state was under U.S. military rule, the Right Reverend Richard Hooker Wilmer, Bishop of Alabama, suspended the prayer for the president of the United States and for all in civil authority. Bishop Wilmer's reasoning was that there was no civil authority, only martial law. On September 20, 1865, Major General Charles Woods, who was not amused, forbade all Episcopal clergy from preaching and conducting divine services in any Episcopal church in the diocese of Alabama. The ban on public worship was not lifted until January 10, 1866, three days before restoration of civil authority. The bishop had upheld the principle that the state cannot interfere with freedom of worship.

Although Montgomery does not have a cathedral to serve the civic and spiritual needs of the whole city, St. John's has often performed that role. For example, on September 2, 1945, after citizens spontaneously went to Court Square to celebrate the end of World War II, hundreds of people of many faiths went to St. John's to give thanks for the end of the war.

The church has ministered beyond its own communicants. It was among the pioneers in social ministry in the city's West End; it led the fight against gross abuse of child labor. At the turn of the century, a quarter of Alabama's textile workers were younger than sixteen years old; the rector of St. John's led a state and then a national campaign to rectify this abuse. St. John's provided a place of worship for gypsies, for wintering circus folk, and for Greek Orthodox and Lutheran congregations before they built their own houses of worship.

During the Great Depression, the rector of St. John's often preached that "a parish that lives only for itself is doomed. Others first." This principle still guides St. John's Episcopal Church.

AROUND 1850, Pickett Chauncey Smith came to Montgomery from Connecticut. By 1859, he had acquired a wife, Edna Terry Smith, and vehicles, livestock, six slaves, and four thousand dollars worth of real estate. Records differ as to his occupation; he may have been a doctor, a lawyer, or even a grocer. (His son was a Commerce Street retail grocer.) Included in his land holdings were six lots on Alabama Street between South Hull and South McDonough streets, which he bought in 1854 for $2,100. Chauncey and Edna Smith lived in an Italianate-style cottage at the east end of the block and Miss Jane E. Smith, who seems not to have been a relative, lived in a similar house, built about 1855, at the west end of the block.

In 1876, the Smiths' daughter, Elizabeth, married Edwin Joseph, a partner, with his father, in the Capital City Insurance Company. From about 1880 until 1885, the Josephs occupied the cottage at 302 Alabama Street. After the deaths of Chauncey and Edna Smith, the Josephs built a two-story house to replace the Italianate cottage on the eastern end of the block. This reflected Joseph's business successes. Edwin Joseph was president of

Smith-Joseph-Stratton House

302 Alabama Street

the Capital City Insurance Company; an original investor and the first president of Montgomery's electric trolley system; a land speculator investing in Highland Park, Montgomery's first suburb; and president of the Highland Park Improvement Company. He also sat on the city council for six years and served as mayor from 1899 to 1903. His health forced him to retire, and he died two years later.

After the Josephs moved, Chauncey Smith, Jr., a Commerce Street retail grocer, his wife, Annie, and their children occupied the cottage at the western end of the block. The cottage passed out of the Smith estate in 1913 when it was bought by Judge Asa Evans Stratton, a man of letters and a referee in bankruptcy cases. In 1899, Judge Stratton had come to Montgomery from Texas, where he had served in the Texas House and Senate and as a district attorney and judge of probate. He lived in the cottage until his death in 1921. Judge Stratton's widow lost the cottage to foreclosure in 1940. It was subsequently partitioned down the center with Elizabeth Gardiner living on one side and Maude Brewer living on the other.

The Smith-Joseph-Stratton cottage is representative of a nineteenth-century and early-twentieth-century middle-class dwelling. Being one of only a few surviving antebellum Italianate cottages, it is also representative of an architectural style.

The frame cottage, five bays wide and two bays deep, is raised on brick piers, originally filled by lattice. Paired brackets support the cornice of the hipped roof. Between the brackets are elongated diamond-shaped saw-work ventilators. The double-hung windows are in the Italianate style with six lights in each sash. The windows have exterior, louvered shutters. The space of three feet between the top of the windows and the fascia is unusual and cannot be explained by the height of the ceilings, as the windows are almost floor to ceiling.

The three-bay attached porch with chamfered columnettes and saw-work balustrade and brackets is not original, but is based on physical evidence and Italianate decorative practices. The Italianate four-panel door and the sidelights and transom, which are not original, are also based on physical and stylistic evidence.

The original cottage, consisting of five principal rooms, may have had other rooms attached at the rear, and certainly would have had several outbuildings.

The entrance hall and the rooms to its right and left have six-inch, quarter-cut pine floor boards that run the entire length of the rooms. Window and door surrounds are very simple. The four-panel doors have long upper panels and short lower panels. The original walls were plaster over lathe. Two internal chimneys originally served back-to-back fireplaces in four rooms. The northwest room has the only original configuration—a simple, cast-iron mantel for a coal-burning fire. The northeast room has a period mantel, not original to the house. The fireplaces in the other two rooms that were once served by the interior chimneys have been closed. The piping for gas lighting was removed during restoration.

The entrance hall opens into a large room, almost square, that was probably in the rear of the cottage when it was built. Because the rear porch was enclosed about 1910, this room is now in the middle of the building.

Because the block on which the cottage is built is only about one hundred feet deep, there is little room for gardens in the rear. Originally, a service yard was behind the house. A one-story, two-room, center-chimney servants' house stands on the southwest corner of the property.

In 1983, the cottage and servants' house were bought, saved from demolition, and restored by Richard Jordan. The cottage is occupied by the law firm of Richard Jordan, Randy Myers, and Ben Locklar, P.C.

Gerald-Dowdell House

405 South Hull Street

PERLEY S. GERALD, a native of New York, settled in Montgomery in the 1830s. He worked as a civil engineer, an Indian trader, and as postmaster at Line Creek, east of Montgomery. He then went to the California gold fields, where he made a small fortune. He returned to Montgomery and by the mid-1850s he and his wife, Camilla, built one of the finest mansions in the city. (This mansion, at the southeast corner of Adams Avenue and South Lawrence Street, was razed in 1964. It was built on a raised basement. Its portico, with six fluted columns and Corinthian capitals, was reached by bowlegged stairs.) By 1856, financial reversals required the Geralds to sell the mansion and build a modest house, which they sold in 1859. In the 1860 census, he is recorded as a stablekeeper, but Camilla is recorded as holding fifteen thousand dollars in real estate as well as a twenty-thousand-dollar personal estate. At the time, three children, ages thirteen, seventeen, and twenty, lived with them.

Subsequently, the house was occupied by a series of owners and renters. One notable occupant who lived in the house from 1940 to 1949 was Robert T. Simson, an associate justice of the Alabama Supreme Court. The house was saved from demolition, which was to have made way for a service station, by Mrs. Annie S. Dowdell.

The Gerald-Dowdell House is one of the few raised cottages remaining in Montgomery. (Before remodeling early in this century, the ca. 1861 Dowe House at 334 Washington Street was an Italianate raised cottage with bowlegged wooden stairs to its second-story porch. Although not recognizable from the street, the ca. 1860 Opp Cottage at 33 West Jeff Davis Avenue is also a raised cottage.)

Raised cottages are usually associated with the coastal areas of the South. In an attempt to accommodate the hot, humid climate, living rooms were on the second floor, whereas work rooms, and perhaps the dining room, were on the ground floor. Consequently, the ground floor would be used during the hotter days, and the second floor during the cooler evenings and nights.

This arrangement also conformed to the mistaken belief that fevers came from the bad air and damp earth at night. It was late in the century that General William Crawford Gorgas was able to establish the connection between mosquitoes and yellow fever. (His parents' house on the University of Alabama campus is a magnificent ca. 1829 brick raised cottage.)

To ensure that the Geralds' cottage's first floor would be as cool as possible, it was constructed of masonry. It is literally the ground floor, as its herringbone-pattern brick floor is laid directly on the ground. The walls and piers of the raised basement are also of brick, which has been stuccoed and scored to resemble stone. The ground floor is further decorated with quoins at each corner.

Today the gallery, which is enclosed with lattice, has five openings, one on either end and three in front. Previously, there were only two openings in the front, one on either side of the central bay. The entrance to the cottage, once shielded by lattice, is by a door opening in the center of the ground floor gallery, rather than by an external staircase as was common in most raised cottages.

The second floor is of frame construction clad in lapped siding. The porch, which extends across the entire front, helps shield the house from the afternoon sun and provides a relatively cooler living space for the evenings. Exterior shutters with movable louvers once provided further protection from the summer sun. Cooling is also aided by the extremely high ceilings on the second floor, the many large windows, and a central hall that facilitates cross-ventilation. Round ventilators between the paired Italianate-style brackets under the eaves helped hot air escape from the attic of the low-pitched, shingle, hipped roof.

The most distinctive exterior decoration is the second-floor porch's Victorian saw-work balustrade and bracket trim for the columnettes. The octagonal columnettes have modified Doric caps. The door on the second floor, like that on the first, is in the Italianate style, with sidelights and a transom. Some of the acid-etched glass is original.

Architectural decoration of the interior of this 42-by-26-foot cottage is confined to the modified Greek Revival design of the simple mantels of the back-to-back fireplaces. Nevertheless, generous dimensions of the four rooms, T-shaped halls on both floors, high baseboards and simple door and window facings, and high ceilings of the second floor, produce an understated, restrained elegance.

The basement's brick floor, the heart-pine flooring, coal grates, six-over-six double-hung windows, and four-paneled doors with rim locks and porcelain knobs are all original. The internal staircase is a reproduction based on an old photograph.

The vertical board-and-batten building at the cottage's rear (412 Scott Street Grocery) was a dependency of the Gerald-Dowdell House.

Fine, Geddie, and Associates, a governmental affairs and legislative services firm, restored the cottage. The Gerald-Dowdell House is now owned and occupied by the law firm of Brantley, Wilkerson & Bryan, P.C., which has constructed an architecturally sympathetic addition at the rear.

IN DECEMBER 1856, Montgomery's *Daily Messenger* gushed with civic pride in its description of the Central Bank building. It likened the new building to the "palatial buildings" of New York's Broadway and noted that "Montgomery is already far in advance of most Southern cities as regards fine storehouses, princely private residences and elegant equipages."

William Knox, president of the newly formed Central Bank, had engaged Stephen Decatur Button, a prominent Philadelphia architect, to design the bank building. A decade earlier, Button had designed the Greek Revival–style 1846–49 State Capitol, for which Knox was a building commissioner, as well as Knox's own "princely private residence" on South Perry Street.

▼

Central Bank of Alabama Building

1 Dexter Avenue

Montgomery's Architectural Heritage

In the 1850s, the Greek Revival style declined in popularity as the Italianate style became more popular. Reputedly, Button used fifteenth-century Venetian palaces as the inspiration for the bank building. Italian-inspired features include the tall arched windows, sculptural ornamentation, and layered wall surfaces.

The contractor of the Central Bank building was George M. Figh, son of John P. Figh, who built many of Montgomery's finest brick antebellum structures. (In the late 1820s, the father built the first University of Alabama, based roughly on Thomas Jefferson's plan for the University of Virginia; from April 1867 to July 1868, the son rebuilt the campus that had been largely destroyed by Union troops.)

The ornate decorative features, including the ornamental window surrounds, were made of cast iron that was attached to a painted masonry structure. The Dexter Avenue elevation was Montgomery's first iron facade. (Some iron facades had previously been erected in Mobile.) Iron decorative features, which were relatively inexpensive ways to simulate stone, were later replaced by pressed metal and terra-cotta. The window surrounds and applied decorative treatments of the upper two stories are relatively unchanged, as are the overhanging eaves supported by paired brackets.

The Dexter Avenue ground-floor facade no longer has its iron decorative work, although it has been restored to resemble its original appearance. The Court Square ground-floor facade, originally almost identical to the second floor, now has projecting show windows with marble bases and handsome metal roofs that were installed after 1923.

The bank, built on a four-foot granite foundation, was originally reached by several steps on either side of a projecting stoop flanked by two lamp standards. The street level has since been raised.

The ground floor, with its twenty-foot ceiling, was the banking house; the upper floors were used for the offices of the president and cashier, and for the living quarters of the latter. No evidence of the appearance of the ground-floor banking house has survived; the only visible reminders of the once elegant second and third floors are the wide window surrounds and the fixed-louver shutters that fold into the window jambs. The second floor's fifteen-foot ceilings and the third floor's twelve-foot ceilings indicate the building's original scale; at sixty-five feet, the bank towered over nearby three-story buildings.

Central Bank, having been a major financial backer of the Confederacy, did not survive the Civil War. The bank failed in 1865 and Knox died four years later. The building was subsequently occupied by other banks, a business college, realtors, insurance companies, and a beauty shop. Rooms were rented on the upper floors.

In 1881, fifteen-year-old Leo Klein emigrated to the United States from his native Hungary. In 1893 he established a firm that became Klein and

Son Jewelers. His first Montgomery store, 7-1/2 North Court Street, was ten feet wide and thirty feet deep. In addition to jewelry, he sold sporting goods and toys. He later moved to the former Central Bank building. Klein and Sons Jewelers occupied the Montgomery landmark from 1923 until 1983.

The first-floor configuration and the display windows on the building's Court Square facade date from Klein's occupancy. Bow-leg stairs rise to the mezzanine that encircles the entire room. The balustrades of the stairs and mezzanine are of delicate wrought and cast iron. The room has applied friezes that use classical motifs.

Klein's eighteen-foot street clock was probably more of a Montgomery landmark than the jewelry store. From about 1940 until 1983, the ornate four-faced clock with large Arabic numerals stood on a Corinthian column just to the southwest of the jewelry store. It is now at Klein's Zelda Place location.

The exterior of the building was restored in 1985. With the exception of the counters and display cabinets, the ground floor was retained as it had been during Klein's ownership. For several years, the ground floor served as the Alabama Artists Gallery, a showcase of Alabama art and artists. The upper floors were used as the offices of the Alabama State Council on the Arts.

At the same time that the former Central Bank building was being restored, the adjoining Maner Building at 10 Court Square was also restored to its nineteenth-century appearance. With its arched dormers and Mansard roof, it is one of a handful of surviving Second Empire–style buildings in Montgomery. The LeGrand Building and the old city hall, both dating to 1871, were also in this style.

Brittan House

507 Columbus Street

IN 1857, ORA BRITTAN acquired the lot at 507 Columbus Street. The following year, she and her husband, Patrick Henry Brittan, built what is today one of the finest antebellum brick cottages remaining in Montgomery. In 1858, it was one of the more pretentious houses in a neighborhood of predominantly frame houses. Today it is the only antebellum house remaining on the block.

Patrick Henry Brittan, son of an Irish immigrant, was born in Virginia in 1815. He learned the printing trade in Washington and then moved to Columbus, Georgia, where he practiced the trade until 1843. After founding a newspaper in Lafayette, he moved to Montgomery in 1847. He was part owner of three newspapers, one of which became the first paper in Alabama to use steam printing (1853). From 1850 to 1856 he was the state printer, and from 1856 to 1859 he was Alabama's quartermaster general. Because he supported the national Democratic Party through the *Daily Messenger*, which he founded in 1856 and which merged with the *Confederation* in 1858, he came into conflict with William Lowndes Yancey and the Southern League. Nevertheless, he became Alabama's secretary of state in 1859 and served in that position until 1865. Brittan died in 1868, shortly after his wife had deeded the cottage to their daughter Kate, Mrs. John T. Simpson. She sold it to Charles W. Norton.

The one-story, red-brick cottage is in the Italianate style, the most fashionable style in Montgomery just before the Civil War. Besides being stylish, the building takes the climate into consideration by being of solid brick construction (except for the hall walls, which are lathe over timber framing). The exterior and interior solid-brick walls rise from the foundations. A porch that wraps around more than half of the house is built on brick piers; wood lattice has replaced the original brick lattice between the piers. Large windows with exterior shutters (now removed) and fourteen-foot ceilings also helped keep the house cool during the oppressive summer heat. Roof ventilators and interconnecting rooms facilitated good cross-ventilation.

The house is T-shaped. The U-shaped porch, with its original boxed wooden columns, covers the five bays on the front of the cottage and two bays on either side. The porch ends, at the crossbar of the T, in French doors that give access to bedrooms. The porch roof has paired brackets. There is a wide wooden fascia with paired drip brackets supporting the eaves. The low-pitched roof is hipped.

Shortly after the cottage was built, it appears that a brick, shed-like structure was added to the rear. It consists of a room on either side of a central porch; the porch was enclosed with wood in the late 1950s.

The aesthetic appeal of the house is its simplicity, proportions, and symmetry. There is, however, some decoration in addition to the brackets. The double-hung windows, with six lights in each sash, have fine jack, or flat, arches, and projecting brick sills. The main door has a bracketed entablature and is flanked with paneled pilasters. The door itself has two long arched panels above two short rectangular ones. The side lights and transom are of etched ruby glass.

The main entrance opens into a central hall that gives access to 17-by-17-foot parlors on either side and to a large central room at the back. The latter was probably the dining room. On either side of the central room are 21-by-21-foot bedrooms. These have access to the porch by French doors, as well as to the front parlors.

The pine floorboards extend from wall to wall. The molded baseboards are very high. Window and door surrounds are wide, but simple. The pine doors, now unpainted, have four molded panels. The simple mantels, also now unpainted, have pilasters supporting a wide shelf; cast-iron surrounds enclose the coal-burning grates. Picture molding in the parlors and entrance hall is gold-leafed. Like the exterior, the interior's aesthetic appeal is really due to simplicity and good proportions.

The cottage has an unusual feature for the period: closets. There are two closets in one bedroom, and one closet apiece in the other bedroom and in the dining room. The four closets are between the dining room and the bedrooms. This wall, which at first appears to be very thick, is shouldered or rounded in the bedroom. (The 1848 Ordeman-Shaw House in Old Alabama Town also has closets.)

The cottage is exceptional because it has been so little altered for a house of its age. Nevertheless, the porch decking is not original, nor is the balustrade, although it probably approximates the original. The bathroom, added early in the century, is a frame structure at the rear. The original kitchen wing has been removed and the chimneys have been cut off below roof level.

After passing out of Charles Norton's hands, the cottage was owned by a conductor of the Western Railroad and by a grocer. From 1957 to 1979, it was an antique shop. In 1979, the house was restored and used as the publishing offices for *Softball Players Magazine*. In 1995, Colonial Bank gave the Brittan House to Landmarks Foundation.

Winter Place

450 and 454
South Goldthwaite Street

COLONEL Joseph Samuel Prince Winter and his wife, Mary Elizabeth Gindrat, built Montgomery's finest Italianate mansion at the northwest corner of Madison Avenue and North Perry Street. This circa 1851 house, designed by Samuel Sloan of Philadelphia, one of the nation's foremost architects, may have been one of the finest Italianate mansions in the country. It was razed in 1919.

The Winters were among Montgomery's most prominent families. They were not, however, planters whose wealth was based on land and slaves. Rather, they had interests in the iron works, banking, railroads, steamboats, and even the ill-fated sixty-mile plank toll road from Wetumpka to Winterboro, which was to have connected the Alabama and Tennessee rivers. Plank roads, an idea borrowed from Russia, did not hold up well in the Southern climate.

The Winters were adversely affected as banks failed and railroad stock fell during the national panic of 1854, which was caused by reckless speculation. The Winters were forced to trade their high-style Italianate mansion for Fleming Freeman's Federal-style clapboard house at 301 Bibb Street. About 1855, the Winters remodeled the house in the Italianate style. This house, now located at 644 Washington Street, is better known as the First White House of the Confederacy.

The Winters then bought, for one thousand dollars, the triangular block bordered by South Goldthwaite, Mildred, and Mobile streets. (After 1890, portions of this tract were sold off.) About 1858, they began building two houses at the southeast corner of their triangular block. Construction was well under way when it had to stop because of the Civil War.

Joseph Winter was one of fourteen children; he and his wife had only three: John Gindrat, Lucy, and Sallie Gindrat. John, who served as a captain of infantry in the Confederate army, was captured and imprisoned. However, Joseph's father, John Gano Winter, had significant business interests, as well as deep family roots, in New York. The senior Winter, therefore, was neutral. He hoped to wait out the war in Montgomery, but conditions deteriorated. In 1863, he took his two granddaughters to Wales for the duration

Montgomery's Architectural Heritage

of the war. They came under fire as they sneaked out of Apalachicola on a blockade runner.

After the war ended, part of the family lived in New York, where Joseph Winter practiced law. In 1871, the family returned to Montgomery, bringing with them James Lahey, a young Irishman whom John Winter had met in prison. Lahey married Lucy Winter.

The Winters' intention before the war was to make the two houses, which they envisioned as being Winter homes forever, into showplaces. Family tradition has it that at one time the entire family, including eleven grandchildren, lived in the two houses, which have eighteen major and twenty-three smaller rooms.

There is physical evidence that the southernmost house was planned to be similar to their Italianate villa on Madison Avenue that financial difficulties had forced them to leave. However, after the war, the houses were finished in the style of the time and to conform to readjusted financial realities. Design modifications for completing the houses could have been done by Samuel Sloan, who worked in the Second Empire style from 1865–70 and who designed houses outside Philadelphia and at Cape May, New Jersey, that resemble the northernmost house.

The asymmetrical southernmost house was finished in the Second Empire style. Its tower, which may originally have been intended to resemble Samuel Sloan's tower on the Winters' Madison Avenue villa, was given a Mansard roof with fish-scale shingles and circular windows. There are fine paired brackets under the eaves of the tower and the main block of the house, which also has a Mansard roof.

The first-floor windows are double hung, whereas those on the second floor are round-headed casement windows. All windows have movable-louver exterior shutters; some windows, in the rear parlor for instance, also have interior louvered shutters.

Some of the windows on the first floor are floor-to-ceiling, to give access to the small porches opening off the front and rear parlors. There is also an L-shaped front porch. The three porches have chamfered columnettes, simple saw-work arched brackets, and delicate, diamond-patterned balustrades.

The round-headed double front door, which has exceptionally fine molded and raised paneling, opens into a vestibule and then into the stair hall. The single-turn staircase is rather narrow but has very fine turned balusters, a mahogany handrail, and tapered octagonal newel post. There are three bedrooms on the second floor.

On the south side of the first floor are double parlors separated by sliding pocket doors and a dining room. The mantels are marbled metal. The doors have four molded panels, and the woodwork is simple.

The front parlor's Belgian damask draperies are believed to date from 1852, having first hung at the Winters' Italianate villa on Madison Avenue, then at the First White House of the Confederacy, and now at Winter Place.

The northernmost house is Italianate. It was not updated to the extent of the southernmost house; it has even retained its antebellum-style six-over-six-light double-hung windows. Although the house is now boxy, massive, and severe, a porch with latticework once softened the front and south side. The house also had an unusual cupola that balanced the tower of the southernmost house.

Because the facade is only four bays wide, the door is off-center. The porch has been removed, and access is by a terrace. On the south side of the house there was an exterior staircase that ended at a door that gave access to the interior staircase landing. It was on this exterior staircase that a Mr. Hendrix, the jilted fiance of Elizabeth Winter Watts, committed sui-

Montgomery's Architectural Heritage

cide. Hendrix shot himself in the head on what was to have been the wedding day of Miss Elizabeth and Andy Bronson.

The two houses are connected by an enclosed hall, or passageway, of five bays; the center bay has doors opening to the service court at the rear and, in the front, to the small garden between the two houses.

The houses seem to have originally been L-shaped. There are identical brick corbels on the sides and backs of both houses, and on the dependencies. However, after the Civil War, and after completing the facades, the two houses became radically different. Both before and after the war, they were painted salmon pink with brown trim; they are now white with green trim.

Although both houses have thirteen-foot ceilings and large rooms, their interiors also differ considerably. The window and door surrounds of the northernmost house are very wide and deeply molded; the windows have panels below and architraves above; the heavy doors have raised and molded panels. There are four bedrooms on the second floor and four major rooms on the first floor. The center two, which cross the house from side to side, are connected by massive double doors. Each of the pine mantels is supported by three brackets in the classical style.

This house is unusual because it has a "moat." More that half of the house's perimeter is surrounded by a masonry dry moat that is approximately eight feet deep and eight feet wide. (Old Alabama Town's 1848 Ordeman-Shaw House has a similiar, but much smaller, moat.) At the back of the house there is a brick barrel-vaulted tunnel connecting the moat with a brick staircase to the service yard.

The basement is well lit, having full-sized double-hung windows. In addition to service areas, there are three fully finished rooms with plaster-over-lath ceilings and plaster over eighteen-inch brick walls. One simple antebellum mantel with Doric pilasters has survived.

Three of the brick servants' houses have survived. Three others and the detached kitchens have not. Adjacent to the kitchen site is a large cistern about ten feet deep; there are numerous wells on the property, including one in the basement of 450 Goldthwaite, the northernmost house.

After the Civil War, the neighborhood centered around the intersection of Mildred and Goldthwaite streets became one of the city's most exclusive. Winter Place was a noted social center, especially for its lawn dances with string bands and minstrel shows. Although the neighborhood began to decline somewhat in the 1920s and 1930s, with the rising prominence of the Garden District, Cloverdale, and Thomas Avenue, it was not until Interstates 85 and 65 were built nearby that the old gentility of the neighborhood was completely lost.

Montgomery Theatre Building

39 North Perry Street

ON OCTOBER 14, 1860, Montgomery saw the opening of a new theater. The Montgomery Theatre was designed by Colonel Daniel Cram, superintendent of the Montgomery and West Point Railroad, and was financed in part by Colonel Charles Pollard, president of the railroad. Construction of the three-story, 75-by-125-foot, solid brick building was begun in 1859. Female slaves of B. F. Randolph, brickwork and plastering contractor, did all the brickwork. After six coats of white paint were applied to the exterior, Montgomery's citizens dubbed the building "The White House."

The Montgomery Theatre occupied the building's second and third floors. The ground floor was occupied by the post office (until 1875, when it moved to the city hall across Monroe Street) and by various businesses, such as The Hole in the Wall, Jr., a saloon. To reach the theater's interior, patrons entered the center door on North Perry Street and climbed the broad flight of stairs on the west wall. Those at the theater's premiere were greeted with an address and a tableau in which the cast sang the "Star Spangled Banner." Then came the doubleheader, a standard feature of the day: Richard Brinsley Sheridan's outstanding comedy of manners, *School for Scandal*, and the now forgotten one-act farce *Persecuted Dutchman*.

The theater's 72-by-95-foot auditorium, with 32-foot ceiling, included on the main floor a plush seating section with a stove on both sides. The U-shaped first balcony was the dress circle. The second balcony was reserved

Montgomery's Architectural Heritage

for blacks and, probably, prostitutes. The auditorium could seat about nine hundred. All seats had good views.

Two tiers of proscenium boxes flanked the stage. The upper boxes were supported by columns, and the lower tier by male and female atlantes figures made of plaster. In front of the stage's apron was an orchestra pit that was large enough to accommodate the small orchestras that accompanied traveling theatrical and operatic companies. The theater was known for its unusually good acoustics.

The auditorium was fitted and decorated with gilt, elaborate plasterwork, wallpapers, and trompe l'oeil painting. This illusionist painting, which gives a three-dimensional appearance, was done by Peter Schmidt and Frank O'Brien. After the Civil War, Schmidt and O'Brien worked in the Capitol. Schmidt had learned the craft in his native Prussia before emigrating to Philadelphia. O'Brien, who apprenticed under Schmidt, eventually moved to Birmingham, where he acquired a fortune and later became mayor.

The auditorium was at first lit by kerosene lamps with ten-inch round reflectors. Some of these were directed at the audience until the curtain rose, at which time they were turned towards the stage. Kerosene soon gave way to gas. It was not until electricity was introduced that spotlights were available.

Famous actors and actresses of the day appeared on the Montgomery Theatre stage. In late 1860, John Wilkes Booth, who would assassinate Abraham Lincoln in Ford's Theater in Washington in April 1865, made his Montgomery debut in R. L. Shiel's tragedy *The Apostate*. Before leaving Montgomery, Booth also played Hamlet, Richard III, and Romeo. Within the first year, Edwin Forrest, Edwin Booth, Mr. and Mrs. James Walleck, Daniel and Emma Waller, and Charles Roberts had appeared.

Just before and during the war, the theater was also used for political meetings and for performances to benefit "The Cause." On December 19, 1860—the day before South Carolina seceded from the Union—Maggie Mitchell, a favorite of the Montgomery audience, presented an impressive flag tableau in which she sang "The Southern Marseillaise."

Shortly before Jefferson Davis's inauguration, Bryant's Minstrels played "Dixie" for the first time in Montgomery. Herman Frank Arnold, the German-born theater-orchestra director and city bandmaster, asked Daniel Emmett, the minstrels' composer, to give him a copy of the score. Because Emmett could not write music, he either hummed the tune or played it on a piano (accounts differ) while Arnold wrote the score on the plaster wall with a piece of charcoal. Later, Arnold's Southern Band played the song at Jefferson Davis's inaugural parade.

Even five months after Appomattox, acts of defiance were continuing. Nightly clashes in the theater between soldiers of Steele's Army Corps and returning Confederate soldiers prevented ladies from attending the theater. To stop an exchange of gunfire between U.S. Indian troops and Confederate veterans, the theater management turned off the house lights. Fighting continued in the streets, where one of the participants accidentally killed his own brother. This event seems to have calmed passions because such clashes ended in late October 1865.

A decade later, several prominent black Montgomerians tested the Civil Rights Act of 1875 when one of them attempted to buy a ticket to the dress circle. This attempt failed, and the subsequent court case eventually overturned the 1875 act by ruling that it did not apply to privately owned public accommodations.

After the war, Edwin Booth was seen again, as were Edwin Forrest; Ole Bull, the Norwegian violinist; and Sarah Bernhardt, the French actress. German, English, and Italian opera companies with casts of more than fifty sometimes performed. Late in the century, some of the traveling troupes used Thomas Edison's vitascope to project large colored pictures on a canvas screen. These were used between acts or in conjunction with action on the stage. On November 13, 1907, the Montgomery Theatre closed with *The Royal Rogue*. The old theater could not compete with Dexter Avenue's lavish Grand Theatre, which opened on November 14.

Today all is silent. Gone are the footlights, the traveling players in greasepaint or blackface, and the rapt audiences. Music, laughter, tears, and gunshots are all gone. The theater auditorium is gone; nothing is left except shadows of the wall decorations, the laths that once held a decorative plaster ceiling, and a few lines on the walls marking where balconies once were. Ghosts and memories remain.

The neighborhood has also changed dramatically. Office workers have replaced the often-raucous patrons of surrounding gambling houses, saloons, and brothels, of street hawkers and fruit carts, of sidewalk displays of produce, chickens, and ducks, and of the nearby fish market and public market on the open ground floor of the city hall. Also gone are the barbershops and bakeries, the offices of black doctors, dentists, and lawyers, the gunsmith, the bowling alley, the Chinese laundry, and Fleming's Restaurant, which was a Montgomery landmark from 1860 to 1904.

The quality of the exterior remains. It is one of the most handsome of the city's antebellum commercial buildings. The building is of modified Italianate style. Under the eaves, there is a blind arcade of brick that forms a cornice extending around the entire building. The windows on the upper two floors have cast-iron hoods supported by brackets. The center windows on North Perry Street differ in that they are rounded and slightly wider. The double-hung windows retain their original sashes with six-over-six lights.

The building's last commercial use was as Walter and Allen James's Webbers department store.

Cast-iron hood molding in the Italianate style

Kahl Montgomery Synagogue (Catoma Street Church of Christ)

100 Catoma Street

SINCE 1902, the Catoma Street Church of Christ has owned and occupied the building originally constructed in 1862 as the synagogue of Kahl Montgomery, or the Montgomery Jewish congregation. The exterior of the building is essentially the same as it was as a synagogue; the interior also retains many features of the Reform Jewish Temple Beth Or that developed from the Orthodox Kahl Montgomery synagogue.

The first Jew known to have lived in the area was a trader, Abram Mordecai of Pennsylvania, who from 1789 to 1815 lived in what is now northeast Montgomery County. Mordecai was a licensed trader with the Creek Indians and, in 1804, he set up the first cotton gin in Alabama. The Indians burned his gin and cut off his ear because Mordecai had offended them.

The nucleus of Montgomery's first Jewish community, however, was formed by German Jews who left Europe because of the revolutions of the 1840s. In 1846, a Jewish religious and benevolent society was formed in Montgomery. Its constitution was written in German and required German to be used as the language of the society. A few years later, the society (*chevra*) was constituted as a congregation (*kahl*). Although this group had no rabbi, Orthodox worship and dietary practices were observed.

Using a bequest from Judah Touro, a Sephardic Jew and philanthropist of New Orleans, construction was begun on a synagogue in 1858. The building was dedicated in March 1862. In the early years when the Montgomery synagogue was one of only two in Alabama, curious Christians came to watch the Friday evening and Saturday morning services.

Over the years, the congregation moved away from Orthodox Judaism. Organ music and a choir were introduced into the services, as was the English language. The reading desk was moved from the center of the room to a dais in front of the Ark on the east wall. Women were no longer required to sit in the balcony, and family members sat together in family pews. Men were no longer required to wear hats during services. Dietary rules were relaxed. In 1874, what had begun as an Orthodox synagogue adopted the Reform ritual of Temple Emanu-El of New York and became Temple Beth Or, or House of Light.

The Jewish congregation used the building until 1902, when a new temple was built on the corner of Clayton and Sayre streets. This grand building—with central dome, four corner cupolas, and classical pediments and columns—was eventually razed. Its stained-glass windows were saved and are now used in a Florala hospital.

The Catoma Street building is in the Romanesque Revival style. As with the Gothic Revival, this style was popular for nineteenth-century houses of worship. Gothic Revival was generally used for Episcopal and Roman Catholic church buildings, and Romanesque Revival for Baptist, Congregational, and Methodist church buildings. This generality does not hold for Montgomery, where Gothic seems to have been more popular. Ironically,

"Christian" Romanesque Revival was no more appropriate for a Jewish synagogue than "pagan" Greek Revival was.

Nevertheless, the synagogue was designed by John Stewart of Philadelphia in the Romanesque Revival style that, in this case, is very loosely based on the architectural style of northern Italy in the early Middle Ages. John Stewart was an associate of Samuel Sloan, one of the nation's foremost architects. Pelham J. Anderson of Montgomery was the supervising architect, and George M. Figh was the brickwork contractor.

Because the building has a raised basement, the main floor is reached by horseshoe stairs to a landing, and then by a broad single flight to the door. The balustrades are of wrought- and cast-iron. The double door is surmounted by a wide, round-headed brick arch.

Montgomery's Architectural Heritage

The central bay with its gabled superstructure dominates the facade. The facade is also decorated with four wheel windows. Fine, intricate brickwork creates rhythmic patterns. The symmetry and rhythm are also evident in the six bays of stacked windows inset into blind round-headed arches on the side walls of the building. Originally there were shutters.

The main entrance, at the top of the exterior staircase, opens to a vestibule. The doors have four panels; the door knobs are porcelain. The ceiling has a plaster cornice. To either side of the vestibule are separate stairwells with curved staircases to the balcony and to the basement.

The auditorium, a large rectangular room with a high ceiling, is surprisingly light and open. The ceiling has a wide cove cornice. A balcony extends across the back of the room and along most of the side walls. It is supported by slender Tuscan columns of wood, painted black, and by Corinthian columns of iron, also painted black. The button-turned balusters of the balcony balustrade, previously painted black, are now antiqued white. The balcony's floor rises in tiers. Although the balcony is no longer used, several old pews remain.

The focal point of the room is its east end. Two tall black columns, without bases or capitals, flank the two large black doors that once covered the Ark where the Torah scrolls were kept. The Church of Christ has retained these features as well as the semicircular painting on glass above the doors. Coincidentally, the painting of God, represented by a single eye, giving the Tablets of the Law, had been painted for Temple Beth Or by Annie Smith, a founding member of Montgomery's Church of Christ.

A baptistry has been built under the dais that was built in front of the Ark in 1874, when the lectern/pulpit was moved from the center of the room. The pulpit is now on a lower dais, in front of the old dais. The pews also date from the 1874 renovation. The floors are of heart pine and the wainscoting of vertical paneling. Plaster, rolled corners abut the jambs of the tall windows.

In 1881, Justus McDuffie Barnes—educator, writer, preacher and railroad entrepreneur—established Montgomery's first Church of Christ. The congregation, which met first in the county courthouse, had a church building on Herron Street before moving to Catoma Street. Although Brother Barnes preached at Catoma Street for more than twenty-five years, he also preached extensively elsewhere in Alabama and in Georgia, Florida, Kentucky, Tennessee, and Texas.

Because the Church of Christ in America grew from a movement to return to Apostolic Christianity, worship practices of the New Testament church are followed. These include observing the Lord's Supper each Sunday and congregational singing. Ironically, the latter corresponds to the original practice of the Orthodox synagogue—congregational singing without a choir and without instrumental music.

WHAT IS TODAY known as Cottage Hill was laid out in the 1830s by Edward Hanrick, an Irish immigrant and Montgomery land speculator known as "Horseshoe Ned." In the 1850s, a significant number of great houses were built there, chiefly on Goldthwaite and Clayton streets. By 1860, Hanrick had retired as a rich man, although Hanrick Plat, which had a rural character, was only sparsely settled at the time.

Facing Goldthwaite Street, at the corner of Herron, was the Andersons' Italianate mansion. At the corner of River and Goldthwaite streets was the city's grandest Greek Revival mansion, with its terraced gardens leading down to the river. It was the townhouse of Thomas Cowles, who was probably the most powerful man in antebellum Montgomery. At the southwest corner of Goldthwaite and Martha streets, and occupying the entire block between Clayton and Martha streets, was the Bibbs' Greek Revival mansion, which had a two-story central block and one-story flanking wings. On Clayton Street facing down Whitman Street was the Randolphs' Greek Revival mansion. At the northwest corner of Clayton and Hanrick streets was the Greek Revival townhouse of Charles G. Gunter, who, after the Civil War, went with a large number of Confederate expatriates to Brazil, rather than submit to United States control. At the southeast corner of

▼

Dowe House

554 Martha Street

Montgomery's Architectural Heritage 101

Clayton and Holt streets on nine acres was Hamner Hall, the Episcopal school for girls. The 124-by-46-foot two-story brick building was not completed until 1862.

All these fine buildings have been lost, although the two Winter houses and the McBryde-Screws-Tyson House stand at the corner of Goldthwaite and Mildred streets as reminders of the lost elegance of the suburb. Even before the Civil War the neighborhood had begun to change. Several very modest frame houses were built at the western end of Martha Street, which seems to have previously been an alley that gave access to the service yards of the big houses on Clayton Street.

Chamfered columnettes supporting porch roof

With few exceptions, Cottage Hill is now characterized by two house types. Five-bay, central-hall plan houses with either low-hipped or gabled roofs were constructed in the mid–nineteenth century, and the more common asymmetrical frame houses with front porches abutting a gabled bay were built late in the century.

The brick cottage at 554 Martha Street was built for Michael and Mary Dowe shortly after the Civil War. The hardware is dated 1863, however, and the style is antebellum. Dowe, who immigrated from Ireland with his parents and three brothers, may have been a grocer and baker, as was his brother John. In any case, the neighborhood was changing from a planter and upper-income neighborhood to one of small merchants and artisans. The Dowes gave the house to their daughter Alice and her husband, James Farley.

The cottage's principal rooms are on the second floor, and secondary rooms are on the ground floor. This is not readily apparent from Martha Street, as the ground floor is not visible because of the slope of the land.

The Martha Street cottage is

five bays wide and four bays deep. The porch, extending across the three center bays, has columnettes with deeply cut chamfers and extraordinary saw-work decorations. The porch railing balusters are also of saw work. The porch has lattice underpinning. The cottage's low-pitched, hipped roof has a dormer on the side elevations. The interior chimneys are unusually thin for wood-burning fireplaces. The double-hung windows have been restored with six lights in each sash. The windows have flat, or jack, arches.

The doorway, with sidelights and transom, features Tuscan pilasters and entablature. The four-panel door opens into a central hall that runs the depth of the cottage to an identical door which opens onto a stoop at the second-story level. The central hall is divided by a wall and double doors, each of which has movable louvers over a molded panel.

The main floor consists of a large front room and a smaller back room on each side of the central hall. These rooms are very plain but well proportioned (16-by-20 and 16-by-16), with 12-foot ceilings. The wood-burning fireplaces have simple Greek Revival mantels with Tuscan pilasters. The baseboards are high and molded, and the door and window surrounds are molded. The doors have four molded panels; box locks with enamel knobs are used throughout the house. The large windows have Venetian blinds in the style of the period: saw-work valances and wooden slats connected by cloth tape decorated with a running Greek-key motif.

The back hall has a steep staircase to the attic and another to the basement; the latter is new. The attic's two rooms are separated by a passageway. The doors are plank; the dormer windows have six lights in each sash. The ceiling is not quite seven feet.

The basement appears to have consisted originally of one room with two fireplaces. The windows, with six lights in each sash, extend almost from floor to ceiling. The floor was brick and the ceiling wood. Tradition has it that the bricks used to construct the Dowe house were baked in a bakery's oven—after regular business hours. Considering that a bakery was in the family, there may be truth in the tradition.

The house has a "moat" on the northeast corner that is approximately three feet wide and five feet deep. This device to allow light into basements is not unusual in the Cottage Hill area.

In 1976, James Loeb bought the Dowe House, which was then in a state of ruin. His meticulous renovation to the cottage's original appearance has served as an example and inspiration to those who have subsequently restored Cottage Hill houses. The neighborhood boasts the city's largest collection of late-nineteenth-century houses.

The Dowe House is now owned and occupied by Larry E. Speaks and Associates, Consulting Engineers and Land Surveyors.

The "Four Sisters"

402, 410, 416, and 420
South Perry Street

FOR ALMOST A CENTURY, one of Montgomery's most elegant addresses was South Perry Street, especially from Washington Street south to where Interstate 85 now cuts its swath through the town. In the early 1860s, Perry Street was called the Fifth Avenue of Montgomery, referring to what was then New York's finest residential street.

Dr. William Owen Baldwin lived on the southwest corner of South Perry and Adams streets in a fine brick mansion designed by the famous John Stewart of Philadelphia. His house was the last great house to be built before the Civil War; in fact, its Italian marble mantels and mirrors were run through the Union naval blockade.

With the exception of the time Baldwin spent earning a medical degree (1837) at Transylvania University, Lexington, Kentucky, and a year in Europe furthering his medical studies, he lived his whole life (1818 to 1886) in Montgomery. In 1843, the young Dr. Baldwin, a nephew of Governor Benjamin Fitzpatrick, married Mary Jane Martin, daughter of Judge Abram Martin and his wife, Mary.

Dr. Baldwin was noted for his learned articles in the *American Journal of Medical Science*. He served as the president of the American Medical Association from 1868–1869 and helped heal the rift in the association that resulted from the Civil War. The physician was also a businessman. He was a founding member and first president of the First National Bank of Montgomery (now Regions Bank), serving as president from 1871 until his death in 1886.

Although Dr. Baldwin was against the war, because he believed the Confederacy could not win it, he did serve as an army surgeon. His eldest son, Buddy Willie, went to war. James Hale, a former slave of Dr. Baldwin, brought the body of Captain William O. Baldwin, Jr., back from Tennessee. He was killed at the age of nineteen, in the bloody Battle of Franklin.

James Hale had been freed before the Civil War. Dr. Baldwin helped him become an independent carpenter, contractor, and designer. Hale and his wife, Anne, prospered. Anne Hale had served as a nursemaid in the Baldwin household and later as Dr. Baldwin's nurse. In 1889, after her husband's death, she opened Hale's Infirmary on the edge of Centennial Hill. This two-story frame structure had a capacity of sixty patients and was the only hospital in Montgomery that would serve blacks. It was built in memory of her husband and her two daughters, one of whom, Sarah, was the wife of Dr. Cornelius Dorsette, the first black physician to be licensed in Alabama. Sadie, their other daughter, was a graduate of Barnard and the Columbia Teacher's College; she married Vertner Woodrow Tandy, a graduate of Cornell University's College of Architecture.

In 1872, Dr. Baldwin engaged James Hale to design and build five houses for his children. Four of these houses, referred to as the "Four Sisters," were built for his daughters; they face Knox Hall on South Perry Street. In the fall of 1880, these houses were deeded to the daughters: number 402 to Mary Baldwin Williams, 410 to Jennie Baldwin Craik, 416 to Cecile Baldwin Maxwell, and 420 to Alma Baldwin Bolton. Alma did not live in the house her father gave her. The fifth house, which faced Scott Street, was built for Marion Augustus Baldwin, one of the four Baldwin sons. It has recently burned.

The "Four Sisters" are close to the street and extremely close to one another. Although the houses take up most of the lots, there was room in the rear for a shared barn and garden.

With minor variations, the four houses use two exterior designs. The two northernmost houses have a Victorian Gothic appearance. With the exception of differing porch supports, they are essentially identical. They are three bays wide; the front doors are recessed from the plane of the two floor-to-ceiling porch windows. These two houses have steep roofs, gables with decorative framing, and unusual gables over some of the second-floor windows. The two southernmost houses, with the exception of a second-floor porch that was added to one, have an Italianate appearance. These two houses are also three bays wide. Rather than steep roofs and gables, each has a sort of pediment surmounting its flat, squared-off facade.

All four houses have porches; they also have identical saw-work balustrades; three have identical columnettes supporting the porch roofs. Each house has two floor-to-ceiling windows opening on the porch, and identical, arched, double front doors. Most windows have two lights in each sash. The windows have exterior louvered shutters.

The interiors, now altered to one degree or another, appear to have been almost identical. To the left of the entrance hall was a straight-run staircase with turned balusters. To the right of the entrance hall were double parlors separated by sliding doors. Behind the double parlors was the dining room. On the main floor, there are porches (some of which have been enclosed) and also three additional rooms.

On the second floor, there are four large bedrooms with closets, several smaller rooms, and porches. On both floors there are twelve-foot ceilings, some of which are coved. There is wide, bold woodwork that frames doors and windows; the doors have four raised panels and single-light transoms. There is a raised panel under each window. The floors are wide heart pine. Most of the coal-burning fireplaces have cast-iron mantels.

Because the lots slope downward from Perry Street, the houses have three stories at the rear. The fronts of the buildings are raised on piers and in-filled with lattice. Each house has a finished basement of brick under the back half of the building. The rooms and lattice-enclosed porches of the basements were probably used for storage, laundry, and food preparation.

The quality of craftsmanship used in these four houses was high. This was unusual for the 1870s, as was the use of wooden pegs and of mortise and tenon joints—practices generally abandoned by the time the houses were built.

Today only two of the "Four Sisters" are residences.

R ICHARD ALLEN founded the African Methodist Episcopal Church in Philadephia in 1787. Montgomery's first AME congregation, which was formally organized in 1871 with the Reverend Christburger as its first minister, seems to have grown out of several small congregations, one of which met in Brother Thorp Williams's house on Dexter Avenue. The congregation of St. John's Chapel Church was dissatisfied with its location at the "bottom" of North Court Street and sought a better site.

Construction began on a new church building in 1873, but it was not until 1888 that the building was completed. The AME church became the "Church on the Hill." Although altered significantly, that original building forms the core of the present church. Originally, the red brick building had round-headed windows, a projecting tower and steeple, and entrance by way of a street-level door in the base of the tower.

In 1885, the city school board noted the deplorable conditions of the Madison Street School operating in the church basement. The floor was

St. John's African Methodist Episcopal Church

809 Madison Avenue

brick; partitions were rough planks; the only pieces of furniture were backless, plank benches; and the 385 students had four teachers.

In 1911, the church's name was changed to St. John's AME Church. In that year, the original building was remodeled based on plans done by Walter Thomas Bailey, a native of Illinois and the first black to graduate in architecture from the University of Illinois, 1904. He was one of the five black architects that Booker T. Washington brought to Tuskegee Normal and Industrial Institute. Bailey had designed the Negro Building at the 1906 Alabama State Fair. In 1910, construction had begun on the First Baptist Church on Ripley Street; it was also designed by Bailey.

Bailey's design significantly altered the building's appearance. The round-headed windows were modified to have Gothic arches. The steeple was removed, two Gothic louvered windows were added to each face of the tower, and the tower was topped with a battlement. The red brick was painted. The most dramatic change was the addition of a two-story porch to the facade of the building. The main entrance through the base of the tower was replaced by two entrances on the second floor. These are reached by two broad flights of stairs. The porch, which has a parapet, also has large openings with Gothic arches.

The auditorium is a large rectangular room on the main floor. At the rear, in the tower, is a wide central staircase that leads to the balcony. Four free-standing and two engaged Tuscan columns support the gently curving balcony. At the top of the two Gothic arched windows of the balcony are exceptional stained-glass portraits of Bishop Richard Allen and Bishop Henry Blanton Parks. The stained-glass windows of the auditorium are decorated with Christian symbols. The room has vertical beadboard paneling and a cornice and boxed beam ceiling of pressed metal. A large old chandelier hangs from the middle of the ceiling.

Separating the auditorium from the sanctuary is a curved communion rail, the top of which is hinged; when opened, it has receptacles for individual communion glasses. Between the communion rail and the rostrum is a wooden communion table. The pulpit is in the center of the rostrum and in front of the choir. Recessed in a large round-headed arch behind the choir is a Hinners pipe organ dating from the 1920s.

In 1909, St. John's AME Church began sponsoring an early morning Christmas cantata. This was the first black church to sponsor such a service, and it became very popular; at the time, there were few cultural events available to the city's black community.

The church has hosted speakers of national prominence, including Julian Bond, Mahalia Jackson, Martin Luther King, Jr., Rosa Parks, and George Wallace.

Dexter Avenue King Memorial Baptist Church

454 Dexter Avenue

THIS CHURCH is probably the most famous building in the city, for it was here that the leaders of Montgomery's black community officially endorsed the 1955–56 bus boycott. That event, which helped energize the civil rights movement, was the beginning of the rise of Dr. Martin Luther King, Jr., to international prominence. But the church had played a leading role in advancement and social justice efforts even before Dr. King's pastorate (1954–60). For example, the church was instrumental in the move of what is now Alabama State University from Marion to Montgomery in 1887.

After separating from the Columbus Street Baptist Church in 1877, the members of Second Colored Baptist Church first met in a private house on High Street, and then in a hall on Market Street (Dexter Avenue since 1885) that had once been a slave traders' pen, where slaves were kept while awaiting sale. Although land was available on the upper end of Market Street because the commercial district had moved down to the Court Square end of the street, controversy surrounded building a black church on the city's main street. The congregation persisted, and after six years of construction, they dedicated the building on Thanksgiving, 1889.

The building was designed by Pelham J. Anderson of Montgomery with William Watkins, a member of the congregation, supervising construction. Members of the congregation aided in construction, including gathering and moving bricks discarded by workmen who were removing bricks on Market Street to lay streetcar tracks. These bricks were used in the building's foundations.

The church building is a rectangular structure, with meeting rooms in the basement, and a vestibule and the sanctuary on the main floor. As the basement is set into the slope of the hill, the building's facade is two-story. The main floor is reached by external double stairs connected by a landing.

The Dexter Avenue church blends Victorian Gothic with other Victorian features. These stylistic features include the Gothic arched windows (with classically influenced keystones) on the facade and on the sides of the main floor, the double staircase with its bold balusters, the Italianate bracketed cornice under the eaves, and the wooden tower and steeple with its Gothic arched windows. These features and, perhaps more importantly, the building's proportions and the rich patina of the red brick, give the building its solidity and its understated, unpretentious dignity.

The sanctuary is reached by three doors opening from a vestibule that also has a staircase to the sanctuary's small balcony and to the basement. The sanctuary is a large rectangular room with high ceiling. The ceiling and cornice are of pressed metal painted white. The walls are light blue above a low, dark wainscot of vertical beadboard. Light from the ten large Gothic windows, the white ceiling, and the light-blue walls gives a serene atmosphere to the room. The pulpit raised on a high podium dominates the sanctuary. This pulpit, which was used by Dr. King, can be moved to

A Sense of Place

reveal the baptistry under the podium. Attention is focused on the pulpit by its central location, its height, and by the apse-like niche that is behind the pulpit. This niche is surrounded by wooden fluted pilasters and a pediment. The pulpit is flanked by two choirs, the larger containing the organ console and backed by Gothic-style, oak-grained paneling. A lattice screen now covers an opening that once contained the organ console and organ pipes. (The old organ was moved to Prattville's St. Mark's Episcopal Church.) The low pews are original. The glass, in rich, mostly primary colors, reproduces the original glass, some of which survives in the windows of the north facade.

Dexter Avenue King Memorial Baptist Church is open to the public. Literature, a civil rights mural, and a short video are available in the basement.

City Water Works

608 North Court Street

EARLY MONTGOMERY depended on individual wells and cisterns, and on several artesian wells, for its water supply. The "big basin" at Court Square was the site of an artesian well; another artesian well was at the intersection of Bibb and Commerce streets. In 1830, John H. Engelhardt discovered mineral waters; for decades his family bottled and sold the water at 100-1/2 North Court Street. In 1854, the city's first water works company was incorporated. It consisted of a series of underground cisterns. In 1873, the second company was incorporated.

But by 1885, water quality and quantity were inadequate. Thanks in part to the campaign that William Wallace Screws conducted through the *Montgomery Advertiser*, the city administration finally relented and agreed to build a new water works. That year, Mayor Warren S. Reese contracted A. H. Howland and Associates of Boston to install and maintain a new water system to consist of mains, water works, standpipe, and pumping station. The system, including the water works building on North Court Street, was completed in June 1886. The 100-foot standpipe was located off Monroe Street at one of the highest points in Montgomery. (This structure, with its exterior spiraled staircase, was a Montgomery landmark until it was demolished in 1990.) The system was capable of supplying about four million gallons a day, from five 700-foot-deep artesian wells, and pumping through sixty-five miles of mains.

The city was to pay Howland eleven thousand dollars a year for use of approximately two hundred hydrants for fire protection and, when necessary, the company was to wet down the streets, which were unpaved, at no cost to the city. Five-room houses were to pay six dollars a year for water; each additional room increased the rate by one dollar.

In 1887, the city boasted that "Its people are invigorated with cool, limpid, delicious mineral water, which comes to us from the bowels of the earth, filtered of all impurities and possessing acknowledged medicinal virtues."

The North Court Street water works building is representative of the civic pride associated with public buildings, including utilities, in the late nineteenth and early twentieth century. A similar building, decorated with round-headed arches and pilasters with Composite capitals, was built about 1905 at 204 Jefferson Street by the Montgomery State Power and Electric Company. (The first electric power in Alabama was initiated in Anniston in 1882. A year later, a small brush dynamo produced electricity for thirty-one Montgomery street lights. By 1902, a power plant on the Tallapoosa River generated power for Montgomery, twenty-five miles away.)

The rectangular water works building, located in the block north of Janney's Foundry, has been expanded several times since its construction in 1885–86. Between 1894 and 1910, the building acquired its present appearance. (By 1910, the street had been paved with granite blocks and there was an iron bridge over Cypress Creek just north of the water works.)

North and south additions and the elegant facade are constructed of dark-red pressed brick with its thin mortar pointing. The building rests on a rusticated stone foundation. Above the large arched door in the center block is a terra-cotta frieze inscribed CITY WATER WORKS. The gable, trimmed with a cement coping and a terra-cotta cornice, has a triple window, above which is a rusticated stone belt course and floral decorative work of terra-cotta. The rectangular windows of the 1885–86 building were altered to match the round-headed windows of the additions. Pilasters with Doric capitals support the door and window arches, which are outlined in egg-and-dart molding. Above three of the facade's paired windows are terra-cotta cartouches. The additions to the original rectangular building have denticulated brick cornices below the eaves. The steeply pitched slate roof of the central block once had dormers.

In May 1945, a very destructive tornado struck the city. Several people were killed in Chisholm. The tornado also destroyed the water works' tower, whose upper stage had paired round-headed windows below a parapet supported by rough granite corbels. The tower had been capped with an octagonal pyramidal roof. The base of this tower survives, to the left of the central block.

Surviving elements of the interior include the steel cross trusses supporting the steeply pitched roof, and three elliptical brick arches separating the original structure and the southern addition. A spiral metal staircase leads to an underground area where there are brick arches and buttresses and a maze of passageways. The station has been powered by coal, gas, and diesel oil, and is now powered by electricity.

The water system, constructed by Howland in 1886–87, was bought by the city in 1895. In 1949, the city transferred the system to the Water Works Board of the City of Montgomery, a public corporation established by an act of the Alabama legislature. Howland's North Court Street facility is now augmented by the Day Street pumping station and water from the Tallapoosa River. Today's daily capacity is more than 75 million gallons, which is distributed through more than a thousand miles of mains.

IN 1864, A GROUP of refugees from Union-occupied Pensacola established Montgomery's second Episcopal parish in a small frame church on South Perry Street. The church building had been constructed in 1834 as the Universalist Church. The Church of the Holy Comforter was led by the Reverend John Jackson Scott and Colonel Samuel Goode Jones. The latter was also instrumental in building the Episcopal university at Sewanee, Tennessee, and Hamner Hall, Montgomery's Episcopal girls' school.

By 1869, the parish lapsed as its communicants returned to Pensacola. The Church of the Holy Comforter was revived in 1886. Funds to build the new church building came indirectly from a Northern Methodist church through St. John's Episcopal Church, and from the sale of a South Perry Street lot given by Colonel Jones in 1869. The Reverend Dr. Horace Stringfellow, rector of St. John's, designed the church.

Holy Comforter's new location on South Goldthwaite Street was on part of the large triangular block that Colonel Joseph Samuel Prince Winter had bought for $1,000 in the 1850s. The church paid $2,500 for their 100-foot square lot—inflation was in full swing.

The new building, located in the city's most exclusive neighborhood, was consecrated in June 1887. Forty families transferred from St. John's, and communicants included members of the city's most prominent families. However, the neighborhood, which had grown rapidly from 1880 to 1890, began to decline in the 1920s. By the mid-1950s, the parish was considering moving to the new suburbs southeast of town. The church moved to 2911 Woodley Road in 1959.

Church furnishings (including the Gothic-style brass lectern, kneeler, and hymn board; oak chairs, altar, and reredos; marble baptismal font; and several stained-glass windows) were moved to the new church building. Architectural elements were copied from the Goldthwaite Street building as well, and the stained-glass windows were placed in the new

Church of the Holy Comforter

432 South Goldthwaite Street

Montgomery's Architectural Heritage

115

building exactly as they had been in the old.

The Goldthwaite Street building is in the Carpenter Gothic style. This type of Gothic architecture was built of wood. It was generally used by small parishes or congregations in towns or rural areas. Carpenter Gothic, especially prevalent with rural Episcopal parishes, was popularized by Richard Upjohn's *Rural Architecture* and, to a lesser degree, by Samuel Sloan's *Model Architect*. Both Upjohn and Sloan were two of the country's most prominent architects. Examples of the Carpenter Gothic style in the Montgomery area are the 1856–57 First Presbyterian Church in Wetumpka, which has a neoclassical, rather than Gothic, interior; the 1857–58 St. Paul's Episcopal Church in Lowndesboro, which was called the Red Church because it was originally painted red; and Grace Episcopal Church in Mount Meigs, which was designed in April 1861 by Joseph W. Pierson of Pennsylvania but, because of the Civil War, was not built until 1892–93.

Like masonry churches in the Gothic Revival style, Carpenter Gothic aspired towards spirituality and the picturesque by variety, irregularity, and contrasts. It is characterized by Gothic pointed-arch door and window openings. Windows, which may be single or grouped, are usually of the simple, long, Early English lancet type. The most distinguishing characteristic of the Carpenter Gothic style is the use of board-and-batten siding. This creates a verticality associated with the Gothic, and distinguishes Carpenter Gothic from horizontal siding used on vernacular, Greek Revival, and Romanesque Revival buildings. Another feature that occasionally distinguished Carpenter Gothic was that some of the buildings were painted brown, dove gray, or red, as opposed to the standard white. This could have been an attempt to make them appear, from a distance, to be made of stone or brick, rather than wood. There is a variety of treatments for belfries. First Presbyterian in Wetumpka has a central, projecting tower with a parapet spire; St. Paul's has a corner tower with an overlapping chamfered spire; Holy Comforter has a bell cote; and Grace has no belfry at all.

The Holy Comforter building presents a high gabled end to the street. The stained glass of the two large lancet windows has been removed to the Woodley Road building. Above the two lancet windows is a *mandorla*-, or almond-shaped, window (now closed). The mandorla is a form of halo, which is appropriate, as the stained-glass window (now on Woodley Road) is of a descending dove, symbolizing God the Holy Spirit. A mandorla-shaped ventilator with fish-scale louvers can be seen in the north gable of the vestry room. Windows in this shape have been incorporated in the Woodley Road church building. The windows of the side walls of the nave are paired, with Gothic pointed arches and leaded glass in diamond pattern, and decorated with fleurs de lis. The siding is of characteristic Carpenter Gothic board-and-batten, the battens being molded. The very steep roof, another feature of Gothic-style buildings, is surmounted by a bell cote capped with a cross.

At the building's northwest corner, formerly opening off the chancel, is a gabled wing that was originally the vestry. This wing, added about 1891, has a small porch, similar to the one protecting the main entrance. Its single door has a modified Gothic arch.

The main entrance double-leaf door is protected by a porch. The porch's sides have chamfered Gothic arches and a steep roof supported by a kingpost, a type of truss dating from the thirteenth or fourteenth century.

Original interior features include the heavy chamfered framing around the central lancet window and mandorla-shaped window on the east gabled wall, the roof trusses and supporting chamfered posts, and beadboard roof and wainscot. Everything else is altered, including the chancel and choir.

Frank Lockwood, the city's most prominent architect in the first quarter of the twentieth century, and a longtime member of Holy Comforter's choir, would often find himself bored during the sermon. At such times he would read Agatha Christie mystery novels, perhaps a harbinger of things to come. After the church building was deconsecrated in 1959, it was converted into Montgomery's Little Theatre. A foyer was made inside the main entrance, at the back of the former church nave, and the floor was reconstructed to slope towards the stage, which was built in the former chancel. Theater seats with interesting cast-iron ends were installed. Because the auditorium was small, there was an intimate relationship between audience and performers.

Montgomery's Little Theatre was founded in 1926. The group built the twin-gabled, Tudor-style building at 130 Julia Street. During World War II, however, the theater lapsed for several reasons: gas rationing made it difficult to attend rehearsals, there was a shortage of male actors, and unescorted ladies did not go out in the evenings.

When the theater group was reorganized in 1949, performances were given in the Grand Theatre on Dexter Avenue (now demolished), the city hall's magnificent civic auditorium (now partially converted into offices), and the Jefferson Davis Hotel ballroom (no longer extant), before the group acquired the deconsecrated Church of the Holy Comforter.

The building served as the Junius Bragg Smith Theatre until 1994. In 1996, the Montgomery Little Theatre transferred ownership to the original owner, the Episcopal Diocese of Alabama. The building is being used as the interdenominational Jubilee Community Center to give spiritual, mental, and physical support to residents of the neighborhood.

Pepperman-Ludlow House

17 Mildred Street

JACOB EDWARD PEPPERMAN, jeweler and pawnbroker, and his wife, Mary Ellen, built the frame house at 17 Mildred Street in 1887–88. At that time, the neighborhood was one of three in the city whose growth reflected the city's booming post-Reconstruction economy.

In October 1888, the Peppermans sold the house to Effingham Wagner, a dentist. Two years later it was sold to Robert and Ida Henderson. Robert was in the grocery firm of Vandiver and Comprey, for which he served as vice-president from 1909 until his death the following year. The house was then owned by Isabella Perry, wife of Francis M. Perry, a contractor. In 1940, it was bought by Willard R. Ludlow, a mercantile clerk, and his brother Richard G. Ludlow, a postal clerk. They did not live in the house, but divided it into apartments. In 1970, Willard R. Ludlow, Jr., moved into the house and operated an antique shop there. In 1979, it was acquired by Aronov Realty Company, restored, and used as offices.

The house is representative of a larger middle-class house of the late nineteenth century and the early twentieth century. Few of these two-story houses from the 1880s survive in Montgomery, and fewer still with Eastlake-style features. The frame house, with novelty wood siding, has Queen Anne–style characteristics and Eastlake-style decorative elements. Both the exterior massing and interior floor plan are irregular or asymmetrical. This trend toward the informal was a reaction against the rigid symmetry of the antebellum Greek Revival style, and even of traditional vernacular houses. It was an attempt to have private homes reflect the actual informal living of ordinary people.

Although the two-story main block has a truncated hipped roof with a flat top, the house does have a gable. It is decorated with brackets and gingerbread. There is a one-story, flat-roofed wing on the east of the main block. The chimneys, which were interior rather than exterior, have been removed. The fascia is of vertical beadboard paneling to which are applied wooden ventilator covers. Under the eaves are brackets with scroll markings.

There is a variety of window treatments, including floor-to-ceiling windows opening from the parlor to the front porch. Most windows are double-hung with two lights in each sash. Pediments cap the second-story windows.

The porch, spanning the five-bay front, is raised on piers that were once filled with metal grills. The porch has Eastlake trim, turned balusters, and columnettes. The front entrance has a molded architrave supported by brackets. The door itself has a single-light upper panel over an Eastlake-style lower panel.

The door opens into a stair hall. To the right are double parlors separated by sliding pocket doors. The front parlor is the only room in the house, other than the stair hall, that retains the original feeling of the house. Its double mantel has Ionic columnettes supporting an entablature. The mirror is beveled glass. The original glazed tiles that surrounded the coal-burning grate have been replaced with white marble. The floor is pine, and the baseboards are very high. Window and door surrounds in the parlors and most of the other rooms are reeded with bullseye or block corners. The older doors have four molded, raised panels, and the newer doors have six. The double-turn staircase has a walnut handrail, turned balusters, and a boxed Victorian newel post. Scroll appliques are on the treads.

The second-floor stair landing has been enclosed. This is one of many alterations for adaptive use since the 1940s. Rooms have been added to the back on both floors.

The house is now owned and occupied by Faith Crusades Fellowship Ministries, an interdenominational Christian outreach ministry devoted to serving the inner city through food and clothing distribution, substance-abuse rehabilitation, and literacy and vocational training.

Mills House

532 Clay Street

COTTAGE HILL is Montgomery's most intact Victorian neighborhood. More than two-thirds of the houses in the historic district predate 1910. Only a few of the houses are early; most were built between 1870 and 1910. Although the lots were laid out by a land speculator, Edward Hanrick, in the 1830s, and the land was incorporated into Montgomery in 1839, the neighborhood was slow to grow.

Before the Civil War, there were at least half a dozen Greek Revival and Italianate mansions in the neighborhood, chiefly on Goldthwaite and Clayton streets. In 1862, Hamner Hall, a large Episcopal girls' day and boarding school, was opened in a nine-acre grove at the southeast corner of Clayton and Holt streets.

In the last quarter of the nineteenth century, the character of the neighborhood changed. The mansions were divided into smaller rental units. Although the majority of the new houses constructed in Cottage Hill were well built, they were simple and unpretentious frame houses of the working class. Here lived railway employees, grocers, carpenters, a gunsmith, a blacksmith, a cabinetmaker, and laborers.

One of the four large houses built in the neighborhood in the last quarter of the century is the two-story, orange-brick, Queen Anne–style house at 532 Clay Street. It was built about 1888 for Alfonso Mills, who had come south after 1879. Mills was a cattleman, timberman, building contractor, and land developer.

However, it is Alfonso Mills's son, John Proctor Mills, who is remembered. He was born in Michigan in 1879 and educated in Montgomery. He composed music at an early age, and in the first quarter of the twentieth century was a noted composer. He gave recitals in Europe and even some in Costa Rica. In Montgomery, he taught voice, organ, and piano. Since Alfonso Mills did not get along well with his eccentric son, he built his son a house two doors to the east.

The Mills House is reached by stairs that rise steeply from the street to a wooden porch whose gingerbread is painted the original colors, gray and white with red accents. The cast-iron urns flanking the steps are original to the house.

The house is symmetrical, unusual for the Queen Anne style. There is a bay window on each side of the central door. Colored glass decorates the upper parts of the double doors and the transoms of all the windows on the main floor of the house. The second-floor facade has one-over-one sash windows on both sides of a central window. Above the brickwork is a wooden bracketed cornice.

From the street, the most impressive aspect of the house is its central tower. The base of the tower has original fish-scale tin shingles stamped with the date March 27, 1888. On closer inspection, however, the most impressive aspect of the house's exterior is not the tower but the fine pressed brick and, especially, the exceptional molded brick for the steps, door and window surrounds, drip course, and several belt courses. There are molded corner pilasters as well as a pilaster in the center of each side wall.

The Mills House was the first brick-veneer house in Montgomery. The structure is of heavy balloon timber construction, with diagonal tongue-and-groove oak sheathing on the inside, and horizontal pine sheathing on

Montgomery's Architectural Heritage

the exterior. The house is also noted for having the first hot-air heating system in Montgomery. Hot air rose from the basement furnace through ductwork in the walls and entered the rooms through circular vents just below the ceiling. There are no fireplaces in the house.

The house has a central-hall plan on both floors. The staircase rises in a single run to the second-floor landing. The staircase has beadboard wainscoting, turned balusters, and a newel post of four turned balusters capped with a stylized acorn. The hall is visually divided by a six-foot-wide semicircular screen of 147 pieces of finely turned pine that hangs from the ceiling. This feature is original to the house.

Two rooms open on either side of the central hall. Originally, these were the parlor and dining room on the left, and the music studio and a guest room on the right, which were connected by sliding pocket doors. The rooms on the ground floor have beaded pine wainscoting and heart-pine floors. Doors and windows are surrounded by molded pine with corner blocks. There is raised paneling under the windows. This paneling, and elements of the door and window surrounds, are of curly pine that has a burled appearance.

At the rear of the central hall there was originally a breezeway that gave access to the detached kitchen. This breezeway was flanked by side porches. The second floor originally had four main rooms, a bath, and a steep staircase to the tower room. When this room's windows are opened, a cooling draft is created throughout the house.

After Alfonso Mills's death, his widow divided the house into apartments. It subsequently served as offices and then as an antique shop. Before Jim and Mary Wallace began renovation in 1991, the house sat empty for about sixteen years. The Wallaces lived in the house and were the proprietors of Sassafras Tea Room and Antiques until the late 1990s.

IN 1877, AT THE age of 33, Archibald Pitt Tyson gave up farming and moved from Lowndesboro to Montgomery. He thrived in real estate and the loan business. By 1886, he had built ten stores in downtown Montgomery, and he had married Ellen Nicholson Arrington, the daughter of Montgomery lawyer Samuel Lewis Arrington. A year later, they acquired property at 465 South McDonough Street. They subsequently demolished the existing structures and, in late 1888, contracted Figh and Williams to build a new house for $12,765. Their house, built in what was then a prosperous neighborhood, illustrates upper-middle-class taste of the post-Reconstruction economic boom.

Although the Tyson-Maner House is Victorian Italianate, it combines elements of various styles. The tower and the overhanging cornice supported by scroll brackets are characteristic of the high-style Italianate that preceded the Civil War. The decorative stone framing of the grouped sash

Tyson-Maner House

465 South McDonough Street

windows with one light in each sash, the double-leaved doors, and the bay windows are characteristic of several styles of the second half of the nineteenth century.

The main block is essentially a two-story square mass of solid brick, faced with red pressed brick with very thin mortar pointing. The foundation is of brick and scored cement. Window sills and lintels are limestone, as are the main entrances' jambs and carved arches, the belt courses, and the water table. The roof is a truncated pyramid. Five paneled, interior end chimneys are on the main structure, and one less-elaborate chimney is on each of the two attached one-story wings at the rear.

The mass of the house is relieved by a three-story tower with a low pyramidal roof, semi-octagonal bay windows, and pedimented gables with semi-circular stained-glass windows. Between the heavy wooden brackets supporting the cornice are circular cast-iron ventilators decorated with floral designs.

The tile-floored gallery on the front and most of the south side was added about 1916. It replaced the original wooden porch that had a great deal of elaborate gingerbread. Such additions and renovations were common at the time of the so-called second cotton fortunes, the first having been made in the 1840s and 1850s. Older houses were updated, often by additions of columns or other features believed to have been "colonial." The gallery's slender Ionic columns are unusual because the upper two-thirds of each column shaft is fluted, and the bottom third is plain. The gallery's style is out of character with the building's style; this is even more evident because the gallery is asymmetrical—a most unclassical feature. This, however, does not detract from the house, which was from its beginning an amalgamation of styles.

At the base of the tower are double doors in the Eastlake style. The fanlight and the upper parts of these doors probably once had clear beveled glass like that in the doors on the south gallery. The main door opens into a small, tiled-floor foyer and then, through a second pair of double doors, into the central hall. The south door opens into a cross hall. Both halls have elaborate paneled wainscoting. The asymmetrical exterior is echoed in the house's irregular room arrangement.

To the right of the central hall is the drawing room or music room, the most elaborate room in the house. The Carrara marble mantel has freestanding columns. Embossed ceramic tiles in a floral pattern surround the firebox; the hearth is also ceramic tile. The elaborate, turned-wood, ivory-painted and gilded overmantel has its original beveled mirror. Between the paired windows is an original beveled-glass pier mirror. Some time after the house was built, the original solid-brass hardware in this room was silver-plated. The drawing room is connected to the central hall by sliding double doors.

To the left of the central hall is the parlor. The mantel and overmantel are identical to those in the drawing room. There is a wooden panel under each window in this room, and under all other windows in the house. The parlor also has a bay window and sliding double doors that open to the central hall and to the dining room.

The dining room features a bay window and a large built-in china cabinet. The mantel is identical to those in the drawing room and parlor, except that it is made of a pink-brown Italian marble. There is no overmantel. Behind the dining room was the butler's pantry and the kitchen. Just outside the door that leads from the central hall into the dining room, in a carved niche under the staircase, is an ornately painted, pink and white porcelain washbasin. Its fittings, even the stopper, are solid brass.

The master bedroom, also on the main floor, has access to the one-story attached wing with a small sitting room and one of the house's two original bathrooms. The relatively simple bedroom has the only wooden mantel in the house.

The oak parquet floors of the drawing room, parlor, dining room, and main floor halls are laid in a basket-weave pattern and bordered by an oak and mahogany Greek key band. Woodwork on the main floor is oak, pecan, and mahogany. Pine predominates on the second floor.

A massive staircase rises from the intersection of the central hall and the cross hall. It has turned balusters and two elaborate, matching newel posts. There is also a steep servants' staircase that rises from the back porch, now enclosed.

The room arrangement on the second floor is almost identical to that on the main floor, although there are no double sliding doors. The four large bedrooms feature the same fourteen-foot ceilings of the main floor and the same wide, unpainted Eastlake woodwork. This woodwork, fanciful in outline, has similar incised designs in addition to applied wooden ornamentation. The unpainted, paneled doors have single-light transoms. The painted slate fireplaces have incised and stencilled decorations, embossed ceramic-tile hearths, and metal fireplace shields.

Solid-brass hardware throughout the house has been removed, cleaned, and replaced. However, the simple, circular ceiling medallions in the main rooms were damaged and have been replaced with elaborate plaster medallions. The entire house had interior louvered shutters. Although these were not replaced during the renovation, they and their solid-brass hardware have been saved. The remaining original metal roof cresting has also been saved.

The original iron fence fronts South McDonough and High streets. At the north of the house, a high brick wall protects a rose garden. The back yard, no longer enclosed by a high brick wall, still has one of the house's dependencies, a brick servants' house.

The Tysons had three girls and a boy. One of the girls, Anne Arrington Tyson, was born prematurely and, although blind, was an accomplished pianist and poet. Anne often played at the grand parties that the Tysons gave. Helen Keller was one of the Tysons' houseguests.

Family tradition has it that, after Mrs. Tyson's death in 1930, ownership of the house was decided by the toss of a coin. Sallie Tyson Maner, one of the daughters, won the house. Archibald Pitt Tyson, Jr., won the small lot at the rear of the house that faces South Hull Street. (In the mid-1990s this lot was reunited with the South McDonough Street lot.) Laura May Tyson Harris seems to have received nothing. A lawsuit ensued, but the decision of the coin toss was upheld.

The Tyson-Maner House has been lovingly restored by Glenda and Von Memory. The entire house is furnished and decorated with period pieces and with contemporary pieces that are sympathetic with the house. The Memory & Gilliland, L.L.C., law office is in the building.

MONTGOMERY has had several disastrous fires. The most destructive one was in December 1838. At that time there was no city fire department, although there was a wagon that had thirty leather buckets and two twenty-five-foot ladders. Leather buckets were passed up and down long lines of people in double rows. In the 1840s, a city ordinance required each drayman, or commercial hauler, to have a 25- or 50-gallon keg of water in his wagon, depending on whether his wagon was a one- or two-horse dray.

There were volunteer fire companies as early as 1847, the same year the city bought its first hand-pumped fire engine. Volunteer companies were manned by prominent citizens who, by volunteering, were exempt from jury and militia duty—perhaps an inducement for prominent citizens to join. (During the Civil War, attempts to exempt members of the volunteer companies from service in the Confederate army failed.) In the 1850s, a

Scott Street Firehouse

418 Scott Street

Montgomery's Architectural Heritage

127

city ordinance required all able-bodied men to report to Court Square when the market-house alarm bell signaled a fire. The mayor commanded these men, and the fire foreman commanded the volunteer companies.

Perhaps the most famous of the "volunteer" companies was one made up of slaves. In April 1865, retreating Confederate forces burned warehouses containing 85,000 bales of cotton to prevent the cotton from falling into Union hands. In the chaos caused by the conflagration, the potential breakdown of order, and the impending fall of the city, this black fire company saved the city from destruction.

As the city expanded up the hills and away from the city center, there were reasons to relocate some of the firehouses to the new residential neighborhoods. This was especially important because of the difficulty of moving heavy, clumsy fire equipment up the hills, once the alarm had been sounded. Until the 1870s, the engines were pulled by the men of the volunteer fire companies. This was extremely difficult, if not impossible, when the streets were muddy.

Horse-drawn fire engines were an improvement. The engine horses were trained to have their harnesses dropped on them from rigs hung from the engine-house ceilings, and to do their work despite the confusion and excitement around them. After they were trained, they were given names and accepted into the fire companies. (Each horse was also given a ten- to fifteen-day summer vacation.)

Lomax Fire Company, originally a ninety-man unit located at 128 Lee Street, was named for Colonel Tennent Lomax, who was killed at the Battle of Seven Pines in 1862. His widow was the company's "mother." In 1887, Lomax Fire Company No. 4 bought land on Scott Street; construction of the new firehouse was completed several years later. The neighborhood was then residential. The immediate neighborhood's most significant surviving houses are the Gerald-Dowdell house at 405 South Hull Street and the Powell-Reese house, which was on the block across the street from the firehouse, and facing South Decatur Street. From 1867 to 1898, this Greek Revival house was the residence of Colonel Warren Stone Reese, mayor from 1885 to 1889—at the time Lomax No. 4 moved from downtown. (In 1975, the Powell-Reese house was moved to 340 North Hull Street, Old Alabama Town.)

In 1898, the volunteer fire companies were replaced by a city fire department. On July 15 of that year, Steam Engine Company No. 2, formerly Lomax Fire Company No. 4, was the first of the city's fire stations to respond to a fire. In 1919, it was equipped with a Continental Second Class Engine (a combination hose-and-ladder wagon) served by four horses and a crew of nine men. In January 1926, the age of the horse-drawn fire engines ended with the retirement of horses named Joe and Ed. The ruins of their stalls are across the street from the former firehouse.

Originally, the Scott Street Firehouse's facade had two wide, segmental-arched, double doors flanking a small round-headed door on the ground floor, and four round-headed and segmental-arched windows on the second floor. This facade had a cornice supported by brackets and surmounted with urn finials on the corners and a segmental arched panel in the center. Behind the panel was an elaborate Victorian belfry. About 1915, a one-bay two-story addition was built west of the original firehouse. Its window treatment matched that of the original arched windows with hood molding. At that time, the elaborate Victorian cornice and belfry were replaced by a simple row of brick dentils and a low, stepped parapet.

The brick facade, originally unpainted, features a belt course, recessed panels, and a marble plaque, on which was engraved "Engine House." (The marble plaque is a reproduction of the original, which is now on the Lagoon Park fire station.) In 1980, the large double doors with glass lights above wooden panels, which had been removed in the late 1920s, were replicated.

The ground floor was originally a large open space supported by cast-iron pillars. The dispatcher's booth in the center has been retained. Although the ground floor has been divided into offices, the original beadboard ceiling has been retained, as have three galvanized poles used by the firemen to respond to alarms.

The second floor, which was one large dormitory, with two sleeping porches added about 1940, has also been divided into offices. One set of louvered shutters was found, repaired, and rehung. The more-than-twenty-foot ceiling has been opened in the reception room, giving access to a new third-floor mezzanine. Some of the original diagonal roof decking, huge roof trusses, and exposed brick walls create atmosphere.

The Scott Street Firehouse remained in service until 1966. It is the oldest surviving firehouse in Montgomery, and the only one associated with the pre-1898 volunteer system. Other old firehouses are Highland Avenue, 1911, and Cloverdale, 1930. The latter was built to resemble a Tudor-style house, at the insistence of residents who wanted to maintain the residential character of their neighborhood.

Ray and Randy Roark restored the Scott Street Firehouse in 1980. The building is now occupied by two law firms and Helms-Roark Inc., a shopping center development company.

Sayre Street School

506 Sayre Street

THE CITY'S FIRST SCHOOL was built in 1818, one year before the unification of New Philadelphia and East Alabama as Montgomery. That private academy, opened by Samuel Patterson, a physician, was short-lived, like most of Montgomery's early private academies. The most respected of these early schools was that of Enoch Childs, a native of New Hampshire and 1840 graduate of Yale College. He served as the principal of Montgomery Academy from 1841 until about 1847. In 1854, the state of Alabama established a rudimentary school system. Montgomery's public schools date from that legislation, but it was not until 1870, with Reconstruction legislation, that the system became firmly established as a city responsibility. In 1885, there were five public elementary schools in the city, three white and two black. In the same year, the editor of a leading New England journal stated that Montgomery's school system was the best in the South and without superior in the North—certainly hyperbole.

The site of the Sayre Street School had been associated with education since before the Civil War, when the Franklin Academy, a private boys' school, was there. In 1871, Lavinia Bradford Chilton opened Montgomery Female College, a private school for girls and young ladies. Late in the decade, when the city was short of funds, the Chilton school was rented by the city. In 1882, the city bought it. (Although a 1910 marble plaque recently attached to the building commemorates Montgomery Female College, that building was demolished sometime after 1891.) By 1890, the old Franklin Academy and Chilton school buildings had deteriorated so much and were so crowded that a new building was needed. The oldest building, probably the antebellum Franklin Academy, was razed.

In 1891, a new school was built for $17,066.90. This building, which was built in what was then a prosperous upper-middle-class neighborhood, still stands at the corner of Sayre and Mildred streets. It is the oldest public-school building in Montgomery. The building had four classrooms on each of its two main floors; the first floor was for grades one through five, and the second floor was for grades six through eight and a girls' high school. The girls' high school moved to the corner of South Lawrence and High streets in 1899, and united with the boys' high school in 1910 as Sidney Lanier High School (today's Baldwin Arts and Academics Magnet School).

The two-story Sayre Street School was built in a modified Richardsonian Romanesque style. Its most distinguishing feature is the polychromatic, pressed brickwork. J. B. Worthington, who soon afterwards worked on the Dexter Avenue United Methodist Church, was responsible for the brickwork. There is an ornamental drip course between the full basement and the first floor, as well as two ornamental belt courses between the first and second floors. Corbels support the parapets. Windows, doors, and pavilions are also decorated with fine brickwork. The gabled pavilions at the center and corners of each side have attached buttresses, decorative stone bands, and polychromatic brickwork accenting their gables and windows. Each of the buttresses was originally capped with a pinnacle. All of the pinnacles were removed after a storm in the 1940s toppled some of them and blew down the school's awkward-looking belfry/clock tower.

Round-headed and segmental-arched windows, which now have six-over-six sashes, originally had four-over-four and louvered shutters. Identical round-headed arches on the east and west facades shelter alcoves with beadboard ceilings and wainscoting. Recessed double doors, with single lights over horizontal panels, are surrounded by delicate reeded molding.

A wide east-west hall and a narrow north-south hall divide each floor into four classrooms. In each of the narrow halls is a staircase with a turned newel post and balustrades of beadboard paneling. The eight large classrooms have high ceilings and large windows. The walls throughout the building are wainscoted with painted beadboard. Door and window surrounds have reeded molding and corner blocks. Floors and ceilings are unpainted pine.

Sayre Street School closed in 1976. The building was completely renovated in the early 1980s. It was sold to Jean Cillie in 1997, and is now occupied by her floral shop, Jean & Co. The school also serves as a venue for weddings, receptions, formal parties, and other special events.

Design elements (from top to bottom):
- round-headed arch;
- decorative polychromatic brickwork and belt courses;
- pressed brick with its thin mortar pointing;
- segmented arch

Montgomery's Architectural Heritage

Steiner-Lobman and Teague Buildings

172 and 184 Commerce Street

IN THE 1850s, business establishments began to move from Dexter Avenue down to Court Square and Commerce Street. Lower Commerce Street locations were closer to the railroad freight depots and the city wharf. In 1890–91, 120-foot-wide Commerce Street was paved with granite Belgian blocks. This was the first project of the newly formed Commercial Club, now the Montgomery Area Chamber of Commerce. By the late nineteenth and early twentieth century, lower Commerce Street was the wholesale center of Montgomery, as well as for the surrounding counties. The eastern side of the two blocks of lower Commerce Street is all that remains of this once-thriving commercial area.

Of the fine commercial buildings that remain, the Steiner-Lobman and Teague buildings at the southeast corner of Commerce and Tallapoosa streets are among the most impressive. They are meant to resemble masonry palaces of the Italian Renaissance.

After nineteen years running a general store in Pineapple, south of Montgomery, Louis Steiner and Nathan Lobman opened a wholesale dry goods firm in Montgomery in the late 1880s. Their success is evident by the grand dry goods emporium they built in 1891. The Steiner-Lobman partnership must have been strong: they were first cousins and brothers-in-law. Their families even have adjoining lots in Oakwood Cemetery.

In 1895, they sold the southern building to Teague Hardware Company. (William Martin Teague had prospered in the mercantile business in Greenville before coming to Montgomery and founding a hardware business. He also prospered in Montgomery, acquiring the Greek Revival mansion on South Perry Street that still bears his name. He served as a city alderman and mayor and, with his son-in-law, built the Teague-Gay Hotel.) Both the Steiner-Lobman and Teague businesses occupied these two buildings until the mid-1970s.

Except for roof ornaments and minor decorative details, the two buildings are identical. The three-story masonry buildings share a common firewall. They have separate hipped roofs. The Commerce Street elevation of each building has six bays separated by cast-iron pilasters that support the masonry of the upper floors, and allow for wide show windows or doors on the ground floor. Originally, each bay had a double door with lower paneled sections, large single upper light, and ten smaller colored lights. There was a large, rectangular single-light transom above each pair of doors. Ground-floor facades of both buildings retain most of the original treatment.

A full entablature of sheet metal separates the ground floor from the second floor. The upper two floors are sheathed in pressed metal embossed with rosettes, rope molding, raised panels, and with egg-and-dart and leaf-and-tongue motifs. Pressed zinc, tin, or galvanized iron provided an inexpensive imitation, very freely adapted, of the stone decorative features of Italian Renaissance buildings.

Second-floor windows are square-headed, and those on the third floor are flat with rounded corners. Both have rope molding and heavy metal hoods topped with small faces. The double-hung windows on the second and third floors originally had two lights in each sash.

The heavy cornice is supported by large brackets. Stepped parapets above the cornice are topped with decorative metal sculptures. The Steiner-Lobman building has an eight-foot goddess, perhaps Athena, who, in addition to being a warrior goddess and protectress of heroes and chastity, also fostered industry, especially pottery and weaving. She also is the protectress of architects and sculptors. The Teague Hardware Company building's symbol is an anvil, not a mythological god such as Vulcan (which is a symbol closely associated with Birmingham, not Montgomery).

The most unusual feature of the Steiner-Lobman building is the fanciful fifteen-foot corner tower with curved Mansard roof capped by a "coffin." This feature has always been ornamental; nothing more, nothing sinister.

The Tallapoosa Street elevation of the Steiner-Lobman building is similar to the Commerce Street elevation, except that the ground floor has windows rather than double doors. A stepped parapet, similar to the Commerce Street parapet, was removed after the late 1920s.

Originally, the interiors of the two buildings were identical. Essentially, each floor was a large, high-ceilinged room supported by a central row of cast-iron pillars. Many of these fluted pillars, with simple capitals of metal leaves, have been preserved. The full basements have a central row of brick piers flanked by two rows of timbers.

To allow for alternative use, the interiors of these buildings have been divided into offices. Woodwork appropriate to the period was used in the renovation of the interiors.

Rushton, Stakely, Johnston, and Garrett, P.A., purchased and renovated the Steiner-Lobman building in 1979–1980. This law firm, which has occupied the building since its renovation, also owns the adjoining Teague building.

ABOUT 1855, Edward Hutton Grant and Emma Jerusha McIntosh Grant built a one-story, four-room Italianate-style cottage at the corner of Adams Avenue and South Hull Street. Grant was born in Scotland in 1815, emigrated to the United States in 1834, and, after first living in Pennsylvania, came to Montgomery in 1841. His wife was born in South Carolina in 1834. Grant, who had a fiery temper, had an altercation with a rival grocer in 1859. Both drew their cane swords. Grant died from complications of the wound he suffered. His widow lived in the house until 1879; she died in 1915.

In 1879, city alderman Thomas Goode Jones, who had married Georgena Caroline Bird in 1866, bought the cottage for $3,300. In 1892, when he was governor, he enlarged the cottage considerably to accommodate his wife and their thirteen children.

Jones, who was born in Georgia in 1844, received his early education in Montgomery. In 1859, he entered Virginia Military Institute, perhaps

Governor Jones House

323 Adams Avenue

because his family had deep Virginia roots. One of his instructors was Stonewall Jackson. With his fellow cadets, he left VMI in 1862 and joined the Confederate army. He rose rapidly through the ranks and ended the war as a major; he carried the truce flag at Appomattox.

On returning to Montgomery, Jones read law under John Archer Elmore, a noted lawyer, and was admitted to the bar in 1868. After serving as editor of the *Montgomery Daily Picayune,* he embarked on a political career. He served as a city alderman, state legislator and speaker of the House, and president of the Alabama Bar Association. In 1890, he represented the so-called Bourbon, or conservative, wing of the Democratic Party as candidate for governor against Reuben Kolb and the Populists, who were backed by the powerful Farmers' Alliance. The Populists wanted direct election of senators, a secret ballot, a graduated income tax, and regulation of the railroads. Although Jones won, with the backing of the large corporations, and probably electoral fraud in the Black Belt, the days of Bourbon rule were numbered. Jones served as governor from 1890 to 1894, and some progressive reforms can be attributed to his leadership. He was a prominent member of the 1901 Alabama Constitutional Convention, where he spoke against the sections of the constitution that were intended to disenfranchise black voters.

Jones, who was noted for his oratorical powers, spoke at the unveiling of the Alabama Confederate Monument in 1892, and attended the 1902 memorial services at Grant's Tomb in New York. Appointed by President Theodore Roosevelt, with the strong recommendation of Booker T. Washington, Jones served as a federal judge from 1901 until his death in 1914. Since there was no official governor's mansion, his own house served that function and, later, as a federal courtroom on several occasions.

The original 1850s Italianate-style cottage consisted of two rooms on each side of a T-shaped central hall. At the front were 18-by-18-foot rooms, and at the rear, 17-by-15-foot rooms. In 1892, a second story with five rooms was added. Several rooms were also added at the rear, if they had not been added previously. Later, a sixth room was added to the second floor. The ceilings on the second floor are eleven feet, whereas those of the first floor are thirteen feet.

The two-story frame house initially appears to be a late-nineteenth-century vernacular house. It has thin chimneys for coal-burning fires, a semicircular window and fish-scale shingles in the west gable, double-hung windows with two lights in each sash, a double-door front entrance with arched frosted lights, and a front porch supported by turned columnettes and decorated by spoolwork. The shallow projection and the brackets between the first and second floors at the southeast corner are reminders of the 1892 remodeling that originally included a short tower with a decorated gable. The steeply pitched roof may have been added when the gabled tower was removed.

Remnants of the antebellum cottage have been retained inside. The T-shaped hall is divided by an arch that springs from acanthus-leaf brackets. The old beaded baseboards, wide pine floors, pine doors with four molded panels, and sliding pocket doors between the double parlors are original to the cottage. The hardware, however, is Victorian. There are two elaborately carved marble mantels and two simpler ones. One of the mantels is original to the house; the others are from Landmarks Foundation.

The house, of course, has late-nineteenth-century features. In the rear hall is a three-quarter-turn Victorian staircase with turned balusters, a walnut handrail, and an Eastlake-style newel post. The woodwork on the second floor is more elaborate; the raised-panel doors have single-light transoms, and there is a variety of mantels with coal-burning grates. One of the mantels is of marbled metal. The semi-detached kitchen was removed early in the twentieth century. Bathrooms were added in the 1920s.

One of Governor Jones's sons, Walter Burgwyn Jones, lived in the house until his death in 1966. Walter Jones, a lawyer and circuit judge, founded Jones Law School in a small house behind 323 Adams Avenue. Judge Jones, a bachelor, lived on the west side of the house. His sister and brother-in-law, Nettie Jones Griffin and William Griffin, lived on the east side.

The Governor Jones House was restored in 1978 by the law firm of Webb and Crumpton. It is currently owned by LuAn Long and J. Edward Parish, and occupied by the law firm of Long & Parish, P.C.

Dexter Avenue United Methodist Church

301 Dexter Avenue

IN 1888, MONTGOMERY's second Methodist Episcopal Church was organized. A lot was bought, at the corner of Dexter Avenue and Bainbridge Street, that was occupied by a five-room cottage and a commercial building—Dotzheim Grocery and Saloon. The cottage became the parsonage, and the grocery and saloon became the church. Two years later, the nascent church moved to the present site and built a temporary wooden "tabernacle" for $724.95.

The cornerstone for the current church building was laid in 1892. Because the congregation was committed to erecting a fine permanent building, it was the turn of the century before the building was completed. They had great difficulty raising the building funds. In 1895, the Reverend T. K. Roberts preached a remarkable sermon that moved the hearers to "willingly part with their money and their jewels so that the new building could go forward to completion."

The Richardsonian Romanesque–style building was designed by R. W. McGrath. Both the Dexter Avenue and McDonough Street elevations are dominated by high gabled ends. There is a variety of round-headed windows and, in the Dexter Avenue gable, a large wheel window. Asymmetrical towers with grouped round-headed windows flank the facade.

These towers have been altered considerably. Originally, the southeastern tower had a Romanesque-style, high-pitched pyramidal roof. This was first replaced with a low-pitched pyramidal roof, and later by the current flat roof. Attached to the east side of this tower is a handsome semicircular stair-tower with a half-conical copper roof. Alterations to the southwest tower and steeple were more drastic. The original tower had another story, the bell chamber, which had two round-headed openings on each face. Above the bell chamber was a very tall, elegant steeple. In the first quarter of the twentieth century, the steeple and bell chamber were damaged by two lightning strikes. Rather than rebuilding in the original design, the truncated tower was capped with a short, heavy steeple. In the early 1960s, this steeple was replaced by the current copper-covered, overlapping, chamfered spire. This seventy-foot-high, five-ton spire fell when it was being erected, and had to be returned to the fabricator for repair.

The most notable feature of the building's exterior is the exceptionally fine decorative brickwork by J. B. Worthington, who also did the brickwork on the 1891 Sayre Street School. The red-brick structure is accented with glazed buff brick; buff terra-cotta belt courses and cornices, with classical egg-and-dart, as well as Romanesque, motifs; a dark-red terra-cotta belt course; rusticated limestone window arches and surrounds; and a limestone drip course. The stonework was by Curbow and Clapp Marble Company.

Between the 1900 sanctuary and the 1948 education building is a small, sunken garden from which the sanctuary's east windows and the semicircular stair tower can be seen. The building's main entrances are round-headed double doors in the bases of the towers. They open into vestibules that have

Montgomery's Architectural Heritage

staircases to the balcony. The circular staircase in the southeast tower is especially elegant. The vestibules are relatively unchanged from their nineteenth-century appearance.

In the major renovation of 1954, however, the sanctuary was completely changed. The very large stained-glass windows, which depict Biblical scenes and Christian symbols, are the only significant reminders of the old sanctuary.

The original interior arrangement was unusual in that the main axis was on a southeast-to-northwest diagonal. Curved pews sloped on a gently raked floor to the northwest corner of the sanctuary. This corner was dominated by a raised pipe organ. Below the organ was a small choir, the pulpit, an altar table, and a curved altar rail. The balcony that today extends along the southern wall in front of the stained-glass windows, originally continued along the eastern wall, partially obscuring the stained-glass windows. Large panels on the north wall could be raised to increase the seating capacity of the sanctuary, by including the space in the adjoining classrooms. This Akron Plan was associated with the expansion of the Sunday School movement. The sanctuary was somber, with dark wainscoting, pews, organ case, and woodwork.

Today the sanctuary is filled with light. One of the balconies has been removed, the wainscoting and woodwork have been painted, and the pews and sanctuary furnishings are of natural oak, as is the refinished organ case. These changes do not, however, explain the complete transformation of the building's interior. After a year's construction, with the excavation of a full basement, a flat floor replaced the old raked floor. The old dome has been transformed into an unornamented, oval dome with indirect lighting. The most dramatic change is the new south-north axis that replaced the old diagonal axis. The pews, now facing north, ended at the wall that originally had the Akron Plan's movable panels. These have been removed to reveal a large, almost cubical room that is today's chancel. On the north wall is an altar, above which is a four-foot brass cross superimposed on a twenty-one-foot red velvet dossal. These changes were made to increase the seating capacity of the sanctuary, because the Akron Plan was unsatisfactory, and because Methodist worship was becoming more formal.

The circa-1900 organ, now on the east wall of the chancel, is a tracker built by Henry Pilcher's Sons of Louisville, Kentucky. It has its original stenciled pipes and a refinished natural oak case.

The members of Dexter Avenue United Methodist Church, many of whom are descendants of the church's early members, are dedicated to the special ministry of a modern urban church. In this way, the congregation is being true to Christ's great commission, and to John Wesley's statement that "the world is my parish."

AFTER THE CIVIL WAR, new styles in architecture were somewhat late in coming to Montgomery. But the economy had recovered sufficiently by the 1880s to see the construction of houses in the latest fashions. These differed from antebellum houses in that they were not in the Italianate style that predominated in Montgomery before the war, or in the Greek Revival style that was also fashionable. Victorian houses of the late nineteenth century tended to be asymmetrical, and anything but classical or restrained. Rather, they were eclectic and exuberant, and emphasized the unusual and the whimsical.

▼

Stay House

631 South Hull Street

Montgomery's Architectural Heritage

It was at this time that Dr. John Hazard Henry returned to Montgomery from Selma. Henry was the scion of an old Montgomery family. When his father, the Dr. H. W. Henry, came to Montgomery in 1820, he was one of the town's first physicians. He ran a drug store and married a daughter of William Falconer. Dr. H. W. Henry founded the Montgomery Hussars, or Henry's Horse Company, Montgomery's second volunteer military corps. As its captain, he and his cavalrymen served as Governor Clement C. Clay's bodyguard in the Creek Indian hostilities in 1836.

John Henry, born in 1829, studied medicine under the famous Dr. J. Marion Sims. He then attended and was graduated from the University of New York City and, later, from the College of Homeopathy in Philadelphia. He was among the first to practice homeopathy in Alabama. On his father's death in 1857, the younger Dr. Henry moved to Selma where he became involved in local politics. Near the end of the Civil War, while serving as mayor of Selma, he negotiated with the Union forces after the fall of the city. After the war, he became a Republican, helping organize the first white Southern Republican convention. But early in the 1880s, perhaps because of the end of Reconstruction, he abandoned politics and returned to Montgomery and to his profession.

In 1893, he constructed a house on South Hull Street in what was then a middle-class neighborhood. On his death in 1906, the house passed to his daughter, Martha Falconer Henry, who married Ernest W. Stay, chief accountant with Alabama Fidelity and Casualty Company. His name is still faintly legible on the threshold at the gate. Three Stay children were born and reared in the house: Mary Stay Buckner of Nashville, Anna Stay Starr of Philadelphia, and Colonel Hazard Stay of Athens, Georgia. The last of the Stays moved away in 1963.

The Stay House is a Victorian house with modest Eastlake trim. The two-story house is asymmetrical, with a gabled wing projecting from a rectangular central block. There is a central tower capped with a steep pyramidal roof. The projecting wing, with its bay window and gable, and the front porch on the left, accentuate the asymmetry.

The most distinguishing exterior features are the horseshoe ventilators in the gables. Each of these large, unusual ventilators once had a small metal trough to catch rainwater for the birds. According to Mary Stay Buckner, her father, who was extremely superstitious, selected the horseshoe ventilators for good luck. The house is often called the Horseshoe House.

Some of the windows are single; others are paired. The right side of the front has a bay window. Each sash in the double-hung windows has one large pane of glass. Lintels and sills are of rock-faced stone. Originally, all the windows had exterior louvered shutters. Some have been rehung.

The pressed-brick veneer walls with very thin mortar pointing are separated from the brick foundation by a rock-faced stone water table or drip

Double-hung windows with one light in each sash

142

A Sense of Place

course. The foundation has small ventilators covered with ornate metal grills. There is a projecting cornice supported by simple brackets. The four end chimneys have corbeled tops.

The front porch, on the northwest side of the front of the house, has marble steps, a wooden floor, and a beadboard ceiling. The balustrade and posts are in the Eastlake style. The solid and paneled double front door in the base of the tower is set in an arch with alternating rock-faced wedges. A four-segment fanlight is set in the arch. The solid double front doors open into a very small vestibule, from which a single door with wood panels and frosted glass panes opens into the hall.

The asymmetrical arrangement of the exterior belies the fact that the house is built on a slightly modified central-hall plan. The double-turn staircase is in an alcove at the rear of the hall. The newel post is very heavy, the balusters turned and very simple. A rear door opens onto the back porch.

To the right of the hall are two parlors connected by sliding double doors. The front parlor has a bay window and the most elaborate mantel in the house. This mahogany mantel has an inset mirror and two inset carved panels. There are also numerous shelves and galleries to display decorative items. To the left of the hall is the dining room. It is open to the hall, except for a surrounding frame and two unusual Victorian columns that help delineate the space. On one wall there are built-in cabinets with clear glass doors.

Round-headed arched doorway with fanlight

Pressed brick with its thin mortar pointing

Montgomery's Architectural Heritage 143

The dining room is connected to the kitchen by a butler's pantry. The kitchen also opens onto the back porch. Kitchen, butler's pantry, and back porch have been altered, the latter now being enclosed in glass. The kitchen itself is in a one-story wing projecting from the northeast side of the house.

Interior trim on the main floor consists of a heavy ceiling molding with dentils, high baseboards, heavily reeded door and window surrounds with corner blocks, and four-paneled doors with single-light transoms. Each of the wide sliding doors between the double parlors has three long vertical panels over three shorter ones. There are raised panels under the windows of the double parlors and the dining room. The floors are made of oak.

On the second floor, there are four bedrooms. The woodwork is simpler, the ceilings are lower, there are no transoms over the doors, and the floors are pine. As on the main floor, all the mantels are different. Some are of wood, others of metal. The hearths are of tile, as are the surrounds of the coal-burning fireboxes. Some of the tiles are original; others are replacements.

The Stays decided to replace the fireplaces with central heating. After the furnace had been on for several days, furniture came unglued, wallpaper peeled off the walls, and everyone in the family came down with the flu. The furnace was removed and the grate fires were restored.

The house is separated from the sidewalk by a low brick retaining wall and the restored original iron fence. A hex-block walk extends to the marble porch steps. The 100-by-138-foot lot is informally landscaped. There were once flower beds and dogwoods. The servants' quarters, greenhouse, carriage house, and barn are gone.

The Stay House was restored by Hoyt Henley, who bought it from the Stay estate. The house is now owned by Walter T. McKee, Jr., and is occupied by the architecture and interior design firm of McKee and Associates.

S PERIDON CASSIMUS waited several years before following his father, Alexander M. Cassimus, Sr., and older brother, Alex, to the United States. Alexander and Alex arrived in Mobile in 1873, moved to Memphis the following year, and came to Montgomery in 1878. They were the first Greeks in the city. (In 1882, there were only 126 Greeks in the United States.) By 1888, they were able to pay Speridon's passage, but he had to leave his wife and two children in Greece. The Cassimus family had a wholesale fruit business on Bibb Street. By 1892, the younger Cassimus was able to return to his native Corfu for his family. He also brought fig trees, flowering Sparta bushes, jujube trees, and several varieties of plum trees. These were for his new house on North Jackson Street. At that time,

Cassimus House

110 North Jackson Street

there were fine Victorian houses on the street, including the houses of two governors. One of these, now replaced by a parking lot, was one of the finest Victorian houses in the city.

The house that Cassimus built in 1893 was intended to proclaim his success as a businessman. It also proclaimed his Greek heritage, because although the house was Victorian in massing and floorplan, it used restrained, somewhat classical decorative elements, rather than the ornate decorative elements of the time. It has been said that the house strongly embodies his personality and "perhaps the fact that he never completely resolved the conflicts of his origins in Greece with the life he had made for himself in America."

The two-story frame house, with a truncated hipped roof that terminates with a pyramidal cap, is Victorian in its asymmetrical massing. The northern, gabled bay projects from the main block. It has a rectangular bay window on the first floor and a paired window on the second. The main block is two bays wide, with the front door and a window on the first floor, and two evenly spaced windows on the second. An L-shaped porch is on the southwest corner of the main block. Nothing is particularly unusual in this massing; it is completely Victorian.

The decorative elements, however, are unusual in their restraint. Even the shallow dome of the curved corner of the porch, not an unusual feature for late-Victorian houses, is restrained. The exterior detailing of cornices, window and door trim, porch columnettes and balustrade are more classical than Victorian. Although the gable is decorated with ornamental shingles, the gable within a gable is unusual—displaying some classical restraint in an era of decorative exuberance. The tall internal chimneys have corbelled tops. The exterior, now gray trimmed with white, with blue-gray shutters and foundation, was originally cream trimmed with white, and with green shutters and lattice between the brick piers. The original metal roof has been replaced.

The front door opens into a stair hall, lit by a large colored-glass window high on the stairwell wall. The stairs rise in two turns to a second-floor landing. The balusters are turned. The Victorian newel posts, now painted, have classical urn finials.

To the left of the entrance hall is a double parlor. The rectangular bay window's corners are protected by turned wooden balusters. The fireplace is decorated with two free-standing turned oak columns with Scamozzi capitals. The oak mantel has applied decorations with both classical and Victorian motifs. There are no two mantels alike in the house, although all are of unpainted oak and combine classical and Victorian elements. Most are double mantels with beveled-glass mirrors. The double parlors are separated by sliding pocket doors, each of which has three long raised panels over three short ones. Other doors in the house have four raised panels. Almost all hardware throughout the house is original.

In addition to the entrance hall, central hall, and double parlors, there is the dining room and a pantry on the first floor. The kitchen, which was once connected to the house by a porch, is now attached.

The original house had three bedrooms on the second floor. There may have been several smaller service rooms, but alterations have obscured the original floorplan at the rear of the house. Additional rooms have been added to the rear of the house on the first and second floors.

Door and window surrounds are of molded woodwork with simple architraves. Most of the double-hung windows have two lights in each sash. The high baseboards are molded. This woodwork is now painted, but the pine doors are still unpainted. The floors are of heart pine, most pieces extending from wall to wall.

Speridon Cassimus and his wife are said to have been excellent gardeners. He laid the octagonal paving stones in the small front yard. It was originally bordered by grass and flowers. The iron fence and the marble threshold with the carved "S. Cassimus" survive from the 1890s. The back yard, now much diminished by the recent construction of an addition, once consisted of an upper terrace of grass and flowers and a lower terrace for vegetables. The brick retaining wall is still in place. None of the plantings that were brought from Corfu have survived.

In 1935, the house was converted into apartments. The 1976 restoration of the house undid the minor changes that were made to accommodate the apartments. Since restoration, the house has been owned and occupied by the Alabama State Employees Association.

Kennedy-Sims House

556 South Perry Street

IN 1856, TWO YEARS AFTER emigrating from Scotland, Absalom Kennedy founded A. M. Kennedy Company at 109 Commerce Street. He dealt in paints, wallpaper, doors, window sashes and blinds, interior woodwork, picture frames, and painters' supplies.

The son of Absalom and Ann McQueen Kennedy, Joseph, remained in Scotland. This young Kennedy (a direct descendant of the Scottish national hero Rob Roy McGregor, who had been romanticized in Sir Walter Scott's 1817 novel) seems to have had a fanciful nature. At twelve, Joseph Kennedy ran away from school with the intention of joining the crew of Admiral Raphael Semmes's cruiser, *Alabama*, which, before being sunk, captured sixty-five Union ships and effectively drove U.S. commerce from the seas. Young Joseph Kennedy was apprehended and returned to his school.

Before leaving Scotland in 1867, the seventeen-year-old served as the youngest bugler in the Queen's Guard. At some time between 1867 and 1877, he served as a ship's painter out of the port of San Francisco when he was "out to see the world." In 1877, he married Mary Irvin, a native of Illinois and daughter of a U.S. Army captain. The Kennedys had a son and a daughter. The former, Absalom, worked in early motion pictures and served as staff engineer of Thomas Edison's laboratory in Orange, New Jersey. In 1902, Joseph, then a widower, married Eunice Estelle Thrash, daughter of a Selma merchant and great-granddaughter of General Edmund Butler, who had served under George Washington. They had one daughter.

Joseph Kennedy was taken into his father's business in 1886; six years later, he became the proprietor of the store, and in 1894 he completed his mansion at 556 South Perry Street. It has been called an example of Victorian exuberance, eccentricity, and even madness. But it was not so unusual a century ago, when it was surrounded by other grand Queen Anne–style houses with their steeples, turrets, tall ornamental chimneys, balconies and rambling porches, gingerbread and spoolwork, and various surface treatments. The Queen Anne style was the culmination of a movement, which began with the antebellum Italianate style, to escape the rigidly formal and coldly rational Georgian, Federal, and Greek Revival styles. The movement was also an attempt at cozy domesticity.

The house is said to have been the fulfillment of Joseph Kennedy's childhood dreams. His romantic nature and artistic talents are reflected in this house, one of the most distinctive surviving in Montgomery. He designed the house and supervised its construction. He is also believed to have designed, cut, and crafted all the stained-glass windows; if this is accurate, he was a superb craftsman.

The porch columnettes, with their almost Oriental capitals, rest on a rusticated sandstone wall. The porch roof is topped with a low balustrade. The scrolled handrails of the steps are brass. One of the seven dormers on the steeply pitched roof is supported by a distinctive corbelling that resembles an inverted beehive. The projecting bay on the facade is a tower whose first story is octagonal; the second story, resting on corbels, is circular. Above a wide frieze is the finial-capped, bell-shaped dome—the feature that makes the house a Montgomery landmark. Other Victorian features are one-over-one window sashes, finials on the dormers, roof cresting, and the fine pressed brick that is said to have been made of molasses, sand, and oil.

Double oak doors, set with stained glass and topped with a round-headed stained-glass transom, open into a small, tile-floored vestibule. Delicate, applied decorations adorn the cove ceiling. The vestibule's walls are decorated with plaster bas reliefs of women with open arms. The double doors that once opened into the stair hall have been removed.

The extraordinary nature of the house's architecture and decorative detail is undeniable in the stair hall. The floors are of quarter-sawn oak banded in mahogany. The raised-panel wainscoting is also of quarter-sawn oak. The sliding pocket doors opening into the parlor are of oak and a burl wood imported from India. The woodwork is unpainted, in contrast to the practice of the preceding Georgian, Federal, Greek Revival, and Italianate styles.

The stair hall is dominated by a ceremonial oak staircase. Its balusters are turned and incised. The stairs rise, past a cloverleaf-shaped leaded window, to a landing with a very large stained-glass window that is decorated with faceted "jewels." The balustrade at the second-floor landing makes a gentle S-curve. An intimate L-shaped banquette is tucked under the staircase.

None of the main rooms are rectangular or square; all have three-sided bays. The front parlor has stained-glass transoms in the bay, Eastlake-style woodwork, a cove ceiling, wall panels made of molding in the French style, and a sophisticated white-marble mantel with console jambs. Sliding pocket doors connect front and back parlors. The latter features a large bay, cove ceiling, wall panels, and a mahogany mantel.

The dining room has the most elaborate floor in the house: parquet squares surrounded by elaborate intertwined banding. The room, with oak raised-panel wainscoting and a large bay, is dominated by a massive fireplace. The mantel is supported by lion's-head consoles with lion's-paw bases. The overmantel's beveled-glass mirror is flanked by columns with Composite capitals.

The 5,300-square-foot house has a bedroom on the main floor, and three bedrooms and a sleeping porch on the second floor. The porch's wide overhanging roof, supported by heavy timber brackets, is an addition to the 1894 house. The house has two bathrooms, one on each floor, plus a servants' bathroom off the back porch. A steep servants' staircase rises from the back hall. The attic, with a high ceiling and seven dormers with colored-glass windows, has a pine beadboard walls and ceiling.

In 1980, William Newell saved the Kennedy-Sims mansion from demolition and restored it. Margo and Jess Jordan of Mansfield, Texas, completed the restoration and interior decoration. The house is owned by John Holloway and occupied by Holloway, Elliott & Moxley, L.L.P.

TODAY, MONTGOMERY does not have a passenger rail service. Amtrak, whose station was in a converted grain elevator in the beautifully landscaped Riverside Park, ended its service in 1995. But before rail service began to decline in the 1920s, the situation was quite different.

Montgomery's early transportation system included overland routes by foot, horseback, and wagon to Savannah and Charleston, and flatboats from Tennessee and Mobile. In April 1821, the first regular stage line between Montgomery and Milledgeville, Georgia, opened. Yet even by the end of the decade, overland travel was very slow, and the roads were notoriously bad. The 150-mile stage journey to Tuscaloosa took 104 hours, averaging a mile and a half an hour, and with a baggage allowance of only fifteen pounds. With the spread of plank roads after 1850, overland transportation improved slightly. The first steamboat arrived from Mobile in October 1821; steamboats were to dominate transportation until the 1880s.

Steam locomotives were introduced into the South by 1830. The first steam railroad east from Montgomery was constructed between 1832 and 1840; it extended 12 miles. By 1851 it extended the full 76 miles to West Point, Georgia, with connections to Atlanta. Yet Georgia had only 185 miles

▼

Union Station

300 Water Street

Montgomery's Architectural Heritage

151

Syrian arch

of track as late as 1840. Not until the late 1850s was there a rail link between Richmond and New Orleans. By the middle of the 1880s, Montgomery had become a major rail junction. A decade later, the city was served by about a dozen railroads.

One of these was the Louisville and Nashville Railroad, nicknamed the Late and Nasty by its employees. Although it was not a major passenger carrier, like the railroads in the northeastern U.S., it did endeavor to increase passenger patronage. Consequently, in the last quarter of the nineteenth century the L&N began to build fine stations, and Montgomery was a beneficiary of this effort to improve the railroad's corporate image. Union Station was the largest railroad station in Alabama, considerably larger than a city the size of Montgomery would otherwise warrant, because the station housed L&N's regional general traffic office, which was second in the company's hierarchy only to the railroad's Louisville headquarters. Passenger traffic was not inconsequential: in 1886, about 585,000 passengers passed through the city, and by 1894 there were forty-four passenger trains a day.

Unlike some large railroad stations, there was no hotel in Union Station. But there were several fine hotels nearby, because, before the development of Florida as a winter resort, Montgomery was popular as a wintering place for Northerners. The city's most fashionable hotels were the Exchange Hotel, on the northwest corner of Montgomery and Commerce streets, and the Windsor Hotel, across from Union Station on the southwest corner of Water and Commerce streets.

In 1893, construction began on the new Union Station to replace the modest station built in 1860. When completed, at the cost of two hundred thousand dollars, it consisted of the main building, that housed waiting rooms on the ground floor and offices on the floors above; the train shed to protect passengers and baggage; and two flanking buildings for baggage and for railroad express. The two flanking buildings were completed about 1913. As the union station, it served as the main passenger station for all railroads, not just for the L&N. There were several other depots to handle freight.

Union Station's architect, Benjamin Bosworth Smith, settled in Montgomery as a result of his work on the station. He may have been inspired by Richard Morris Hunt's neo–French Renaissance designs. He certainly was influenced by Henry Hobson Richardson's Romanesque. For a time in the late nineteenth century, Richardsonian Romanesque was the dominant style for public buildings and, to some degree, for major commercial buildings. The Richardsonian Romanesque style is characterized by numerous features that are evident in Union Station. These include the building's general massiveness or solidity, repetition of arched openings, bands of closely spaced windows, massive pyramidal roofs, towers and turrets, and the low, wide, heavy Syrian arch for major openings.

The main building has a three-story central block with symmetrical two-story hyphens that end in smaller three-story blocks similar to the central one. The central block and the two end blocks have high-pitched pyramidal roofs with projecting gables and miniature corbeled turrets. The intervening hyphens also have projecting paired gables. The ornate building, constructed of pressed brick with very thin mortar pointing, rests on a rusticated Georgia-granite base. Limestone is used on window trim, gables, finials, corbels, and belt courses.

The main street entrance is under the projecting porte cochere. Its wide, brick Syrian arch is enhanced by seven large stone insets. Above the door is an arched segment filled with stained glass; terra-cotta work, with fleur-de-lis motif, covers the wall surrounding the door. An identical door is on the opposite side of the central block, opening to the train shed platform. Main entrances from the street and the platform open into the large waiting room that is two stories high. Large brackets, clad in decorative, pressed metal, support a shallow balcony with oak balustrade that encircles the entire waiting room. From this balcony, train arrivals and departures were announced. The four large windows at the balcony level have their original stained glass. There is a boxed-beam ceiling, oak raised-panel wainscoting, and a mosaic tile floor.

The asymmetrical east flanking building was the baggage house. Although constructed later than the main building, it is identical in style and construction. The two-story building has a gabled attic. Interior walls are

Train shed

of exposed brick, as they were originally. When the wooden floor was replaced, a layer of charcoal was discovered under the floor. This practice, also discovered under the basement floor of Old Alabama Town's 1848 Ordeman-Shaw House, may have been to control moisture or rising dampness.

The west flanking building was the railroad express agency depot. The exterior of the one-story building with gabled attic is identical in style and construction to the main block. Its interior, however, was open to the rafters. An exceptionally elegant interior has been constructed in this formerly utilitarian building.

To many architects, certainly to most engineers, the chief interest of Union Station is not the Richardsonian Romanesque–style building, but the 1897–98 train shed that was constructed to protect passengers and baggage. Only a few of these structures, whose popularity began in the 1870s, survive today. They are examples of how bridge-building techniques could be adapted to building construction. In fact, some 1868–85 iron bridge parts are incorporated in Montgomery's train shed.

The train shed, which was designed by the L&N engineering department, covers an area measuring 600 by 95 feet. This does not include the sloped-roofed portico that previously connected the train shed to the station. The roof is supported by twenty-five tri-composite Pratt trusses of timber, wrought iron, and cast iron, with cambered bottom chords. The roof, originally metal covered with slate, has a twenty-foot-wide central monitor that runs the entire length of the shed. The monitor has louvered sides for ventilation, and once had a glass roof to admit light. There is still colored glass in the gables at either end of the train shed. There was competition between railroads and cities regarding the size of their train sheds. Gable-roofed sheds, like Montgomery's, were supplanted by arched balloon sheds in the 1890s.

Union Station was restored in the early 1980s as four separate projects, all of which were the results of Mayor Emory Folmar's leadership in saving and restoring this, one of Montgomery's most familiar buildings. Landmarks Foundation sponsored an auction that raised $100,000 for the restoration of the train shed. Jim Wilson and Associates restored the main building, SouthTrust Bank restored the east flanking building, and the Frazer Lanier Company, investment bankers, renovated the west flanking building.

Today, Union Station is not only a fine example of late-nineteenth-century commercial architecture, and one of the largest and most ornate railroad stations remaining in the Southeast, but it is also a fine example of alternative use of historic buildings. Union Station's center building, now owned by the City of Montgomery, houses several firms, agencies, and businesses, in handsome offices, as well as the Montgomery Visitor Center in the former waiting room. Some offices are elaborate and sophisticated, while others emphasize the building's original woodwork and interesting windows, and others focus on exposed brickwork and the huge trusses that support the roof. The east flanking building is owned and occupied by SouthTrust Bank, and the west flanking building is owned and occupied by The Frazer Lanier Company. The train shed is used for a variety of private and public functions, including housing one of the Jubilee CityFest stages.

In the past, Court Square was the heart of the city. After the demolition of four blocks in front of Union Station, and the closing of Lee Street, which once terminated at the station's main entrance, the great open space (albeit a parking lot) served Montgomery as its living room. Two sides of this square are very handsome: the station's south facade and the facades of the late-nineteenth- and early-twentieth-century mercantile houses of lower Commerce Street. Until the summer of 1994, the uninterrupted view of Union Station and the east side of lower Commerce Street presented the finest streetscape remaining in the city.

Great Western Railway of Alabama Freight Depot (Riverfront Center)

200 Coosa Street

THROUGHOUT HISTORY, cities that have thrived have been located on important transportation routes. Land speculators selected what is now Montgomery as a town site because it was on high land near the northernmost limit of navigation on the Alabama River. Numerous ancient trails crossed here or nearby, and the Federal Road from Milledgeville, Georgia, to St. Stephens, Alabama, passed only a few miles to the southeast. In the beginning, mail came to the isolated frontier village of Montgomery only once a week. Goods came by wagon or on horseback from Savannah and Charleston, or were poled upriver from Mobile. Flatboats from Mobile took from fifty to seventy days. In March 1821, the *Republican* arrived. This fifty-foot keel boat had traveled nearly a thousand miles, including ten by portage, from West Point in east Tennessee.

In October 1821, the village became less isolated with the arrival of the steamboat *Harriet*, which took seven days, excluding stops, from Mobile. Eventually, the city wharf became the most important source of city government revenue, reaching $50,000 in one year. A tunnel was built from lower Commerce Street to the wharf so that cotton wagons did not have to cross the railroad tracks and make a steep descent to the wharf. The city depended on steamboats to take its cotton, the basis of the city's economy, to Mobile and markets beyond. Gradually, the railroads displaced the steamboats, and significant river traffic ended in the 1910s.

Although construction of Montgomery's first railroad began in 1832, connections were not made with Atlanta until 1851; not until later in the decade were connections made with Richmond and New Orleans. The Confederacy's war effort suffered because of the underdeveloped Southern railroad system. After the Civil War, Southern traditionalists opposed extension of the railroads, which were already underdeveloped by Northern standards. New South advocates, however, promoted railroad development—with Northern capital and Northern control. Consequently, Atlanta and Birmingham thrived, while formerly important centers, like Milledgeville, declined. By the 1880s, Montgomery had become a major rail junction. In 1893, the Louisville and Nashville railroad began construction of Union Station, which served as the passenger station for the numerous railroads serving Montgomery.

In 1898, the Great Western Railway of Alabama, a descendant of Alabama's first railroad company, built a new Montgomery depot. Although this depot did serve passengers, it was primarily a freight depot. At one time, there were some half-dozen freight depots in Montgomery, but the Great Western's is the only one that has survived.

The complex is composed of the two-story main building that fronts on Coosa Street, and two one-story wings (now renovated as two-story) extending from the rear of the main building to the east, parallel to Tallapoosa Street. The main building of lightly glazed tan brick has a low hipped roof with wide, overhanging eaves supported by brackets. Although primarily utilitarian, the main building does have several decorative features, most of which have been incorporated in structural elements. For example, the drip course is of granite. The most distinctive of the decorative features is the unusual paired wall chimneys that spring from corbels. There are two of these paired chimneys on the facade, and one on either end of the building. Another distinctive feature is the escutcheon bearing the name of the railway on the southwest corner of the building. The second floor's grouped windows are round-headed with one light in each sash. The wide arches enclosing the windows on the first floor are much larger than those on the second. A similar large arch shields the alcove at the main entrance. The alcove is reached by granite steps and is paved with one-inch red, brown, and white marble squares.

The two red-brick (now painted) wings at the rear have protective shed roofs supported by heavy wooden brackets. The U-shaped wings (which once had railroad tracks and loading platforms on the inside of the U, and access for delivery vehicles on the outside) have large, segmental-arched freight doors. In 1981, after a $6 million renovation, the buildings were opened as a 131-room hotel. The interior renovation exposed the orange-red brick laid in common bond, and retained the pressed metal ceiling of the lobby, enormous railway safes, solid-brass fittings on the windows, pine doors, and floors of quarter-sawn long-leaf yellow pine.

Each of the two one-story wings, originally freight warehouses, was modified as a two-story guest-room wing. The rooms on the second floor had cathedral ceilings with exposed wooden roof trusses. The bottom cord of each of these mortised and tenoned trusses is eight inches square and more than sixty feet long—each made of a single timber. In an age of mass production and look-alike buildings, the Great Western Railway of Alabama Freight Depot's renovation, which was sympathetic to the building's original construction, gave the hotel a distinctive, unique atmosphere. This hotel was a far cry from the double log cabin that James Vickers built in 1818 as Montgomery's first hotel, or the elegant 1847 Exchange Hotel that served as the unofficial capitol of the Confederacy in early 1861.

In 1996, the hotel's 131 rooms were converted into 60 apartments. The front part of the Riverfront Center was converted into office suites.

AT THE TURN of the century, Burtonville was a prosperous middle-class suburban neighborhood. There are still fine late-Victorian houses, especially on the south side of Noble Avenue. The large two-story house at the corner of Noble Avenue and South McDonough Street is representative of the taste and way of life of a prominent business family at the turn of the century. The house on the tree-shaded, terraced hill dominates the neighborhood. Originally, the complex was much larger. There were flower gardens behind the house. Servants' quarters and the vegetable garden were on the north side of Noble Avenue.

Charles Linn Gay of Montgomery and Ida Belle Smith of Tallapoosa County were married in 1888. They first lived on Holcombe Street. Gay was originally in the wholesale grocery business and later in the wholesale drug business. (He eventually sold his shares in the drug business to the Durr family.) Gay also opened the Farmer's Compress Warehouse Company, which included a gin, grist mill, and commissary. He discovered a method to compact cotton into even smaller bales. However, because there was a danger that the bales would expand violently if they got wet, railroad and steamboat shippers refused to accept the compacted bales. Mrs. Gay was the founder of the Montgomery Woman's Club.

▼

Gay House

230 Noble Avenue

Montgomery's Architectural Heritage

In 1883, Charles Gay was graduated from the State Agricultural and Mechanical College of Alabama, now Auburn University. Because he had been trained as a civil engineer, he must have felt himself competent to design his own house after his marriage. (Actually, his course of instruction included road, bridge, and canal construction; there was no instruction in building design.)

In 1900, Gay contracted Hugger Brothers Construction Company to build the house. Robert and Emile Hugger had come to Montgomery from Ohio in the mid-1880s and had become well-known builders, working in more than fifteen states. Their most ambitious project was the 1928–29 Jefferson Davis Hotel.

Montgomery's finest high-style Queen Anne houses (e.g, the Davidson, Farley, Nicrosi, O'Connell, and Thomas houses) were built about 1890; they have all been demolished. Nevertheless, the Gay house is a good example of late Queen Anne–style architecture. Combining Victorian and classical elements, it is more subdued, less exuberant than high-style Queen Anne.

The irregularly shaped house, with its central truncated hipped roof, has projecting gables and dormers, a bay window supported by brackets, a wrap-around porch with octagonal corner, second-story walkout porches, tall corbelled chimneys, and a variety of materials (such as fish-scale shingles in the gables, stone and brick foundations, and clapboard siding) that are associated with the Queen Anne style. It also has classical elements, examples of the so-called Colonial Revival style that was then supplanting the Queen Anne style. Classical elements on the Gay house include a porte cochere, pedimented portico at the entrance, modified Tuscan columns, fluted pilasters, denticulated cornice, and Palladian windows and attic vents. There is a variety of window treatments, including upper sashes with frosted glass and patterned muntins above lower sashes of a single transparent light. The house is painted yellow, its original color.

The main door is recessed in a tiled and wainscoted alcove. This double-leaved door has round-headed, beveled lights above molded panels. The interior has an irregular floor plan. Both the main entrance on the north and the entrance from the porte cochere open into a large wainscoted stairhall, the most impressive feature of the house. The woodwork, now painted, was originally stained dark. The triple-turn staircase has turned balusters, paneled newel posts, and paneled wainscoting. The large second-floor stair landing is graced by a long, curved balustrade. There is also a servants' staircase at the rear of the house.

The living and dining rooms are connected by sliding pocket doors. There is no window to the right of the living-room fireplace because a huge gilt-framed mirror originally covered that wall. On the main floor, there is also the master bedroom and adjoining dressing room and bath, the butler's pantry with original fitted buffet-china cabinet, the kitchen, and service rooms. On the second floor there are three bedrooms, a bath, closets, a large stair foyer, and two small walkout porches.

The house is noted for its fine interior detailing and woodwork. Window and door surrounds vary, but all are elaborately molded; some have corner blocks. There are molded panels under the windows in the principal rooms. The six fireplaces are treated differently. Four have free-standing columns that support mantel shelves. One of the overmantel's beveled mirrors is oval, and another is shield-shaped. The coal-burning grates are surrounded by decorative cast iron and embossed ceramic tile. The interior walls are plaster over wood lath; cove ceilings grace the principal rooms on the main floor. Original lighting fixtures and door hardware are in several of the rooms. The floors are heart pine, and the baseboards are molded. The doors have a variety of paneled configurations.

Charles and Ida Belle Gay had four children who survived to adulthood. The house remained in the Gay family until 1975.

Davenport-Harrison Shotgun

911 Hutchinson Street

AFTER THE CIVIL WAR, large numbers of freedmen left their plantations and came into Southern towns and cities. Although there was no economic basis for this migration, there was the protection of Federal troops and the Freedmen's Bureau, access to political activity, and new black institutions and schools. For those who did find jobs, a very difficult thing for black men, wages were better than on the plantations.

Urban whites viewed this migration as a threat to the social order, and rural landowners viewed it as a threat to a cheap labor source. Poverty was severe; in the winter of 1865–66, the Freedmen's Bureau issued rations to more than twice the number of whites as it issued to blacks. The Montgomery City Council passed an ordinance that tried, but failed, to force white and black paupers to leave the city.

Urban blacks, both freedmen and those who were free before the Civil War, probably also viewed the migration of former plantation slaves into the towns as a threat. There were 439,000 slaves in Alabama in 1860 and only 2,360 free blacks. More than half of Alabama's free blacks lived in Mobile; there were very few in Montgomery.

Antebellum urban and rural blacks were significantly different. In general, the former had daily contact with whites, and most often with the more-affluent whites. Many of these blacks, slave and free, had marketable skills that they exercised relatively independently. Plantation blacks, however, had minimal or only superficial contact with their masters. Their lives were dependent on their masters, and they lived and worked in communal relationships. What skills they had were of little economic value in urban areas.

Although many of Montgomery's black servants continued to live in small houses in the back yards of their employers, many blacks skilled in the trades and the slowly growing professional and commercial classes lived in Centennial Hill, their own community in the southeast part of the city. Their ideals and values approximated those of middle-class whites.

Freedmen from the plantations, however, had few skills and no personal relationships with Montgomery's white population. Their lives were very difficult. Having little financial wherewithal, they tended to congregate on undesirable, especially low-lying, land. Hundreds lived in shanties, in caves dug in the Alabama River bluffs, and even in the old furnaces and ruins of the burned-out Confederate arsenal. Newtown, on the flood plain north of the city, was a new home for freedmen who came into Montgomery from the surrounding plantations and farms. Some of them built their houses of the charred timbers of the railroad depot and warehouses that had been burned by Union troops in the closing month of the Civil War. By necessity their housing was rudimentary.

The shotgun house became the predominating house type. It is associated with plantations, mill villages, and the poorest urban neighborhoods. Although whites lived in shotgun houses, for example in Montgomery's West End industrial area, the house type is generally associated with blacks. The shotgun house is turned perpendicular to the street. Its facade presents a gable, a front porch, and one door and window. The house is one room wide and two or more rooms deep, the rooms connecting to one another without an internal hall. Shotgun houses are invariably frame, and raised on piers.

Several explanations have been given for the origins of this type of house: marsh dwellers, American Indians, and maximal use of land. While the latter is certainly a plausible explanation, and may be a reason why shotguns proliferated in poor urban neighborhoods, shotguns appear to have been built in rural areas before they were built in urban ones.

There is another explanation of the shotgun's origin. This house type's first appearance in the United States was in New Orleans in 1809. It was imported from Haiti when 2,060 free blacks fled the island's slave revolt. (Consequently, the population of New Orleans was approximately one-third black slave, one-third free black, and one-third white. By 1860 there were 10,939 free blacks in New Orleans.) The house type may have been developed in Haiti by combining elements of West African, Caribbean Indian, and French-peasant building practices. From West Africa, especially the Yoruba, came the customary nine-by-nine-foot room size. From the Arawak Indians of Haiti came the door and porch at the gable end. The building techniques of heavy timber structure, with double-shuttered door and window, seem to have come from French peasants. These houses, called *caille* in Haiti, were common by the late seventeenth century and have not varied significantly from the mid-eighteenth century. Although first built on plantations, the *caille* became the predominant house type of Haiti's urban free-black population. Room size was increased to twelve-by-twelve feet before the house type was brought to New Orleans.

The house's name, shotgun, is usually explained by the fact that if a shotgun were fired through the front door it could go through every room in the house and exit the back door without hitting a wall. On the other hand, shotgun may be derived from the Yoruba word for house, *to-gun*. This explanation, however, seems strained, as the terms *to-gun* or shotgun are not used in Haiti.

The shotgun has been associated with the communal nature of African life and of slave life in the New World. Reputedly, Africans did not value privacy, or perhaps even individuality. (Europeans, at least from the Middle Ages, moved progressively towards increasing privacy and individuality.) The shotgun house allows little or no privacy, no individual space, and demands constant interaction and intimacy with others in the house or, the only alternative, with those in the street. The porch links the house and family with the street and larger community.

Some authorities connect the shotgun house's proportions and asymmetry to the so-called African aesthetic, with its emphasis on novelty, improvisation, whimsy, and spontaneity. This is contrary to the so-called Anglo-American aesthetic, with its emphasis on order, balance, bilateral symmetry, and especially on a two-to-three proportion.

Hutchinson Street is at the bottom of Centennial Hill's southern slope. (Houses on the southern side of the street were demolished to make way for Interstate 85, a graphic example of how destructive the construction of a highway through the middle of Montgomery's residential neighborhoods has been to community life.) The shotgun house at 911 Hutchinson Street is representative of the hundreds of shotgun houses that were once in this neighborhood and in other poor neighborhoods. The 14-foot-wide housewas built on its 31-by-175-foot lot sometime before 1901; at that time, Florence Davenport owned the house.

The wood frame house presents a gabled end to the street. The porch extends across the front, which has two bays: a door on the right and a window on the left. The door is new, but the double-hung window, with four lights in each sash, is probably original. The attached porch is supported by three box columns that replaced the original turned posts. The porch and gable bargeboards are decorated with saw-work. The gable also features a louvered rectangular attic ventilator.

The house appears to have originally had two rooms connected by a four-panel door. Both rooms are fourteen feet square with eleven-foot ceilings. Except for the west wall in each room, which is of horizontal beadboard, the walls and ceilings are of plain boards. The two rooms share a brick chimney and have back-to-back fireplaces. The identical coal-burning fireplaces have cast-iron round-headed surrounds and simple wooden mantels with Tuscan pilasters. The chimney is paneled with plain boards laid horizontally.

Attached to the back of the house is what appears to be an addition that accommodates the kitchen, bath, eating area, and a bedroom. The addition is the same width as the front two rooms, but slightly offset to the east. The addition has considerably lower ceilings. Both the front two rooms and the addition are two bays deep.

In 1930, Maria Harrison willed the house and another house on South Jackson Street to St. Peter's Roman Catholic Church to be used for the "furtherance of education" at St. Peter's Boys School. Because the rents did not cover taxes and maintenance, in 1933 St. Peter's sold both properties to Albert Kohn for seven hundred dollars.

Today, 911 Hutchinson Street is used as a rental unit.

Carnegie Building

131 South Perry Street

EARLY IN 1843, a Library Association and a Lyceum Association were founded through the efforts of Colonel Francis Bugbee; Enoch Childs, a native of New Hampshire, graduate of Yale College, and principal of a Montgomery school; and the Reverend A. A. Lipscomb, pastor of the Protestant Methodist Church. Books were bought and donated. For a short time, the nascent library flourished in its back room over a drug store. It then faded and died.

In 1898, a subscription library was founded as the Montgomery Library Association. Three years later, the Reverend Edgar Gardner Murphy, rector of St. John's Episcopal Church, secured a $50,000 gift from his friend Andrew Carnegie, the great steel magnate and philanthropist. The gift was for the construction of a free library on land that Montgomery was to acquire by public subscription. Between 1881 and 1917, the Carnegie Library Program funded 2,509 free public libraries. Of these, 1,600 were in the United States and 14 in Alabama.

The Reverend Mr. Murphy, who as a social reformer fought against the gross abuse of child labor, and fought for improved race relations, secured another contribution: $21,000 from George Peabody to build and equip the city's first Young Men's Christian Association building. The YMCA movement, which began in London in 1842, came to Montgomery in 1868. At first it was devoted almost wholly to Bible study. When the first YMCA building was built in 1906 at the northwest corner of Washington and McDonough streets, the program had been broadened. Although there was some local opposition to accepting "Yankee charity," the YMCA and the library were built.

The cornerstone of Montgomery's Carnegie Library was laid in 1902, and the library opened in 1904. It came under city-county control in 1949, and served as the public library until the current High Street library was built in the early 1960s.

The Carnegie Library was built in the Beaux Arts Classicism or Beaux Eclectic style. This style, which was widely popular from 1890 to 1920, was used in the Chicago Columbian Exposition (1893), the New York City Public Library (1895–1902), and New York City's Grand Central Terminal (1903–13). Although the Beaux Arts style was not particularly popular in Montgomery, the return to classicism did influence the 1894 Montgomery County Courthouse, razed in 1958. The old governor's mansion (1911–50), constructed in 1906 and demolished in 1963 to make way for construction of Interstate 85, was also in the Beaux Arts style.

Beaux Arts Classicism is named for the Ecole des Beaux-Arts, or Paris's school of fine arts and architecture. The style was popularized in the United States by Richard Morris Hunt, Charles Follen McKim, and Stanford White, three of the country's most prominent architects. Beaux Arts is a form of classicism, a synthesis of Greek and Roman architecture, but it is heavily influenced by the Baroque with its emphasis on drama, movement, and the unusual. Beaux Arts features in the Carnegie Building include multiple planes (two on the facade, for example), paired columns, and a variety of classical ornamentation—presented for a somewhat theatrical effect.

The Carnegie Building is well sited on a quarter block. Complementary landscaping, a low limestone wall, three flights of wide limestone steps, and a marble walkway with limestone coping contribute to the overall effect that the building makes.

The rectangular symmetrical building is raised on a terrace and has a full, sunken basement. The foundations, columns, entablature, projecting cornice with modillions, and ornamental carvings are limestone. The walls and parapet are glazed cream-colored pressed brick with very thin mortar pointing. The low, slate Mansard roof has several round dormers that are louvered for ventilation. The roof proper is of copper. The building's front has three recessed bays that are defined by engaged columns with Scamozzi capitals embellished with floral swags. Above the arched door and windows with their console-like keystones are spandrels with carved limestone wreaths and oak leaves. A limestone belt course with running Greek-key motif separates the first and second floors. The second-floor windows are capped with floral garlands. The front doors and the iron balustrades use a Roman motif. The building's sides are identical to the front, except they have two bays rather than three.

The foyer is the most impressive interior space. The floor, two monolithic Tuscan columns, four monolithic Tuscan pilasters, and staircase wainscoting and steps are white marble. The plaster cornice is painted. A divided staircase of marble and cast iron gently rises to a landing immediately above the front door and then divides again to rise to the second floor. The landing is lit by an arched window over the building's front door. The staircase also incorporates the Greek-key motif. There is a cove ceiling at the top of the staircase.

There are two large rooms on each floor. The library's reading room and the reference room were on the main floor. Tuscan columns are used in the mantels of each room. The arched windows are floor-to-ceiling. The two large rooms on the second floor, which were the trustees' room and the assembly hall, are similar to the first floor rooms, but they have cove ceilings. The handsome woodwork and single-panel doors, now painted, are of Flemish oak. The framing over the doors has a shouldered, or eared, architrave.

The Carnegie Building was designed by the New York firm of York and Sawyer. Philip Sawyer attended the Ecole des Beaux-Arts and worked for McKim, Mead, and White, as did Edward Palmer York, before the two formed their own architectural firm in 1898. They were especially noted for their banks, but they also designed the Department of Commerce Building in Washington. Frank Lockwood, Montgomery's most prominent architect of the period, was the Carnegie Building's consulting architect. (He used Beaux Arts principles for the 1906–12 additions to the Alabama Capitol.) The library's initial design, which had a semicircular bay at the rear for book stacks, had to be returned for revision to keep the building within its budget.

The Carnegie Building is currently occupied by the Montgomery County Appraisal Department.

Highland Avenue School

2024 Highland Avenue

THE AUTOMOBILE, and government-backed home loans for World War II veterans, fueled the spread of suburbs and the remaking of the American urban landscape. But it was the streetcar that allowed the first suburbs to be created. Real-estate development went hand and hand with the extension of streetcar lines.

Highland Park was Montgomery's first streetcar suburb. It was platted in 1887, the same year the city's entire streetcar system was converted to electricity. Streetcar tracks ran down the center of Highland Avenue to Panama Street, the 1910 eastern limit of the city. Service was inexpensive and frequent—a car every ten minutes during the heyday of the two lines serving Highland Park. Businesses, churches, a movie theater, and a fire house were built along Highland Avenue. In 1903, a school was built on the street.

Highland Avenue School, a two-storied square building, displays some characteristics of the Richardsonian Romanesque. This style, named after Henry Hobson Richardson of Boston, flourished from the 1880s to the early 1900s. The Richardsonian Romanesque elements are the solid mass

Montgomery's Architectural Heritage

of the building, its pyramidal roof with wide overhanging eaves, the round-headed front door, and the arched windows grouped in twos and threes.

Originally, the second-floor windows had glass in the arches. The terra-cotta hoods or brows on the arches employ the classical egg-and-dart motif and spring from foliated corbels. Yellow-brick quoins at the corners are definitely not Romanesque. Yellow brick is also used to outline three diamonds over the front door. The school, of finely laid red pressed brick with very thin mortar pointing, is raised on a half basement, making the building all the more imposing.

At the top of the front steps, which have depressions made by thousands of children's feet, is a landing paved with black and white hexagonal blocks. Double doors open into a wide central hall with high beadboard wainscoting. The ceiling is of the same material. On each side of the hall are two classrooms separated by a staircase that divides at the landing.

There are four classrooms on each floor. The classrooms have wooden ceilings, crown molding, and wainscoting. Each classroom originally had six large windows. The classrooms also have cloakrooms. The principal's office was originally on the second floor, directly over the main door. There were outhouses until restrooms were built in the basement.

The building was designed for the climate. It has a raised basement, high ceilings, wide overhanging eaves, and it had exterior shutters. The many windows, transoms over the doors, wide halls, two divided staircases, and central halls facilitated cross-ventilation.

The 1903 schoolhouse now has several red-brick additions; the newest addition is architecturally sympathetic with the first building. The school still fronts on a broad avenue, the old streetcar tracks now replaced by a median that is planted with trees. The school grounds now occupy an entire city block, and many turn-of-the-century houses survive in the neighborhood.

And, fittingly, Highland Avenue School is still a neighborhood school. After almost a century, the original schoolhouse, dignified and imposing, still conveys its builders' message that education is an important community responsibility.

SOUTH PERRY STREET, once the address of many of Montgomery's richest and most influential citizens, has the city's finest surviving collection of domestic architecture, especially houses of the mid-nineteenth to early twentieth century. The Sabel-Cantey House is one of the finest.

The limestone mansion at 644 South Perry Street was built about 1903 for Samuel and Jeanette Sabel. Several doors to the south was the home of his brother, Moses Sabel. His 1906 Beaux Arts–style house, which served as the governor's mansion from 1911 to 1950, was demolished in 1963 to make way for Interstate 85.

▼

Sabel-Cantey House

644 South Perry Street

Montgomery's Architectural Heritage

171

The Sabel brothers' business dated from about 1869 when their father, Marx Sabel, came from Louisville to sell leather goods and wagons to farmers trying to reestablish themselves after the Civil War. Because the farmers did not have cash, they bartered furs, hides, scrap metal, etc. Sabel Steel, now in the fifth generation, grew out of this barter business.

Samuel and Jeanette Sabel, who had no children, sold their house to Moses and Hattie Sabel. Hattie Sabel subsequently sold the house, because it reminded her of the deaths of her husband and of her daughter, who died in the Spanish flu epidemic after World War I. The collapse of the demand for leather after that war, and the resulting decline in the family's fortunes, may also have influenced the decision to sell.

In any case, the Sabels sold the house to Mr. and Mrs. Hardie Bell. After their divorce in 1926, it was sold to Dr. and Mrs. Gibson Reynolds. Following her husband's death, Ethel Reynolds sold the house to Lucy Rice Naftel Cantey in 1938.

The Sabel-Cantey House was designed by T. Weatherly Carter of Montgomery, who also designed the 1907 Ligon house, which has been the governor's mansion since 1950. The Sabel-Cantey House is said to have been inspired by a house on New Orleans's St. Charles Avenue (Jeanette Sabel was a native of New Orleans).

The two-and-a-half-story mansion is the only Chateauesque-style house in Montgomery, and one of only a few surviving in Alabama. Houses built in this late-Victorian style, although related to the Queen Anne–style houses, are likely to be more stately, and their facades more symmetrical, than are Queen Anne houses. The Chateauesque style, which was also influenced by the Beaux Arts style popularized by Richard Morris Hunt after he studied architecture in Paris, is named for sixteenth-century French chateaux that combined elements of Gothic and Renaissance styles.

Chateauesque characteristics evident in the Sabel-Cantey House are the evenly spaced windows with stone mullions, grouped gable and roof dormers, flattened or Tudor arches, steeply pitched roofs, and grouped chimneystacks.

The symmetrical facade is composed of a central block flanked by recessed wings. The central block's steep, slate pyramidal roof, capped with a copper finial, is decorated with two dormers. The gabled ends of the recessed wings also have dormer windows.

Attached to the front of the house is a porch that is flanked by terraces. The porch roof is supported by grouped columns with Gothic floriated capitals. Above the round-arched openings of the porch are Gothic pointed coping and a parapet wall of Gothic blind tracery. The hood molding of the two windows over the porch terminates in human masks. The porch and flanking terraces are paved with white hexagonal tiles and trimmed with blue tiles. The terrace balustrades are of Gothic pierced tracery. French doors set in Gothic arches flank the double front door, which is also set in a

Gothic arch. Each of the doors, with elaborate Gothic hardware, has a single beveled light above dark oak panels.

A porte cochere, attached to the north side of the house, has arches that are similiar to the front porch. The high steps of the porte cochere were to accommodate carriages. The Sabels maintained carriages, horses, and a stable at the rear of the 225-foot-deep lot. There were also gardens behind the house.

Unlike the exterior, the interior is not symmetrical. The front door opens into a large reception hall with high raised-panel oak wainscoting, originally ebonized. The room is dominated by a very large fireplace whose overmantel extends to the beamed ceiling. The mantel, originally in ebonized oak, is decorated with four turned columns with Corinthian capitals, and with a gallery at the top that features open Gothic tracery.

To the left of the reception hall is the large winter parlor. Rather than doors separating the two rooms, there are two octagonal columns with Gothic capitals. The enormous, magnificently carved, teak mantel is in the French Renaissance style. The ceiling has box beams. At the rear of the house is the oval dining room, with a high stained-glass window in a large bay. The cornice is decorative plaster and the high wainscoting is oak. The dining room is separated from the reception hall by sliding pocket doors that have paneling to the height of the wainscoting, and clear beveled glass above. The doors are flanked by fluted pilasters with Corinthian capitals. To the right of the reception hall is the summer parlor. This room, with a cove ceiling and inlaid floor, is separated from the reception hall and the side hall by doors identical to those of the dining room.

The main rooms have floors of inlaid parquet surrounded by wide geometric entwined bands of walnut. In addition to these formal rooms, there are a breakfast room, butler's pantry, kitchen, servants' hall, and storerooms.

To the right and rear of the reception-hall fireplace is a broad staircase with wainscoting. There are four balusters on each step of the gently rising staircase. On the second floor there are two bedrooms, two bathrooms, a sitting room, a sleeping porch (not original to the house), and several service rooms.

The mansion was restored in 1989 and is owned and occupied by McAlpine Tankersley Architecture.

Moses-Haardt House

670 South Perry Street

THE MOSES-HAARDT HOUSE is one of the surviving mansions on South Perry Street—an address of the city's elite after the downtown became predominantly commercial. It originally sat on a seven-acre lot. The mansion is a silent witness to how grand Perry Street once was.

Although the house dates to the 1850s, what is visible today dates from the first decade of the twentieth century. In the 1850s, the original house was occupied by Richard Jones, president of the Montgomery Insurance Company.

The house, however, bears the name of Alfred Huger Moses and his wife, Jeannette Nathan of Louisville, who bought the house in 1883 from the Jones estate for $6,000. Alfred Huger Moses came to Montgomery from Charleston in the late 1850s. As commercial opportunities were better in booming Montgomery than in Charleston, he was soon followed by his parents and several brothers and sisters. During the Civil War, Alfred Moses served as clerk for the Confederate District Court. After the war, the Moses brothers did extremely well, buying up real estate at bargain prices. In 1888, Moses Brothers Banking and Realty Company built the city's first skyscraper, the high-Victorian six-story Moses Building on the northern side of Court Square. Alfred Moses was founder and first mayor of Sheffield, one of the twenty-four new iron boom-towns founded in north Alabama between 1885 and 1893. The Sheffield Land, Iron, and Coal Company collapsed in 1891 and brought Moses Brothers down with it. Subsequently, all the Moses family left Montgomery. Alfred Moses and his family moved to St. Louis. They never regained their fortune.

Alfred and Jeannette Moses owned the antebellum house from 1883 until 1891. But it appears they and their five children actually lived in their new mansion at the head of Montgomery Street in Sheffield from 1884 until 1888, when Alfred resigned as president of the Sheffield Land, Iron, and Coal Company. (A portrait of Alfred Moses hangs in the conference room of the House of the Mayors, the 532 South Perry Street house that was the home of Mordecai Moses from 1868 until 1893.)

In 1892, Simon and Bettie Gassenheimer bought the house for $12,500. He was a prominent businessman and civic leader, who founded the Capitol Clothing Company, a leading men's store. He also was instrumental in the construction of the new Exchange Hotel (1906) and the First National Bank (1907). The latter replaced the Moses Building, which in less than twenty years was judged obsolete. Gassenheimer served on the board of the Alabama Reform School, the board of education, and as a director of the Exchange Bank. He was a charter member of the Chamber of Commerce. In 1921, he sold the house to James M. Williams, secretary of the American Cotton Association. John Haardt bought the house in the early 1960s to use as his realty office.

The Moses family is believed to have put in the grand staircase, parquet floors, elaborate plasterwork, and stained-glass windows. Between 1900 and 1910, the Gassenheimers converted the asymmetrical antebellum house into the mansion that it is today. The wooden porch, which extended across the entire front and most of the north side of the house, was removed. The two-story red-brick house (built on a full basement) was plastered.

The original double-hung windows, with six lights in each sash, and exterior shutters were replaced. Two of the original windows with cast-iron hoods decorated with Greek motifs have survived on the north elevation. Today's casement windows have two vertical lights under the single-light transom. The window surrounds have extended keystones.

The rectangular central block is flanked by a set-back wing on the north and a set-back sun porch on the south. Since the central block is four bays wide, the front door is not centered. An L-shaped terrace is wider than the central block, and connects to the enclosed sun porch on the south. The terrace has masonry balusters and marble flooring. The sun porch has wooden balusters and Tuscan columns. Both the sun porch and the portico protecting the main entrance are supported by heavy, high-relief masonry piers and a pair of Tuscan columns. Both porches are surmounted with a simple entablature decorated with dentils.

A parapet encircles the house and obscures the roof. The cornice, which is actually a metal gutter, is decorated with dentils and modillions.

The raised-panel double doors are enclosed in an arch with keystone and archivolts. The stained glass from the elliptical transom and sidelights has been removed. Behind the exterior double doors are interior ones, each with a large single light of beveled glass.

The interior floor plan is irregular. There are three very large rooms on each floor, plus numerous smaller rooms. Opening from the entrance hall on the south is a large parlor. It is separated from the dining room by a wide doorway. The dining room has access to the sun porches by two pairs of French doors. The entrance hall, stair hall, parlor, and dining room are ornamented with high-relief plaster cornices, parquet and banded-oak floors, molded wainscoting, and recessed doorways. The doorway between the parlor and dining room is surmounted with an arched entablature that is supported by console brackets decorated with classical motifs. Centered over the door, in the arch of the entablature, is a circular medallion with a high-relief carved head.

The broad, gently rising two-turn staircase, one of the most handsome and monumental in the city, has three delicate turned balusters on each step, a heavy hand rail, and corresponding paneled wainscoting. The landing was once lit by four large stained-glass windows. The fireplaces in three of the bedrooms have cast iron around the coal-burning fireboxes and marble hearths and surrounds. One of the baths has marble wainscoting and a decorative tile floor.

In addition to the main house, there are two brick dependencies: a two-story, three-bay house and a carriage house. Each of these buildings has been remodeled as an apartment.

In 2001, the Moses-Haardt House was bought by Sterne, Agee & Leach. The investment firm will use the complex as offices, after restoration and renovation.

MONTGOMERY'S BAPTISTS experienced several financial and organizational setbacks in their formative years. There was even a political problem: Lee Compere, a founding member of the Baptist congregation and eventually its pastor, had previously been an English missionary to Jamaica, and then to the Creek Indian nation in what was about to become eastern Alabama. His stand with the Creek chiefs and United States government was not very popular in land-hungry Montgomery; his position even split the Baptist congregation. (The Creeks were removed in 1836.)

However, First Baptist would not always have membership problems. For example, during the six-year pastorate of Dr. Morton Wharton (1884–90), the church's membership more than doubled. During the revivals of 1886, it was even necessary to rent a warehouse because some services drew as many as three thousand people.

First Baptist Church

305 South Perry Street

Montgomery's Architectural Heritage

The church also became a great force for moral reform. Dr. George Eager (pastor, 1890–98) tirelessly campaigned against Montgomery's thriving gambling and prostitution establishments, the exploitation of child labor, and the restrictions that Southern traditions put on women. The campaign for moral and social reform was not an easy one. It was continued by Dr. Eager's successor, Dr. Charles Stakely, and by the Montgomery Ministerial Association. During the 1920s, the church's prison ministry was so successful that it was said that half the membership of First Baptist would soon be in Kilby Prison. The church also condemned the convict-leasing system; it was ended in 1928.

First Baptist Church's buildings have reflected the needs and the resources of the congregation. The first meeting house of Montgomery's Baptists, like that of the Methodists and Presbyterians, was the shared Union Church building (construction begun in 1823) on Lee Street. After the Methodists bought out the shares of the Baptists and Presbyterians in 1830, the Baptists met in the new Presbyterian Church building on Adams Avenue until they were able to construct their own building.

The First Baptist Church's South Perry Street building was preceded by two other Baptist church buildings, both of which stood in the small triangular block bounded by Bibb, North Court, and Coosa streets. The first (1833–54) was a very small frame building that could be described, stretching the point slightly, as vernacular Greek Revival.

The second (1854–1908), however, was an extremely handsome brick building with a Renaissance Revival facade and belfry. (It was designed by Thomas Ustic Walter, a founder of the American Institution of Architects, whose work includes the 1851–65 extension of the national Capitol and its world-famous cast-iron dome.) First Baptist sold this Bibb Street building because the congregation had outgrown it. Demolition of this fine building was a major loss to Montgomery's architectural heritage.

The new building on South Perry Street was constructed during the twenty-nine-year pastorate of Dr. Charles Stakely. The fortress-like Romanesque design of Frank Lockwood and Benjamin Smith of Montgomery was rejected. Dr. Stakely may have believed that Richardsonian Romanesque, a style favored by his denomination at the time, was forbidding.

In 1904, the design of George Norrman of Atlanta was accepted. Construction began the following year, but the building was not dedicated until 1923, because work was undertaken only when funds were available. The church did not want to borrow funds for construction.

Norrman's design was loosely based on Florence's great Italian Gothic cathedral, whose dominating feature is Brunelleschi's red-tiled ribbed dome and classical cupola. His 348-foot high, 140-foot diameter dome built between 1420 and 1434 was a marvelous engineering feat.

In 1964, after a light fixture fell during a service, First Baptist's dome had to be taken down because of dry rot, and rebuilt with steel girders. The congregation insisted that the dome be re-covered with its distinctive red tiles.

Besides the distinguishing dome and glistening white rough-finished Georgia-marble exterior, the church building exhibits blind arcading, parapets, and battered foundations (the stone walls flare outward at their base, giving the building an even greater sense of solidity). The simple, Gothic-style facade is dominated by two large pinnacles. On Gothic structures, pinnacles were engineering devices used in conjunction with buttresses to redirect outward forces downward to prevent the structure from collapsing. The facade also has three round-headed doors, each with decorative hinges. The center door's carved wood tympanum features two high-relief angels.

Originally, there was a tower with a parapet and a pyramidal red-tile roof at the southeast corner of the church building. This and a shorter tower on the north side were taken down to make room for a larger education building. This addition altered the curved lines of the original church building and gave it a more massive, boxy appearance.

The building's interior architecture and decorative schemes have never corresponded to the Gothic style of the exterior. The foyer, with its marble wainscoting and floor, has a classically decorated ceiling. A Tiffany-glass screen separates the foyer from the auditorium.

The auditorium has been redecorated several times. The original Greek-style baptistry of Alabama marble has been replaced by painted wood. Mahogany woodwork has been painted. Decorative motifs, generally classical and Baroque, are gilded. The walls are now off-white. The neoclassical-style choir and rostrum have been enlarged and extended several times. After considerable controversy, choirs became common in Protestant churches during the nineteenth century. Rostrums with lectern pulpits replaced older tub pulpits in order to accommodate the new revival-type services that required chairs for several service leaders.

The Italian cathedral's eleven brilliantly colored *occhi*, or eye, windows, as well as the windows on the lower level of the cathedral, also inspired the design of First Baptist. Although different in coloring and subject matter from those in Florence, First Baptist's windows are very interesting. The windows on the lower level depict hope, light, victory, praise, purity, harvest, reward, resurrection, guardianship, and faith. Above the apex of the interior dome (sixty feet above the floor of the auditorium) is an unusual stained-glass dome within a dome. It is surrounded by decorative plasterwork of classical and Baroque motifs. Together, the windows and the gold and off-white decorative scheme fill the auditorium with light.

While originally an engineering necessity to cover a large square space, the dome has come to symbolize the sphere of heaven embracing the Church, the body of believers. Inspired by the great dome of the cathedral of Florence, the First Baptist Church building of Montgomery, with its unmistakable red-tile dome and white-marble walls, is an inspiration in its own right.

Tulane Building

800 High Street

Tulane-Simmons House

470 South Union Street

JUST AFTER the end of the Civil War, the neighborhood centering on Union and High streets became the heart of Montgomery's black community. Since 1876 it has been known as Centennial Hill. The American Missionary Association, nominally nonsectarian, but predominantly Congregational, built a school and a church. The 1868 Swayne School, at the corner of Union and Grove streets, was one of the first primary schools for blacks in Montgomery, and was supposed to have been one of the finest black institutions in the South. It was named for General Wager Swayne, who directed the Freedmen's Bureau in Alabama, and who was the Reconstruction military governor of Alabama from July 1867 to July 1868. (The First Congregational Christian Church's 1872 building was struck by lightning and burned in 1995.)

The Swayne School and the Congregational Church formed the nucleus from which grew other institutions in Centennial Hill and elsewhere in Montgomery. At 515 South Union Street was the Montgomery Industrial School for Negro Girls. Founded in 1886 by Alice White, it was also under the sponsorship of the American Missionary Association. Although the federal government's Freedmen's Bureau efforts ended in 1873, Northern philanthropic efforts in the South were maintained until about 1900. These efforts were dominated by Protestant mission societies, notably the American Baptist, Congregational, Methodist, and Presbyterian mission societies. Because the missions provided social, educational, economic, and political opportunities, they were particularly attractive to those with ambition.

James Rapier, Alabama's first black congressman, came to Centennial Hill. But his background was unusual, if not unique. The son of a white slaveowner and a free black mother, he was born free. Because antebellum state law forbade the education of mulattos and blacks, his father sent him to Montreal College in Canada, and then to the University of Glasgow in Scotland.

Another ambitious man who came to Centennial Hill was fifteen-year-old Victor Hugo Tulane. He arrived in Montgomery in 1888 after walking barefoot from Wetumpka; in his pocket was $13.60 he had earned picking cotton. In a year, he saved $100 and was ready to set himself up as a grocer. This he did with a fifteen-by-twenty-foot store, a rusted set of scales, a broken meat knife, a lamp, a peck measure, and his stock, including a five-pound bucket of lard and ten cents' worth of salt. He prospered, not only in the grocery business, but also in real estate, as the cashier of the Montgomery

180

A Sense of Place

branch of the Penny Savings Bank (a Birmingham-based black bank), and as manager of Dean's Drug Store on Monroe Street.

Between 1904 and 1908, he built the store at the corner of High and South Ripley streets, in the center of Centennial Hill, the most prosperous black neighborhood in Montgomery. He and his wife, Willie, ran the grocery and lived in a large apartment on the second floor. They bought close to margin and sold goods reasonably, and they prospered. Tulane Grocery was noted for Tulane's Pride, a special blend of high-grade coffee sold in cans. The grocery also sold charcoal and coal.

The two-story building with its corner entrance and corner turret is not only the neighborhood's most distinctive building, but it is also one of the city's most distinctive small commercial buildings. The fifteen-inch solid-brick walls on High and South Ripley streets are made of white face brick. The narrow buff-colored bricks were brought from Texas, and were laid in common bond with thin pink mortar pointing. Window placement is irregular, apparently conforming to interior needs rather than to aesthetic considerations. The windows, with masonry sills, have several muntin configurations, including unusual second-floor sashes with four vertical lights. A ground-floor, triple show window is divided by cast-iron posts.

The ornamental corner turret was not an unusual Victorian feature, but is now unique in Montgomery. (The 1884 post office at Dexter Avenue and Lawrence Street had a corner clocktower; it was demolished about 1958.) The turret has a conical metal roof with ornamental cap, previously painted red. The turret is supported by foliated brackets and is decorated with egg-and-dart molding of pressed metal. The turret and the main block of the building have a metal frieze decorated with dentils and garlands.

The grocery consisted of the large shop and a smaller rear room that, until recently, had the meat blocks and large built-in icebox used by Tulane. One door of the freezer display unit had a beveled-glass mirror. The floors are pine; the ceiling is beadboard. Coal for sale was kept in the basement.

On the southwest side of the building is the entrance and stairway to the second floor. It is sheltered by a pediment supported by two turned columnettes that once had Ionic capitals. The door originally had a single light above a molded panel with applied decorations. The interior staircase has turned balusters and paneled newel posts. At one time there was an exterior stair on the south side of the building.

The second-story floorplan originally consisted of five major rooms, two baths, and several service rooms. The principal room today features a circular bay in the turret, double doors with molded panels that open into what probably was a sitting room, and a double mantel with a beveled-glass mirror. Both the mantel and the overmantel are supported by unfluted columns with Composite capitals. The room has picture molding and high molded baseboards.

Tulane's businesses prospered, and he became a prominent civic leader as well. In 1908, the Tulanes entertained Booker T. Washington in their second-floor apartment. Tulane was a member of the board of Swayne School, chairman of the trustees of Old Ship AME Zion Church, a member of the executive committee of the National Negro Business League, the first black trustee of Tuskegee Institute, and, in 1919, the only black member (honorary) of the Montgomery Chamber of Commerce.

After the Tulanes vacated their apartment, it was used as the clubroom for the Imperials, a prestigious social club that included among its members George Washington Trenholm and his son Harper Councill Trenholm, both presidents of Alabama State (1921–25 and 1925–61). The Chesterfields, a group of younger men, also used the clubroom. In 1942 the building was bought by Florence and Elver O. Wright, mother and son. The Wright Grocery operated at 800 High Street for almost sixty years.

ABOUT 1921, TEN YEARS before Victor Tulane's death, he and Willie moved into the red-brick house at 470 South Union Street. The house, with neoclassical front porch supported by paired Roman Doric columns, large high-ceiling living room and dining room (both with neoclassical mantels and classical cornices), interior glass doors, study, two bedrooms, tiled bathroom, and kitchen and butler's pantry, was a long way from the apartment over the grocery. Their neighbors were the elite of the black community, including Dr. Cornelius Dorcette, the city's first black physician, at 422 South Union Street, and Nathan Alexander, editor, bank president, and Republican Party activist and officeholder, at 503 South Union. Willie Tulane lived at 470 South Union Street until her death in the 1950s.

The house was restored by John Baker for the Alabama Democratic Party headquarters. It is now owned and occupied by the Alabama Parent-Teacher Association.

THE HOUSE at 1142 South Perry Street is Alabama's second governor's mansion. The first, a 1906 Beaux Arts–style mansion with strong French architectural influence, that had been built for Moses and Hattie Sabel, served as the governor's mansion from 1911 to 1950. It was sold in 1959 and, after serving as The Montgomery Academy, was demolished in 1963 to make way for construction of Interstate 85.

The second mansion was purchased in 1950 from Emily Ligon Foley, wife of the undersecretary of the United States Treasury. The house had been built in 1907 for her parents by T. Weatherly Carter of the Montgomery architectural firm of Benjamin Smith and T. Weatherly Carter.

The executive mansion is in the so-called Colonial Revival style that began in the Northeast and became popular after the national centennial celebrations of 1876. This style is eclectic, in that it makes liberal use of various period details; it bears almost no resemblance to colonial or antebellum architectural styles. On the East Coast, this style included the so-called Dutch Colonial and Cape Cod, as well as the Classical Revival. In the South, neoclassical elements dominated.

The Colonial Revival style, although an inaccurate representation of any previous style, conformed to turn-of-the-century romantic views of the Old South. The style of the house, and its location in the fashionable southside, was fitting for the clerk of the Alabama Supreme Court and

▼

Governor's Mansion

1142 South Perry Street

Montgomery's Architectural Heritage

183

Fluted column with Composite capital

Fluted corner pilaster with Composite capital

adjutant general of Alabama, and for his wife, Aileen Means Ligon, daughter of a former president of Emory University. Brigadier General Ligon, a title he retained throughout his life, lived in the house until his death in 1939.

Mrs. Ligon, who lived in the house until her death in 1950, had an understanding with Governor "Big Jim" Folsom that the Ligon house would be an ideal residence for Alabama's governors, because, in Governor Folsom's words, "it looked so Southern."

Several other houses, including three of the city's finest antebellum mansions, have been proposed to serve as Alabama's executive mansion. One proposal was the high-Italianate-style villa, with its unusual octagonal tower, that Thomas Hill Watts had built about 1850. Watts served as Confederate attorney general and then as Alabama's governor from 1863 to 1865. His city estate had exceptionally fine grounds. From 1902, St. Margaret's Hospital occupied the old Watts estate.

The Seibels-Ball-Lanier House, once the home of John Jacob Seibels, United States minister to Belgium, was more recently proposed as a potential governor's mansion. It was the first mansion in Alabama to deviate from the symmetrical arrangement used in the Federal and Greek Revival styles. And, with its demolition in 1988, it was the last of Montgomery's antebellum high-style Italianate mansions. This villa may have been designed by one of the nation's greatest architects, Samuel Sloan, or perhaps by his partner, John Stewart. Sloan and Stewart, both Philadelphians, designed buildings in Montgomery. The former significantly influenced the taste of the elite of the antebellum South. This villa, like that of Governor Watts, also had fine, large grounds. The Adams Avenue site is now occupied by the Alabama Center for Commerce.

A third proposal was Knox Hall, one of the finest mansions ever built in Montgomery. It was designed by Stephen Decatur Button, architect of the ill-fated 1847–49 Capitol. Of the few antebellum mansions surviving today, it is the most magnificent. Its grand suites in the Greek Revival style are without equal in Montgomery. Today it is a private business.

The Ligon house has been altered somewhat over the years to conform to changing fashions, and to make it more functional for the state's chief executive. For example, the kitchen has been enlarged, a marble-floored terrace has been added on the back of the house, and two porches have been enclosed. Three stained-glass windows have been removed. The originally dark-finished woodwork of the interior is now painted.

The grounds have undergone more extensive changes. The formal gardens have given way to paved parking, tennis courts, and a swimming pool in the shape of the state of Alabama. Nevertheless, the structure itself, exterior and interior, remains much as T. Weatherly Carter designed it.

The facade of the mansion appears much as it did originally. The recessed main entrance is through a portico whose four fluted columns, with

184

A Sense of Place

Composite capitals, support a pediment. There is a central balcony at the second-floor level. It and two flanking balconies are supported by large scroll brackets. The entablature, supported by fluted pilasters with Composite capitals, has dentils, egg and dart, and modillions in the classical style. The stucco walls are scored to resemble stone. The roof was originally red tile.

A porte cochere flanks the center block on the south. The porte cochere's roof, entablature, and wood balustrade are supported by fluted columns with Scamozzi capitals with their angular volutes. An enclosed sun porch flanks the center block on the north. This was originally a screened porch. A marble-floored terrace wraps around much of the house, and French doors give access to the terrace from the principal rooms.

Scamozzi capitals

The outstanding feature of the interior is the grand entrance hall with its exceptionally wide staircase that divides at the first landing. This is a grand hall with Composite pilasters, a decorative plaster ceiling medallion, and an oak floor inlaid with cherry and mahogany. But it is the wide staircase, the wide sliding doors opening into flanking rooms, and especially the scale of the hall that create the illusion that the house is much larger than it actually is.

Other than the stair hall and the sun room, there are only three principal rooms on the main floor. The large drawing room is the least altered. The crystal chandeliers, wall sconces, three large gilt mirrors, and pink-marble fireplace surround and hearth are original. The cornice and ceiling are decorated with elaborate plasterwork. In the library (or music room), the fireplace's tile surround and hearth have been replaced with marble; wooden scroll brackets embellished with carved fruit support the mantel. The dining room has simple pilasters and two free-standing fluted columns. The boxed-beam ceiling is decorated with egg-and-dart and running Greek-key motifs.

Putting aside the romantic notions of the Old South held earlier in this century, Alabama's executive mansion is a dignified residence for the governor as the state, and the house, begin a new century.

Bell Building

207 Montgomery Street

WHEN THE BELL BUILDING was constructed (1906–10), Montgomery was undergoing rapid expansion. Although cotton was still vital to the city's economy, there was diversification into manufacturing. The city boasted of its economy, construction boom, and population (about 35,000). Among the major construction projects underway at the time were three skyscrapers, although not of the height of those in Chicago and New York.

Skyscrapers were made possible by replacing load-bearing masonry walls with skeleton steel frames. Masonry and glass skins covered the steel frames. But it was the Otis steam elevator (1857) and especially the von Siemens electric elevator (1880) that made taller buildings practical. (Montgomery's first elevator was in the 1884 federal building at the southwest corner of Dexter Avenue and South Lawrence Street; that fine Richardsonian Romanesque building was demolished about 1958.) Skyscrapers changed the urban landscape. Cities, such as London, that experienced great expansion before the advent of skeleton steel construction and the elevator, expanded horizontally. Major cities that expanded later, such as New York, expanded vertically.

Technology made the skyscraper possible and practical, and Newton J. Bell was a practical man. The native South Carolinian prospered as a Lowndes County planter and as an entrepreneur. He wanted to build a municipal status symbol for Montgomery, and he wanted it to be beautiful and practical. In 1906, he engaged Frederick Ausfeld, a prominent Montgomery architect, born and educated in Austria, whose work includes the Jefferson Davis Hotel and Sidney Lanier High School, both from 1928–29. Consulting engineers were Westcott and Ronneberg of Chicago. Bell died while his building was being constructed, and his son saw the building through to completion in 1910.

Ausfeld designed a twelve-story building faced with stone on the first two floors and with pressed brick on the upper floors. The vertically stacked windows are separated vertically by brick, and horizontally by decorative terra-cotta panels. The flat roof is surrounded on the Montgomery and Lee street sides by a two-and-a-half-foot parapet over a galvanized-iron, bracketed cornice that protrudes six feet, creating an overhang. The vertical effect is quite similar to St. Louis's 1890–91 Wainwright Building by Louis Sullivan, who is credited with developing the vertical, rather than the traditional horizontal, emphasis. Buildings of this type have been likened to a column: the base being formed by the stone-clad first two floors, the fluted shaft by the body of the building, with its vertically stacked windows, and the capital by the cornice and parapet.

The Bell Building's two street facades are very similar. The main entrance on Montgomery Street is flanked by four twenty-six-foot pilasters with Corinthian capitals. The spandrels over the arch are filled with bas

Montgomery's Architectural Heritage

relief sculpture in the classical style. The ground-floor show windows, considerably altered, had beveled glass, brass surrounds, and granite sills.

The building's interior was practical and handsome. The small entrance hall has a granite floor, marble walls, marble pilasters with Composite capitals, and a classically decorated cornice and ceiling. Doors, hardware, and brass fittings are original. The ground floor has several businesses, with internal and external entrances. When the three high-speed Otis elevators were converted to self-service in the mid-1970s, the old brass and polished-wood cabs were modernized. The upper floors have been altered considerbly. Most of the marble walls in the corridors remain; some of the red and white ceramic-tile corridor floors remain. Originally, each floor had a water fountain with piped cold water and a restroom with marble partitions.

For its time, the Bell Building featured technological innovations. The 100-by-100-foot building has an inset light-well to the south, making the building U-shaped. This inset facilitated cross-ventilation, and ensured that all 259 offices above the ground floor had windows. The 160-foot building was heated by coal-fired furnaces in the basement. There was a central vacuuming system throughout the building.

The Bell Building is Alabama's finest example of a Sullivanesque skyscraper, and is the finest remaining early steel-frame building in Montgomery.

▼

Belser House

103 North Lewis Street

IN 1904, THE Capitol Heights Development Company bought the 200-acre Vickers plantation and established a new suburb. As the land was 150 feet higher than Court Square, it was advertised as being considerably cooler in summer. At that time, there were only about 3 automobiles for each 100 families in Montgomery. By 1929, there were 62 cars for each 100 Montgomery families—greater than for Philadelphia (59), Baltimore (50) and New York (49). However, growth of the town depended on the streetcars, not on the automobile.

Capitol Heights was incorporated in 1907 and became part of Montgomery in 1926. The developers' intention was for Capitol Heights to be "deluxe, majestic, and exclusive." Most construction was on a smaller scale, although some large, expensive houses were built, such as the Colonial Revival–style Morning View and the Tudor-style mansion of James S. Pinckard, president of the land development company.

One architect who seems to have done considerable work in Capitol Heights, including many houses on Capitol Parkway, was Richard S. Whaley. In 1908, he designed and built a house for himself at 103 North Lewis. His house was in the Craftsman style, a style for which he was noted but which was not well received for upper- and upper-middle-income housing in Montgomery, although an early Montgomery Country Club was built in the style.

The Craftsman style may have been too avant-garde for Montgomery, or perhaps not grand enough during a time in which historical-revival styles were also in vogue. Richard Whaley went to California to study the California-bungalow style, which was considerably less expensive to build than the Craftsman, which emphasized fine workmanship. The bungalow style became very popular for middle- and lower-middle-income housing in Montgomery. The Whaleys eventually moved to California, and their house was acquired by the Belser family who lived there until 1993.

Craftsman was more than a style; it was an ideology that affected architecture, furnishings, interior design, and landscape architecture. William Morris and the Arts and Crafts movement that he started in England in the second half of the nineteenth century sought to reestablish the connection between aesthetics and utility that was believed to have prevailed before the Industrial Revolution. The movement sought not only to "reintroduce" beauty into everyday household items, as opposed to the mass-produced Victorian bric-a-brac, but also to "reestablish" the quality of craftsmanship that had preceded the machine age. Consequently, the movement had a built-in contradiction: high quality hand-craftsmanship, no matter how simple, could not be produced at affordable prices for the masses.

The movement found support in the United States with the establishment of the American Society of Arts and Crafts in Boston in 1897. Gustav Stickley of New York was the style's most famous promoter. It was his two *Craftsman Home* books and his *Craftsman Magazine* that gave the style its name, and made its designs and ideology widely available. He was also able to manufacture relatively high-quality furniture at affordable prices. He did it, however, by mass production, not hand-craftsmanship. Furniture in this style is frequently called Mission, not because of any connection with California's Franciscan missions, but because the furniture had a "mission of usefulness."

At a time that most Americans rented, rather than owned, their homes, Stickley and others holding the Craftsman ideology advocated well-built, affordable houses designed to conform to the new, informal life-styles of most Americans. Craftsman houses eliminated superfluous ornamentation, infrequently used formal rooms, and even elaborate furnishings. Craftsman emphasized finely crafted built-in closets, window seats, bookcases, and chests of drawers. Beauty, according to the Craftsman ideal, was in line, craftsmanship, utility, comfort, and simplicity. Stickley advocated the "great room" where the family would gather around the fire. Fire and family had an almost spiritual meaning.

The house that Whaley designed for himself is probably Montgomery's finest Craftsman house. The informality, and perhaps some of the house's practicality, is evident from the exterior. The house of stucco over lath has a high-pitched roof and several gables. There is no symmetry, no ostentatious display of ornament. A weak argument could be made that the ornament that does exist—the porch's flat arches with wooden "keystones," chamfering on the posts supporting the porch roof, half-timbering on the second floor, curved brackets in the eaves, and curved rafters supporting the eaves—is not superfluous, but integral to the construction, or at least useful. The house is built on two terraces to allow for a basement. The altitude of Capitol Heights, promotional hyperbole notwithstanding, did not dispel the long, hot summers. However, wide eaves and the front porch and terrace helped make the summers more bearable.

The front door, which is not in the Craftsman style, has an oval, beveled glass surrounded by a classical molding. The clear, leaded-glass window over the front door gives the house's street number. The door opens into a large stair hall whose ceiling has finished oak beams that are rather close together. To the left is the staircase with bold, oak newel-post and square oak balusters. Opening from the stair hall are the dining room's double doors in oak veneer, a door leading to a hall and the rear of the house, and the living room's double doors, also of oak veneer.

The living room is the only room in the house that has features that are not Craftsman. The room is separated from the rest of the house in a conventional, formal way—much unlike the Craftsman preference for an open or free-flowing floor plan. The room has a wide, heavy cornice of plaster. Although the woodwork is Craftsman, it is painted.

The dining room is probably the most thoroughly Craftsman room in the house. Opposite the double doors leading into the entrance hall is the fireplace. The room has a bay window with large, long windows on both sides. The small, high window in the middle formerly had leaded glass; this was removed by the last Belser owner. The ceiling has four oak beams that intersect to form a large square in the middle of the room. At each of the four intersections of the beams is a simple light fixture.

Also on the main floor are the kitchen, a rear stair hall that also functioned as a butler's pantry, a large bedroom, and a bathroom. The bathroom is actually two rooms—a separate water closet and a tiled bathroom with tub and shower, separated by a washbasin. An identical arrangement is directly above on the second floor. There are large closets in each bedroom and also under the front staircase. These features are indicative of Craftsman's interest in functionalism.

The second floor exhibits another Craftsman feature: the "great room." The front staircase rises directly into this 19-by-32-foot irregularly shaped room. A sloping ceiling, many angles, several types of windows, a fireplace, and the Craftsman bookcase (original to the house) make this room very appealing, and very much in conformity with Craftsman ideology. Some neighbors recall the parties in this room during the first and second World Wars. Two bedrooms and the sleeping porch open off this room.

The house has finely crafted woodwork throughout. With the exception of the living room, the woodwork is unpainted. Many rooms have low, oak picture moldings. The floors are heart pine. The five-panel doors are oak on the main floor and pine on the second. The octagonal doorknobs are clear glass. The large windows are double hung, with a single light in the bottom sash and a turned square pattern in the top sash. The second-floor windows under the wide, overhanging eaves are unusual in that they have a single sash that lowers into the wall. Although the house is heated by hot-water radiators, the main rooms have Craftsman fireplaces. All the mantels are oak, but all have different bold, rectilinear, and straightforward designs. All have marble hearths but different brickwork surrounding the coal-burning fireboxes.

The Craftsman style lasted from 1900 until 1920, when the historical-revival styles triumphed. Even in its heyday, it was more popular in the South for beach cottages and mountain summer houses than it was for upper- and upper-middle-income urban residences. But its ideology has been borne out in today's mass housing: today's house, without servants and with both husband and wife working outside the home, must be functional. Few resources can be devoted to nonfunctional rooms or furnishings.

The Belser House is currently the home of the Reverend and Mrs. Larry T. Self.

CONSTRUCTION OF John Jefferson Flowers Memorial Hall began in November 1909. Named after a devout Methodist who was interested in higher education for young women, and whose family contributed a large sum towards its construction, Flowers Hall was the first building on the new campus of the Woman's College of Alabama.

The college that had been founded in Tuskegee in 1854 was on the southeastern edge of the town of Cloverdale, which was incorporated into Montgomery in 1927. The college was forced to admit male students because of the Depression. In 1935, the name was changed from Woman's College of Alabama to Huntingdon College in honor of Selina, Countess of Huntingdon, one of the first influential persons to be connected with the early Methodist movement.

The college was beyond the end of the relatively new Cloverdale electric streetcar line, which then ended near the intersection of Felder Avenue and Cloverdale Road, both unpaved country roads. The streetcar line reached the college in 1913. The southeastern terminus was at the intersection of Narrow Lane and Woodley roads. With the exception of several bungalows in College Court and Edgewood on what is now Thomas Avenue, few other buildings were nearby.

For the first several years, Flowers Hall was the entire college. As well as being the dormitory, it housed classrooms, offices, the library, an infirmary, the dining room, the college's president and his family, and even a swimming pool and a kitchen in the basement.

Of all Huntingdon College's buildings, Flowers Hall is the most faithful example of the English Tudor Gothic style. The Renaissance came late to England. In the sixteenth century, English architecture was in transition.

John Jefferson Flowers Memorial Hall

Huntingdon College
1500 East Fairview Avenue

Montgomery's Architectural Heritage

England's Renaissance style was Tudor, which was essentially late Gothic with an overlay of Renaissance decorative motifs. This overlay is most evident in larger windows, skylines confused with decorative chimneys, and ornamental details.

The academic-revival, or pseudo-historical, architectural styles of the early twentieth century were departures from the so-called Colonial Revival of the late nineteenth and beginning of the twentieth century. Flowers Hall was the first building in Alabama to use a pseudo-historical style.

Judge William Thomas, the most active member of the building commission, was impressed with the Collegiate Gothic style being used on East Coast campuses. He led his fellow commissioners to reject the proposed Spanish architecture and to adopt the Tudor or Collegiate Gothic style for Huntingdon. Consequently, H. Langford Warren and F. Patterson Smith of Boston were engaged as designing architects. Warren, a native of England and a professor of architecture at Harvard, maintained that the building "will compare favorably with the old Gothic buildings at Oxford and Cambridge." Montgomery architects Benjamin Smith and T. Weatherly Carter were also retained.

The Tudor Gothic, pseudo-historical elements of Flowers Hall's exterior include the cupola at the crest of a high-pitched, multiple-gabled roof; tall chimneys; red brick accented with black brick; and a uniform facade broken by an oriel window over the north door, arched windows with stone tracery, rectangular windows with heavy stone mullions, and two large bay windows. Ornamentation includes heraldic devices, animal and human figures, obelisks, and other decorative elements of the English Renaissance.

Flowers Hall's interior has several impressive rooms. The entrance hall has a fine vaulted ceiling with limestone ribs and bosses and red brick fill. The chapel, modeled to a degree on the old chapel of St. John's College, Cambridge, resembles the great halls of medieval and Tudor college dining rooms, chapels, inns of court, and great houses. The chapel's most striking feature is its hammerbeam roof of seven large wooden arches that spring from limestone corbels. Between these arches, and at the south end of the chapel, are large Gothic windows with stone tracery. The original transparent green glass was replaced in 1953 by Belgian and French stained glass, designed by a German working in North Carolina. The painted paneling below the windows was originally stained dark, creating a unifying effect with the dark hammerbeam roof. The balcony is an addition, to increase the hall's seating capacity from approximately five hundred to approximately seven hundred.

The chapel's exterior has engaged buttresses and cloister-like porches whose Gothic arched windows with stone tracery are without glass. Until the building was extensively renovated in the late 1990s, the brick paving of the porches was well worn—evocative of generations of students who have, to modify Huntingdon College's motto slightly, "entered to grow in wisdom and gone forth to apply wisdom in service."

Although the architect's assurance that the hall would "compare favorably with the old Gothic buildings at Oxford and Cambridge" has not been exactly borne out in brick and stone, Flowers Hall is very impressive. This is due, in part, to siting. And this is attributed to Frederick Law Olmsted, Jr., also a professor of architecture at Harvard, and noted landscape architect of Biltmore Estate at Asheville. As the college's landscape architect, he insisted that the building face Fairview Avenue, rather than Woodley Road, so that there could be a "dignified and impressive treatment of the immediate approach to the grounds." What Olmsted wanted to be a "noble wide avenue" is today's College Avenue.

Huntingdon College, which is related to the United Methodist Church, is a four-year coeducational liberal-arts college.

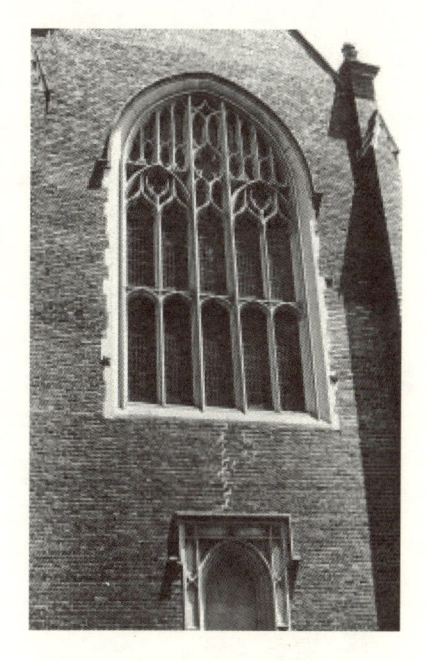

Decorated Gothic-style window with tracery

Day Street Baptist Church

861 Day Street

IN THE FALL OF 1882, a new Baptist church was organized by members of Bethel Baptist Church. Only thirty-two members of Bethel chose to move to the new site, at the corner of Day and Davidson streets. By 1908, membership had grown to about four thousand.

It was then that the congregation began building a new brick structure around the original frame church. The new Gothic-style building was 92 by 47 feet, considerably larger than the old. It was completed in 1910 at the cost of $36,000, in addition to the thousands of bricks that individual members brought to build the two-foot-thick walls.

The architect was Wallace A. Rayfield, a native of Macon, Georgia. After being orphaned in his teens, he attended Howard University's preparatory school. He was graduated from Howard University with a Bachelor of Science degree in 1896, and then he attended Pratt Institute in Brooklyn. He was the first black to obtain an architecture degree there (1899).

Rayfield was then recruited by Booker T. Washington, and taught architectural drawing at Tuskegee Institute until about 1907, when he established a private practice in Birmingham. About 1909, he became the African Methodist Episcopal Zion Church's official architect for church buildings in the U.S. and Africa, as well as the general supervising architect of the Freedman Aid Society, an agency of the Methodist Episcopal Church. Rayfield did not confine his ecclesiastical work to the AME and AME Zion churches, but also built Baptist, Congregational, and Episcopal churches. Perhaps his most famous church building is the 1909–11 Sixteenth Street Baptist Church in Birmingham, famous for the September 1963 bombing that resulted in the death of four girls at Sunday School. Rayfield also built numerous residences in Birmingham's Smithfield suburb.

The Day and Davidson street elevations of Day Street Baptist Church are red pressed brick with thin mortar pointing. The church building rests on a raised basement of scored cement that the architect intended to have painted to resemble stone. Its facade is dominated by two towers, a tall bell tower on the west and a smaller tower on the east. The elegant bell tower has a Gothic-style window with simple tracery and hood molding, paired lancet windows with louvers, and a single Gothic window with louvers. The tower, which may have originally had pinnacles, is capped with a crenellated parapet. The shorter, east tower also has a crenellated parapet.

Between the two towers is the gabled end of the sanctuary, with one large Gothic-style window with simple tracery. The gable is decorated with step brickwork. Also between the two towers is a porch with three pointed Gothic arches; the porch was enclosed with glass doors in the 1970s. The sides of the church building have high gables and six Gothic-style windows of various sizes. The gables are decorated with step brickwork.

Access to the sanctuary is through the bases of the towers. Like the exterior, the interior is relatively unchanged. Original features include the gallery at the back, supported by two grained, wooden Tuscan columns.

The balcony does not obstruct the huge stained-glass window of the facade's gable. The two staircases to the balcony are unusual in that they are open to the sanctuary. They are delicate with square balusters and newel posts.

The sanctuary floor is very gently raked toward the rostrum. On the right side of the rostrum is the tiled baptistry with marble surround. Behind the central pulpit is a large Gothic arch that frames the choir. The pipe organ that was once in the arch has been replaced with an electric organ. The new oak pews have ends that echo the Gothic arches of the windows. The memorial windows of opalescent glass are decorated with floral designs, figures, and Christian symbols. The most unusual feature of the interior is the pressed metal ceiling. It is unusual because it is not flat, but vaulted in the Gothic manner. An old chandelier hangs from the intersections of the two vaults. The white ceiling, pale yellow walls, and the light filtered through large windows create an open and airy atmosphere.

Day Street Baptist Church sponsored the first black Girl Scout troop in Alabama and one of the first black Boy Scout troops. The former parsonage on Davidson Street adjoins the rear of the church and serves as an education building.

Montgomery's Architectural Heritage

Church of the Ascension

315 Clanton Avenue

BEGINNING AS EARLY AS 1897, St. John's and Holy Comforter recognized that another Episcopal parish was needed in Montgomery. In May 1909, the Church of the Ascension was organized. The forty-nine communicants of St. John's that lived south of South Street (Interstate 85) were supposed to attend Ascension, which was to be located in the fashionable suburb now called the Garden District. Although streetcars and automobiles made it possible for families to move away from the city center, they had not yet formed strong attachments to their new suburbs. Consequently, families went to whichever parish church they preferred. Several times a year, divine intervention did encourage those living in Cloverdale and the Garden District who were still clinging to St. John's to attend Ascension. This was when rain-swollen Genetta Ditch, which ran east and west near what is now Julia Street, overflowed and churchgoers could not get into town. Even if it was possible to get to Ascension, however, the basement classrooms were likely to flood—complete with floating furniture.

Construction began on the nave in November 1909. Four months later, at Easter, the first service was held in the nave, the only completed part of the building—and even then the windows were not glazed. From the beginning, the parish vestry was committed to the finest in design and construction, and to raising a building that would stand indefinitely. Because such construction was expensive, it took time. For several years there was no indoor plumbing, and until 1921 the young children's Sunday school met in the tool house left by the construction workers. In the 1920s, the transepts, crossing, and chancel were built. The building was finished in 1927 with the completion of the tower. The tower's three great bells, which are capable of English change ringing, were not installed until 1965.

The church complex has been expanded, most significantly after the 1984 fire, and again in 1999–2000. Additions and renovations have been done in keeping with the Gothic style of the original building. In fact, the original architect's designs have been used in two columns and capitals in the new chapel—the design was taken from All Saints, Peterborough, New Hampshire, another church designed by Ascension's original architect.

The Church of the Ascension was designed by Ralph Adams Cram of Boston, whose numerous Gothic ecclesiastical works include the Cathedral of St. John the Divine in New York, and the chapels at Princeton and West Point. Ascension is his only building in Alabama. As the foremost church architect of the first third of the twentieth century, his aesthetic and spiritual ideas dominated fine ecclesiastical architecture. This was a time of significant church building; nationally, spending more than tripled between 1900 and the beginning of the Great Depression.

Cram thought that he followed the architectural and spiritual ideals of the Middle Ages. He believed that the impressiveness, power, and dignity of the Gothic could inspire and motivate the faithful. He wrote, "Build in stone or brick; plan with rigid simplicity; design both interior and exterior with reserve, formality, and self control; have the mass simple, the composition equally so; imitate no form or detail of larger structures, but work with the dignity and the reverence that are theirs. Above all, let the spirit be that of the unchanging Church. . . ."

Gothic, referring to a Germanic tribe that had helped destroy classical Rome, was originally an Italian Renaissance term of derision. In the nineteenth century, it came to be widely accepted as "Christian" architecture, as opposed to the "pagan" architecture derived from classical Greece and Rome. Ascension was not only fortunate to have been designed by the greatest ecclesiastical architect of the day, but also to have been designed at a time when American Gothic building was most closely following the aesthetic of the Middle Ages. Ascension therefore missed the picturesque romanticism of mid-nineteenth century Gothic Revival and the daring, eccentric Victorian Gothic of the late nineteenth century, as well as the neo-Gothic, which began in the 1920s and increasingly deleted historical architectual detail.

The parish also was fortunate to have as its senior warden Algernon Blair, a great churchman and a giant in construction. He came to Mont-

Gothic capital

gomery from Macon, Georgia, in the late 1890s but really began his career here in 1902 with the construction of the Standard Club at Molton and Montgomery streets. His buildings include Baldwin and Sidney Lanier schools, Huntingdon College's Bellingrath Hall, the Regions Bank building, and Montgomery's city hall, veterans' hospital, and federal courthouse. But his pride was the Church of the Ascension. He believed that "God's house should embody the noblest, finest, and fairest conception of which the human mind is capable." The tower and great north transept window were dedicated to his memory. This window, whose central figure is the resurrected Christ in an attitude of blessing and invitation, also includes King Solomon, builder of the Temple in Jerusalem; Nehemiah, builder of the walls of Jerusalem; St. Thomas, patron saint of builders; and symbols of the building trades.

Cram ensured that the building would embody the Christian faith by echoing the unity of the arts of the great Age of Faith. Blair ensured, with masonry construction faced with gray Indiana limestone, that the building would withstand the passage of time.

The building is in the style of an English parish church of the twelfth and thirteenth centuries. Its mass and solidity, simple engaged buttresses, steeply pitched roof, and low, massive tower evoke the Norman style, which was England's version of Romanesque architecture—the style that preceded Gothic. But the building's arched doors, double and triple narrow pointed lancet windows, deeply molded crossing arches, rich stained glass, and simple hammerbeamed nave roof evoke the Early English style, the first period of English Gothic architecture. Cram preferred the sobriety of this period to the continental Gothic styles or the more elaborate Gothic styles that were to develop later in England.

Surprisingly, the elevation that most evokes the medieval is the rear—with the assortment of planes, angles, heights, windows, roofs, and gables that characterize buildings that were built over centuries. Were it not for the weathered slate roof, landscaping, and variety in the complex of parish buildings, the church building would be rather severe in its simplicity.

The interior is not at all severe. It is rather small, seating about four hundred. It is intimate, yet grand. This is achieved, in the Gothic tradition, by combining the practical requirements of engineering and liturgical worship with spiritual requirements that appeal to both the senses and the intellect. A dominant spirituality is achieved by uniting art and theology.

On the intellectual level, Biblical stories and concepts, especially the life of Christ, are presented in stained glass and sculpture. The building's cruciform plan, based on the Latin cross, also has theological significance. In the ancient tradition, it is oriented to the east; that is, worshipers facing the altar in the east end of the building are facing Jerusalem and, for morning services, the rising sun. Christ's sacrifice and God's plan for man's redemption are represented by the altar. Symbolically, it is the objective of the Christian life. This journey begins with baptism. Consequently, the baptismal font is at the church's entrance, at the west end. A single aisle connects font and altar. The fine oak reredos behind the altar, designed by Cram, presents Christ's ascension and four of his miracles. This conscious, intellectual symbolism and spirituality are complemented by the subconscious spirituality that derives from the senses.

In significant ways, the worshiper's subconscious can be focused on God by the rich sounds of organ, choir, and ancient liturgy, by timeless stone and aged dark wood, and, especially, by the light filtered through stained glass in deep, rich colors. Ascension's stained glass conforms to the French practice of using very deep colors, because the sunlight here in Montgomery is strong, as it is in France. This is especially evident in the deep blue of the large, triple lancet window of the south transept and in the deep red and blue of the chancel's triple lancet window, which is in a thirteenth-century configuration, and whose glass was inspired by a twelfth-century window from the French cathedral of Poitiers.

Early English Gothic lancet windows above carved wooden reredos

In June 1984, fire almost destroyed the church building. It was so badly damaged that rebuilding took a year. The walls, most of the stained-glass windows, and much of the carved woodwork was saved. Neighbors and friends rushed in and out of the burning building saving furnishings. Among these friends was Rabbi David Baylinson of Temple Beth Or. Before he left that morning, he had offered the use of the Temple. His offer was accepted, and the Church of the Ascension worshiped there until September. They then worshiped in Huntingdon College chapel, until returning to the rebuilt church in June 1985.

The fire was a more significant spiritual event than a physical event. The parish quickly realized that Ascension was not the building, but the body of believers. One communicant remarked that "the building has been burned, but the Church is alive."

St. Andrew the Apostle Roman Catholic Church

441 Clayton Street

IN 1910, MONTGOMERY'S second Roman Catholic parish was organized. The church building is a memorial to Catherine Harrison Connor, wife of Martin Connor of Troy, who donated the church building and the adjacent rectory. Connor also built a Roman Catholic church in Troy that is similiar, but smaller.

The exterior of the building is in the Italian Romanesque style. The facade is dominated by the bell tower that projects from the central block. The main entrance, reached by a flight of stairs, has double doors surmounted by a semicircular tympanum that memorializes Catherine Harrison Connor. Above the door is a stained glass window depicting St. Andrew with his distinctive X-shaped cross. On each face of the bell chamber is a rectangular opening flanked by Tuscan columns. The tower's pyramidal roof is supported by heavy brackets, and is covered with red tiles and capped with a cross. On both sides of the main entrance are single doors sheltered by shed-type, red-tile roofs supported by heavy brackets. These doors open directly into the rear of the aisles flanking the nave. The roof of the nave is considerably higher than the roofs of the aisles. Elaborate scrolls once masked the half-gables of the aisle roofs. (The scrolls, made of metal, rusted out and have not been replaced.) This architectural screening device is Italian Renaissance rather than Romanesque. The building is of red pressed brick with thin mortar pointing, and is trimmed with buff pressed brick. The contrasting trim, and especially the quoins at the corners of the tower and main block, are not Romanesque features.

The church is built on the basilica plan: a rectangular room consisting of central nave flanked by two aisles. The vaulted ceilings of the nave and aisles have been lowered slightly. The clerestory windows in the upper walls of the nave are possible because the nave's roof is considerably higher than the roofs of the flanking aisles. The clerestory windows are small, rectangular, and paired; those of the aisles are large and round-headed. All are filled with stained glass, but only the four aisle windows closest to the chancel have elaborate figures.

In the traditional basilica plan, the entrance is on one short side of the rectangular building, and the chancel with altar is on the opposite short side. The chancel is raised from the floor of the nave. Before changes made by Vatican II in the late 1960s, the main altar was even higher and was against the south wall. Although the original marbled altar has been removed, its reredos has been retained. It has recently been marbled, as have the metal Tuscan columns separating the nave and aisles, and supporting the upper nave walls.

A large painting of St. Andrew, which was on the chancel wall above the altar, as well as two other wall paintings on the chancel's side walls, have been plastered over. The altar rail has been removed, and the main altar has been moved towards the pews so that worshipers can see the priest at the celebration of the Holy Eucharist. Vatican II also required that the baptismal font be moved from the rear of the nave, its traditional location, to the front. The original font, now to the right of the altar, is an elaborate affair of painted plaster, marbled metal, and fine mosaics. It is topped with a full-round sculptural group of Jesus being baptized by John the Baptist.

Romanesque capital

The church has numerous other devotional aids, including polychromatic high-relief stations of the cross and polychromatic full-round statues. The Gothic-style accessories for the chancel are very fine.

In the large balcony at the rear of the nave is the original tracker organ, which is in full working order.

To the east of the church building is the former rectory, now the parish hall. Like the church building, the rectory is constructed of red pressed brick and trimmed with buff pressed brick. The central door is protected by a pedimented porch supported by two Romanesque columns. The double-hung windows have three lights in the upper sashes and two lights in the bottom sashes. The house, although only three bays wide, is massive. The wide eaves supported by heavy brackets and the red-tile low-pitched pyramidal roof contribute to its solidity. This large building is subordinated to the church building because the latter is raised on a terrace, and because its raised basement is higher than that of the house.

St. Andrew's is the mother church of St. Bede's in east Montgomery (1940s) and St. Joseph's in Prattville (1960s). At one time, there was often standing room only at divine services. However, the large parish was dismembered by the construction of Interstates 65 and 85. Consequently, today's parish roll is considerably diminished. Many of the remaining communicants, although they no longer live in the neighborhood, were baptized, confirmed, and married at St. Andrew's.

BLACK MEMBERS of Montgomery's First Baptist Church initially sat in the pews behind their masters, then in the balcony, and finally in the basement. In 1867, the black members established their own church, the Columbus Street Baptist Church, under the leadership of the Reverend Issac Tichenor, white pastor of the mother church. When approximately seven hundred members of First Baptist moved their letters from the old Bibb Street church to the new Columbus Street church, the old church lost the majority of its members. Yet the old church bought the lot and assisted in construction of a handsome frame building with round-headed windows, exterior shutters, and a belfry. In many ways, the building was similar to today's Dexter Avenue King Memorial Baptist Church.

▼

First Baptist Church, Colored

347 North Ripley Street

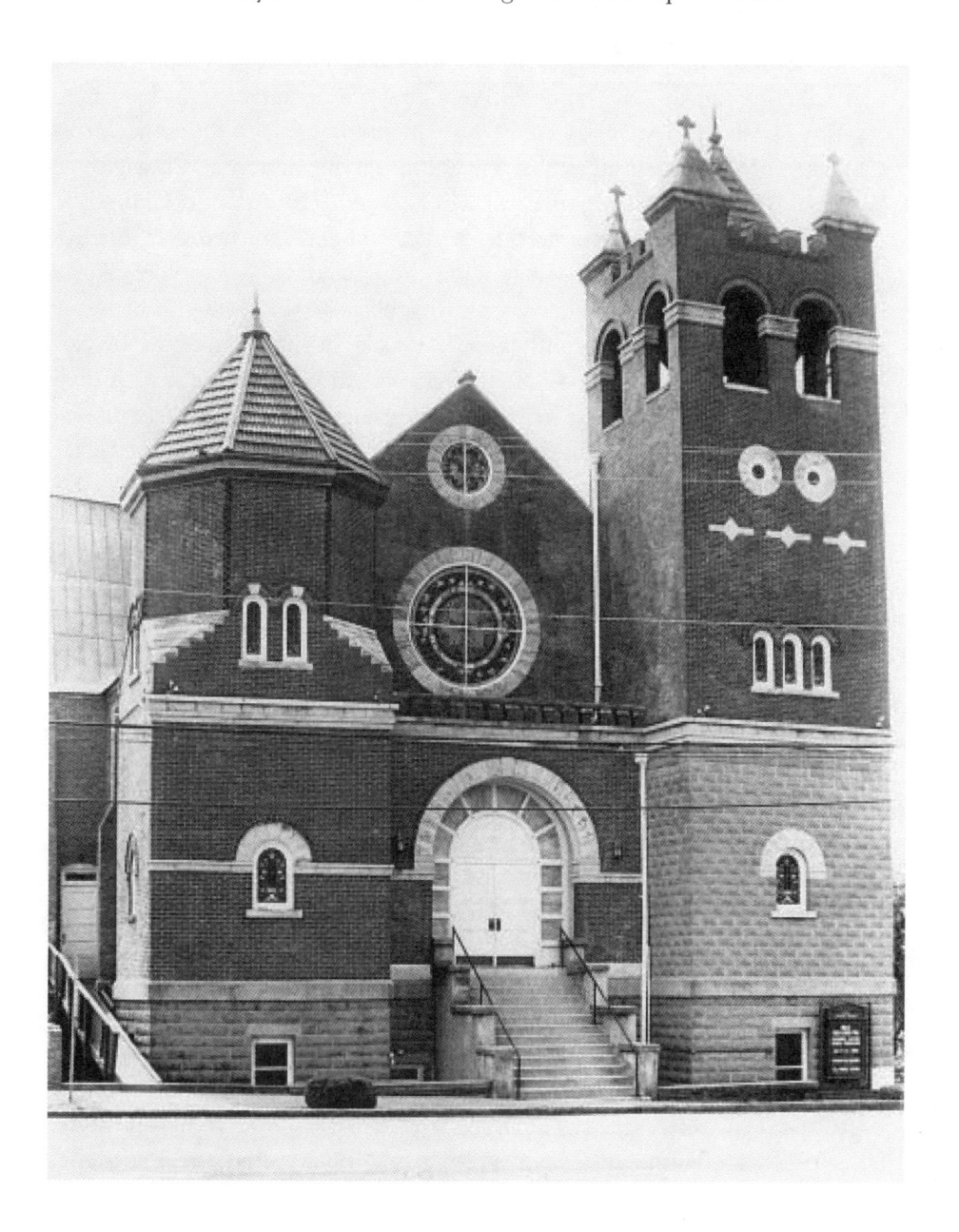

Montgomery's Architectural Heritage

By 1910, the Columbus Street congregation had grown tremendously. Construction of the present building began on an adjoining lot, facing North Ripley Street. The original church building burned in 1912, three years before the new building was completed. The new building cost more than $60,000, as well as the thousands of bricks that members brought. Each member was expected to bring a brick for every service attended.

The church's third pastor (1892–1924), Dr. Andrew Jackson Stokes, inspired the building of the new church. A man of great energy, vision, and courage, he also built the Montgomery Baptist Institute and made a fortune in real estate. He was the first black person in Montgomery to own an automobile. He was banned from driving it on Dexter Avenue, because he got dust on some white women; he did not adhere to this restriction.

With the new building came a new name—First Baptist Church, Colored—still the church's name, although it is often referred to as First Baptist Church, Ripley Street. In 1915 the church, with five thousand members, was the largest church in the country. One church in Chicago was composed entirely of members of Montgomery's First Baptist Church.

The building was designed by Walter Thomas Bailey, one of the five architects that Booker T. Washington brought to Tuskegee Normal and Industrial Institute. Tuskegee was the first black school to offer a certificate in architecture. Washington believed that blacks should not only be carpenters, but also architects—that blacks should not only work with their hands, but also with their heads. Bailey, a native of Illinois, was the first black to graduate in architecture from the University of Illinois, 1904. He was head of Tuskegee's architectural department from 1905 to 1914. He then practiced in Memphis and, by 1925, in Chicago. His greatest work was probably Chicago's seven-story Pythian Temple. This 1925 structure, built at the cost of $695,000, was reputed to have been the largest structure in the country that was financed, designed, and built by blacks.

First Baptist's Richardsonian Romanesque–style building is built on a modified Greek-cross plan—more evident from the belfry than from the street or interior. The ends of the cross are marked by broad, high gables.

The building is constructed from a variety of materials. Red brick predominates, but rusticated concrete blocks that resemble sandstone are also used. Sandstone trim is used for belt courses and for window and door surrounds. The original red-tile roof of the main block was replaced by a copper roof in 1981. Engineers advised that the roof timbers (some apparently from the Columbus Street Church, because they were charred) might not be able to support the weight of the tile if it were reinstalled.

Two corner towers dominate the facade. The southeast tower rests on a square, rusticated basement. Its first story, also square, is red brick. The transition to an octagonal tower is marked by large sandstone triangles. (Octagonal ecclesiastical structures are associated with Romanesque architecture.) The southeast tower's high-pitched roof is red tile with a copper finial. The second tower is the bell tower. Its basement and first story are of rusticated cement, and its upper part is red brick. The bell chamber has two round-headed openings on each face. The tower is capped with a sandstone pinnacle at each corner, and a pyramidal roof of red tile with a copper finial.

The large bell, mounted on a wooden frame and with a wooden wheel, is capable of both tolling and ringing. It tolls when a hammer-like device strikes and remains against the interior rim of the bell. When the wheel is turned, the bell rings as the clapper rapidly swings from side to side. Tolling is to signal a death or an emergency. Ringing is for celebration.

The double doors at the top of the front steps were installed after klansmen bombed the church on January 10, 1957. At the time, Dr. Ralph Abernathy was the church's pastor and the vice president of the Montgomery Improvement Association.

The round-headed sandstone arch originally sheltered a porch. This porch, now a vestibule, opens into the auditorium through a single, round-headed door with a (replaced) stained-glass transom.

The auditorium is filled with light from the stained-glass windows. In the north and south arms of the Greek cross are enormous round-headed windows flanked by smaller round-headed windows. The balcony at the rear of the auditorium is lit by the large rose window that is centered in the Ripley Street facade. Three banks of curved oak pews slope gently to the rostrum across the western arm of the Greek cross. Three round-headed arches dominate the western wall. The 1922 pipe organ, built by Henry Pilcher's Sons of Louisville, is behind the middle arched opening, and the choir stalls are on both sides. The Victorian Gothic and Eastlake-style walnut lectern-pulpit is centered on the rostrum. In front of the pulpit, on the floor of the auditorium, is the carved oak communion table.

In 1868, the Alabama Colored Baptist Convention was created in this church. It was also the birthplace, in 1880, of the National Baptist Convention, the main association of black Baptist congregations in the United States.

First Baptist Church has played a major role in the life of the city. It has had a lasting influence on Missionary Baptists throughout the country and, through the civil rights movement, has influenced the nation as a whole. (The second of the city's Freedom Riders riots, in May 1961, occurred at the church, and in the park that was then across from Ripley Street. Four hundred U.S. marshals could not contain the rioters. The governor declared martial law and called out the Alabama National Guard, which restored order. This, and similar violence elsewhere, directed against churches and parsonages, helped prompt federal authorities to enact legislation that desegregated all interstate bus transportation.) Today the church is thoroughly committed to ministering to the special needs of the inner city, and of the hungry and homeless.

Dexter Avenue King Memorial Baptist Church Parsonage

309 South Jackson Street

DURING RECONSTRUCTION, a black neighborhood developed in what was then southeast Montgomery. It came to be called Centennial Hill, as its development coincided with the celebration of the centennial of the United States. Centennial Hill was the neighborhood of the black professional and business class. Its principal streets were High and South Jackson. In 1887, what is today Alabama State University relocated from Marion, where it had been founded in 1866. Its new campus was at the southern end of South Jackson Street. To the west, centering on the corner of High and Union streets, were several schools and the First Congregational Church. In many ways, Centennial Hill was the heart of Montgomery's black community.

It was natural that the parsonage of Dexter Avenue Baptist Church, one of the most prominent churches in the city, would be in Centennial Hill. In 1919, the church acquired the house at 309 South Jackson Street, which had been built about 1912. It represents a typical home of the prosperous black families in the first decades of the twentieth century.

The unpretentious frame house, now clad in vinyl siding, is dominated by a modified pyramidal roof. These high, steep roofs visually increase the mass of the house. Pyramid-roof houses, which may have developed along the Carolina-Georgia coast, were built extensively in the lowland South in the late nineteenth and early twentieth centuries. The facade features an offset gable decorated with a round-headed window and an attached porch that extends across the full front. The balusters are turned, and the ceiling is beadboard. The porch's roof is supported by four Tuscan columns and small brackets. The brackets are repeated under the eaves of the main block of the house. The porch's original wooden decking and steps have been replaced with concrete. Following the fashion of the time, the double-hung windows have one light in each sash, or the more stylish diamond-shaped lights in the upper sash. The front door's sidelights and transom also have diamond-shaped lights. The door itself has a large single light outlined by egg-and-dart molding.

Although the house was slightly remodeled in 1966, many original features have survived. The narrow crown molding and high baseboards have survived, although narrow-strip hardwood has replaced the original floorboards. All walls are plaster. The window and door surrounds have simple block facing. The doors have five horizontal raised and molded panels, with the exception of the pair of French doors, with transom, that lead from the entrance room into the living room. The living room's double mantel has a beveled-glass mirror. The mantel is supported by console brackets and the overmantel by Doric columns. Sliding paneled pocket doors separate the living and dining rooms. The two bedrooms are separated by a bath. Adjoining the back bedroom is a large study. In 1966 the back porch was enclosed for a second bathroom, and the kitchen was modernized.

The parsonage was the home of Dr. Vernon Johns from 1947 to 1952.

Dr. Johns was a man of great intellect and learning. He was admitted to Oberlin College after astounding college administrators with his oral translations of German poetry and Greek scripture. He was also a man of courage, challenging both his congregation and the socioeconomic system that then dominated the city. A man of many interests and talents, he even organized a cooperative supermarket. Dr. Johns was succeeded by the Reverend Martin Luther King, Jr. The Kings lived in the parsonage from September 1954 until February 1960.

As president of the Montgomery Improvement Association, Dr. King was completely involved with the 1955–56 bus boycott. It launched the modern civil rights movement, as well as Dr. King's career as the movement's foremost advocate. The MIA was formed, at the suggestion of the Reverend Ralph Abernathy, because whites were so traumatized by the NAACP. Baptist ministers predominated in these organizations because ministers were among the few blacks who did not work for whites, and because the Baptist denomination was the only black institution that could organize a mass movement.

Montgomery's Architectural Heritage

At 9:15 P.M. on January 30, 1956, the parsonage was bombed. Coretta Scott King, ten-week-old Yolanda Denise King, and a church member, Mary Lucy Williams, were in the house. No one was hurt. The hand grenade or half stick of dynamite merely broke some windows and made a small hole in the concrete floor of the porch. This hole, now marked with a brass plaque, is still visible.

A large angry crowd gathered at the parsonage. Dr. King returned from a bus boycott meeting, comforted his wife and infant daughter, talked with the mayor and police commissioner, who were at the scene, and calmed the crowd. Rather than intimidating the leaders of the civil rights movement, the bombing helped focus national attention on the movement in Montgomery, and on Dr. King's firm stand on nonviolence. The city's tarnished reputation also retarded economic growth; in 1954–55, five manufacturers, including DuPont, reversed their decisions to locate in Montgomery.

After leaving Montgomery in 1960, Dr. King served as first president of the Southern Christian Leadership Conference (founded in Montgomery during the boycott), led the 1963 Washington march, was awarded the Nobel Peace Prize in 1964, led the 1965 Selma-to-Montgomery march, and led the 1967 New York anti–Vietnam War march. He was assassinated in Memphis on April 4, 1968.

Until August 1994, the house served as the parsonage of Dexter Avenue King Memorial Baptist Church. It will be opened as a house museum. The dining room and bedroom suites, and some study and living room furniture used by the Kings, have been preserved.

THERE WERE several attempts to develop the land that is now South Capitol Parkway. The first was in 1856, when lots of five to seven acres were platted. After 1887 it was replatted for Albert and Mary Jane Elmore. At that time, what is now South Capitol Parkway was called Central Street.

In 1904, Colonel James S. Pinckard and Henry L. Davis of Philadelphia bought the adjoining 200-acre Vickers plantation and, in 1907, incorporated it as the Capitol Heights Development Company. At the request of the company, the city of Montgomery extended Madison Avenue east to intersect with Mt. Meigs Road. Madison Avenue and Mt. Meigs Road were connected by South Capitol Parkway, which was first known as Lasseter Street, after Frank S. Lasseter, who was an investor in the development company, a builder, and first mayor of Capitol Heights. Capitol Heights, like Highland Park to the south, had easy access to downtown Montgomery by the electric streetcar system; the Madison Avenue line's eastern terminus was Electric Park, an amusement park on the Atlanta highway.

South Capitol Parkway, the name first appearing around 1915, was modeled on Green Street in Augusta, Georgia. This attempt to design a parklike neighborhood in the Frederick Law Olmsted tradition was more fully developed in Old Cloverdale, and on the campus of Huntingdon College. The 108-foot-wide street has a median of grass. The large old trees that once graced the median were removed in the late 1980s because they were interfering with the utility lines.

Lewis House

18 South Capitol Parkway

For some reason, the intention of the land developers for Capitol Heights to become an exclusive suburb were not realized. Nevertheless, some very substantial houses were built. The circa-1913 M. P. Wilcox house at 4 South Capitol Parkway, with its landscaping by Olmsted Brothers of Boston, and the 1912 A. O. Clapp house at 11 South Capitol Parkway were among them. The latter, which was the first house to be built on the parkway, was constructed of concrete blocks made to resemble stone; these blocks were made on the site. Most houses in the neighborhood, however, are more modest.

The predominating house type on South Capitol Parkway is the bungalow, named after the veranda-adorned low houses of Bangla, now Bengal and Bangladesh. Using the philosophy of the Arts and Crafts movement (informality and simplicity, as opposed to the formality and pretentiousness of historical revival styles), British designers combined this traditional Indian house type with the English cottage to make the bungalow. The style was popularized in the United States by Charles Sumner Green and Henry Mather Green of California; in fact, this one-and-a-half-story house type is frequently called the California bungalow. Most bungalows, however, were not designed by architects. As they were generally low-cost, small-scale mass housing, bungalows were built from published builders' plans.

Bungalows are common in most of Montgomery's older suburban neighborhoods. The bungalow at 18 South Capitol Parkway is an outstanding example of this house type that was popular between 1900 and 1920. (Very similar bungalows are at 1551 Gilmer, 949 Park, and 1100 Felder avenues.) The original 100-by-200-foot lot was bought in 1913, but the house may not have been constructed until as late as 1919. It was built for C. D. Lewis, for whom Lewis Street, one block to the west, was named. Frank S. Lasseter was the contractor; in 1914, he had built his own house at 34 South Capitol Parkway. Richard S. Whaley, who was the architect, had built his own house at 103 North Lewis Street in 1908. From 1913 until the 1920s, Whaley was the architect for many houses built by Lasseter on South Capitol Parkway. Whaley, who had previously studied the bungalow and Craftsman styles in California, eventually moved to that state. Because of its fine craftsmanship, the Craftsman style was beyond the resources of most Montgomerians who favored bungalows. The Craftsman style was more popular in California than it was in Montgomery, where historical styles were favored for upper- and upper-middle-income houses.

The Lewis house is among the finest examples in Montgomery of a bungalow, because it also has numerous Craftsman features. The asymmetrical front elevation has triple gables that are irregularly massed. The rafter tails that support the wide eaves have decoratively cut ends that once supported gutters. The deep, L-shaped porch is paved with small hexagonal blocks, and has a balustrade of delicate pickets and wider slats featuring heart cut-outs. The roof of the porch and attached porte cochere is supported by graduated brick piers topped with square columns and by battered piers. The rough brick is painted a dark purple-brown that approximates the original, unpainted brickwork. The deep-profile wooden siding was originally painted pumpkin. The siding is cypress, and the original shake roof was probably cedar. The house has single-, paired-, and triple-window configurations. All windows are double hung, with six lights in the upper sash and a single light in the lower sash. Screens only covered the lower half of the windows. The gable end to the left of the porch is decorated with a double window with an unusual Egyptian surround: an exaggerated battered and eared surround surmounted with a turned urn.

The main door and flanking windows make a unit. They open directly into the living room. This generously proportioned room, with vertical box beams and dark-brown woodwork, is dominated by a massive fireplace of rough brick. Carved brackets support the heavy mantel shelf. There is an original built-in bookcase to the right of the fireplace. French doors separate the living room and the dining room. The box beams in this room form a large square. The shallow bay has triple windows. The breakfast room has an original built-in buffet-china cabinet, and the kitchen and pantry also have some original cabinets and shelving. What was a screened back porch has been enclosed. The house has two bedrooms separated by a hexagonal, tiled bath with original tub and pedestal sink. In addition to the two bedrooms, there is a sleeping porch. Floors throughout the house are of narrow-width oak, but those of the bedroom are particularly handsome, because they have borders. The house also has numerous built-in closets and cupboards. Many of the house's original light fixtures and push-button light switches have also survived.

Cooling is enhanced by broad overhanging eaves, deep porches, eleven-foot ceilings, and a thirty-five-foot hall. (Curiously, the transoms never were movable.) The house was originally heated by a coal-fired furnace in the basement; hot air was conveyed to the rooms through ducts. One of the two basements was originally a laundry room.

The large back yard retains an early chicken house (a customary feature in pre-war Montgomery) and seven large pecan trees. The lot was once a pecan grove.

The Lewis house was never neglected and therefore did not require renovation. Since 1991, it has been owned by C. A. King and comfortably accommodates the large King family. Early twentieth-century family pieces, as well as collected Mission furniture, enhance the Craftsman features of the house.

Old Ship African Methodist Episcopal Zion Church

483 Holcombe Street

OLD SHIP African Methodist Episcopal Zion Church is the oldest black congregation in Montgomery, and the nucleus of its church building is the city's oldest surviving church building.

Most of Montgomery's churches divided along racial lines after the Civil War. Court Street Methodist Church was an exception, in that it had divided before the war. In the early 1850s, white members of the church decided to build a large masonry church building. They offered the black members the old wooden building that had been built about 1835 as the Union Church—if they would remove it from the Court Street site.

Thomas Wilson, a free-black contractor, supervised the move. He was assisted by Sol Brack, Solomon Hannon, Emmanuel Noble, and a number of other slaves. Part of the 60-by-45-foot frame building was moved half a mile uphill to the Holcombe Street site on wooden rollers, while other parts of the building seem to have been dismantled, moved, and reassembled. In 1852, Holcombe Street was sparsely settled, but by the end of the century, it was part of a prosperous, white middle-class neighborhood.

There are several versions of how the church was named. In one version, a bystander who asked, "What do you have there?" was answered by a laborer moving the church, "It's the Old Ship of Zion moving on." In another version, an onlooker remarked that "She has landed many a thousand [souls]. Let's call her the Old Ship of Zion." This 1835/1853 building is depicted in a stained-glass window to the right front of the sanctuary. The only portion of this wooden building now visible is the rear (east) gable.

For ten years after the building was moved, the black congregation was served by white ministers. In 1862, Allen Hannon, a slave of Thomas Hannon, assumed the duties as minister of the church. After Emancipation in 1865, the church's name was changed to Clinton's Chapel, in honor of J. J. Clinton, African Methodist Episcopal Zion bishop. He came to Montgomery and convinced the congregation to withdraw from the Methodist Episcopal Church, South, and join the AME Zion Church. There have been several name changes since then.

In 1888, the first commencement in Montgomery of the Alabama Colored People's University (changed to Normal School for Colored Students in 1889, and now called Alabama State University) was conducted in the church building. The church had been involved in moving the school from Marion to Montgomery.

The church grew and prospered. In the late nineteenth century, the exterior of the building was modified by replacing the short wooden tower and steeple with a central projecting tower and steeple, and by putting up orange brick veneer. The remodeled building is pictured in a stained-glass window to the left of the sanctuary.

In the first quarter of the twentieth century, AME Zion congregations erected fine church buildings. The Montgomery congregation decided to build "a structure commensurate with the national reputation and historical greatness of this institution."

Among those on the building committee was Abraham Calvin Caffey, a carpenter by trade. He was well respected by blacks and whites. From 1894, until white officers replaced blacks in the Spanish-American War (1898), Caffey had served as commander of the Capital City Guards, a militia unit organized in 1885 during a time of prosperity and relaxed racial tensions.

Between October 1919 and June 1920, the church building was completely remodeled, to the extent that it now bears no resemblance to the 1835 white wooden church with a steeple. Remodeling cost $80,000. The old Mount Zion AME Zion Church building at the northeast corner of Holt and Stone streets, which was founded from Old Ship in 1869, has a similiar facade; it dates from 1921.

Old Ship's impressive, dark-red brick facade was added to the old building. Between wings with simple stone corner pilasters, four Ionic columns support a central pediment that is decorated with modillions and a lunette window. Broad sandstone steps lead to the recessed portico with its marble floor. Three doors on the portico are surmounted by stained-glass transoms and architraves supported by curved brackets. The rectangular windows on the facade have one-over-one sashes filled with stained glass. Windows on the sides of the building have brick arches and stone sills and keystones. Below the stone belt course, the raised basement windows with camber or flattened arches have two lights in each window sash. The facade and two sides have a wide cornice with modillions; the rear or east elevation reveals the only remaining evidence of the 1835 church building. The exterior is dominated by truncated twin towers with arched louvered openings. These towers, which replaced the late-nineteenth-century central tower, have corner pilasters with Corinthian capitals.

The portico's three main doors open into a marble-floored vestibule that opens into the auditorium that seats twelve hundred. The light filtered through stained glass windows gives the room a serene atmosphere. Dark, painted wooden pilasters topped with white Corinthian capitals encircle the room. An anthemion rosette is above each of these exceptionally fine capitals. The cornice is decorated with dentils, egg-and-dart molding, water leaves, and modillions. Box beams support the cove ceiling. Behind the choir on the east wall is a pipe organ; Old Ship was the first black church in Montgomery to have one. Curved chancel rails, wainscoting, door and window surrounds, and exposed ceiling beams are of dark painted wood. The curved oak pews have Gothic-style ends. The quarter-sawn pine floor is laid diagonally.

In 1898, President William McKinley spoke in the church after having addressed the Alabama General Assembly. Frederick Douglass, Booker T. Washington, Governor Thomas Kilby, and Dr. Martin Luther King, Jr., also spoke in the church.

Old Ship AME Zion Church's membership roll is revealing. It includes Montgomery's first black dentist, post office employee, undertaker, probation officer, silversmith and watch-maker, organist, principal of Swayne School, and even taxicab owner. The roll includes many entrepreneurs, businessmen, and professionals. This vibrant church still maintains its active role in the life of the city.

BETWEEN 1915 AND 1932, a large number of fine houses were built in the Garden District, Old Cloverdale, and on Thomas Avenue. More than thirty were designed by Frank Lockwood, a favorite architect of Montgomery's wealthiest families. Lockwood worked in a variety of styles, but his houses fall into three broad historical styles of the academic revival popular from about 1910 to the early 1930s: the Georgian-Colonial, Tudor, and Mediterranean–Spanish Colonial.

The Whitfield House is Montgomery's grandest example of the Mediterranean–Spanish Colonial style. Other examples are the Blair House at 161 Felder Avenue, the Moulthrop House at 2001 South Hull Street, and the Alvin Weil House at 1639 Gilmer Avenue; all were designed by Lockwood. Period stylistic features, however, masked modern building materials and techniques such as poured concrete, stucco on metal lath, concrete cinder blocks, and hollow tile. The houses also had modern conveniences such as central heat, tiled kitchens, showers, and concrete basement floors.

The house was built about 1920 for L. B. Whitfield, Sr. The family's fortune was based on the "pickle with the perfect pucker." Large numbers

Whitfield House

1506 South Perry Street

of the cucumbers for the Whitfield Pickle Company were raised on the Mount Meigs Reform School farm. The elegant house has been known by the inelegant name of the "Pickle Palace."

The eclectic Mediterranean–Spanish Colonial style is characterized by stucco, tile, wrought iron, balconies, round-headed arches, irregular fenestration, asymmetrical massing, and low-pitched tile roofs with wide, overhanging eaves. The two-story Whitfield House has all of these features, plus a great deal of quality detailing—such as the carved rafter tails and the arcaded gallery that balances the south facade of the house. These details make the house exceptional.

Curved marble steps, flanked by marble lions, lead from the motorcourt to the terrace paved with decorative ceramic tile, bordered in marble and with a marble balustrade. The South Perry Street entrance is through an arcade of three round-headed arches supported by marble columns with Corinthian capitals. The door, with two decorated wooden panels and leaded glass, is surmounted by a semicircular transom of leaded glass. In addition to the South Perry Street entrance, there is another formal entrance from the courtyard on the west side of the house. The porte cochere has round-headed arches supported by piers and marble columns with Corinthian capitals. A wrought-iron balustrade surrounds the terrace on the roof of the porte cochere.

Both formal entrances open into a cross hall that is paved with dark and light marble squares. The vaulted ceiling springs from corbels in the form of Corinthian capitals. A grand staircase with wide marble steps rises from the cross hall. Its balustrade of wrought iron is accented with gilding. A landing door in the Palladian style opens to a small loggia framed with pilasters and four marble columns, and onto the terrace over the porte cochere.

To the north of the hall is the living room. The arched window alcove is echoed by a low-relief arch over the large, Italian Renaissance–style stone mantel. The most remarkable decorative feature of the room is the painted beamed ceiling, also in the style of the Italian Renaissance; the painting has been meticulously restored to its original appearance. (The main courtroom of Montgomery's Federal Building, also designed by Lockwood, has a similar ceiling.) Two arched French doors open onto the entrance arcade.

Double doors of bold mahogany paneling open into the study. As elsewhere in the house, arches are used to give depth to the wall, and those of the study have a faux leather finish. The stone mantel is in the Italian Renaissance style. The small, built-in bookcase is original. The plaster ceiling is in the eighteenth-century British style of the Adam brothers: squares and circles with bas relief classical figures.

The sun room also adjoins the living room. Its original marble mosaic floor, with a running Greek-key border, has been complemented by the addition of faux marbled finishes on the room's baseboards and pilasters.

The ceiling is vaulted, as are some of the seven round-headed windows.

Across the entrance hall from the living room is the dining room. The five round-headed windows are glazed with 390 circles of glass. Legend has it that these are the bottoms of the champagne bottles used at the Whitfields' wedding reception. The stone mantel is in the Italian Renaissance style. The floor, like those in the living room and study, is of two widths of wide quarter-sawn oak, anchored with screws hidden by contrasting pegs, and tied together with butterfly pegs. Again the most remarkable decorative feature of the room is the ceiling. Red squares with gilded rosettes and elongated blue hexagons create an elaborate geometrical pattern around a red, blue, and gilt central hexagonal medallion. This plaster, coffered ceiling was originally monochromatic; it is now more appropriate to its historical antecedents. The breakfast room is octagonal, a signature Lockwood feature. Its floor and small copper-hooded fireplace are bordered with original tiles.

Like many of Montgomery's mansions, the Whitfield House had been divided into apartments. This practice was intensified because of the housing shortage during and after World War II. The second floor of the Whitfield house was divided into five efficiency apartments. The original features were hidden, damaged, or destroyed. Consequently, the second floor was thoroughly redesigned to conform to modern needs and the requirements of the owners. There are four bedrooms and four sitting rooms. The floors are of quarter-sawn, narrow-width oak. The fine cornices and the door and window surrounds have been restored.

In 1987, Pat and Milton McGregor bought the mansion and began restoration. The project took sixteen months; a marble craftsman came from Italy, but most of the artisans came to Montgomery from elsewhere in the Southeast. The project, which included new construction, complements and enhances the original Lockwood design. In addition to restoration of the main house and carriage house, with its second-story apartment, a swimming-pool complex was constructed. The pool house has a loggia of five round-headed arches supported by unfluted columns with Scamozzi capitals. The grounds were landscaped so as to enhance the house and to create an Italian Renaissance villa. Palms, Italian cypresses, fig vine, and oleander are especially appropriate. The house, although on a grand scale, makes an intimate home because of the skill of designers and the vision of the McGregors.

Agudath Israel Synagogue (The Ephod Church)

507 South McDonough Street

MONTGOMERY'S JEWISH COMMUNITY did not form a congregation (Kahl Montgomery) until 1849, although one of the first settlers in the area was Abram Mordecai, who lived east of Montgomery from 1783 to 1815. Unlike Mordecai, who was born in Pennsylvania in 1755 and had deep roots in Norfolk and Charleston, most early Jews in Montgomery, who were relative newcomers to America, came from Germany. Kahl Montgomery began as an Orthodox synagogue but, in 1874, it adopted the Reform ritual and became Temple Beth Or. At the turn of the century, when a new temple was being built, part of the congregation that adhered to Orthodox rather than Reform practices withdrew from Temple Beth Or and formed Congregation Agudath Israel, or Brothers of Israel. The differences were not only between Reform and Orthodox Judiasm, but also between American-born and foreign-born.

From 1904 until 1914, Orthodox services were held in private houses. Services were conducted in Hebrew or Yiddish, whereas, in the early years of Kahl Montgomery, German had been used. In 1914, a stone and brick synagogue was built at 510 Monroe Street. A decade later, the state of

Alabama wanted the site for construction of a government building. Consequently, property was acquired at the corner of South McDonough and High streets, and a new synagogue was built in 1927. The congregation used this synagogue until 1957, when it sold the McDonough Street facility and moved to Cloverdale Road. At that time, the cornerstone and the metal Star of David that capped the facade were moved to the new synagogue. The move coincided with the congregation's change from Orthodox to Conservative Judaism.

Historically, there were no synagogues before the mid–second century B.C. There had been several Jewish temples until 620 B.C., when all except King Solomon's Temple, which had been built in Jerusalem about 955 B.C., were suppressed. Gradually the Jerusalem temple priesthood and sacrificial worship lost influence to the Pharisees. This transition was completed after A.D. 750, when Herod the Great's Temple (built 20 B.C.) was destroyed by the Romans. Judaism then became congregational and diffused, rather than hierarchical and centralized.

Unlike the Jerusalem temple, synagogues were not for sacrifical worship, but for congregational worship, study, and community meetings. Consequently the only necessary features for synagogue worship and teaching were the ark, for storing scriptures, and the reading desk, or *bimah*.

Nevertheless, reminders of the arrangements and practices of Herod's Temple have been retained. An entrance vestibule, a prayer hall, and a recess for scripture storage recall the arrangement of that temple. Synagogues also included a ritual bath, or *mikva* (which is used for conversions, ritual purification of women, and marriages) as a reminder of the ritual hand-washing basin in the court of the Jerusalem temple. Following temple practices, synagogues also separated women from men—behind a screen, in a balcony, or in a separate part of the room. There was no need for an equal number of seats for women and men, because women were not required to attend synagogue worship services, learn Hebrew, or read the Torah; their duties were at home.

Under the influence of American Reform Judaism, separating women and men has been abandoned. Although the McDonough Street synagogue had a women's balcony, it was never strictly used as such. Rather, single women sat on the south side of the worship hall, single men sat on the north side, and couples and children sat in the center. Reform Judaism also influenced the location of the reading desk, which had traditionally been in the center of the building. The reading desk has been moved to the east end of the room to be with the ark on a rostrum, from which the rabbi officiates rather than teaches. This is exactly what had happened in the synagogue/temple on Catoma Street, and this was also the arrangement at the McDonough Street synagogue.

Two generalities can be made about the historical architecture and decoration of synagogues. There have been periods of strict adherence to the proscription against making images (usually interpreted as human images), and there have been periods of freely using images for decoration, and as teaching and worship aids. There have been no distinctive architectural styles; rather, synagogues have conformed to the dominant styles of the time and place, although they have tended to be small and unostentatious. This was not only because Jewish congregations were usually small and synagogue worship and teaching were intimate, but also to avoid provoking jealousy in the predominantly Christian or Islamic populations.

The McDonough Street building, designed by Joseph Hirsch and Associates of Boston, is octagonal. This was one of several central plans used from the fourth century for synagogues and churches. Central-plan synagogues with Byzantine or Islamic architecture and decoration were popular in the nineteenth century. This architectural form may have been selected for Montgomery's orthodox synagogue because it was an ancient form, and one no longer associated with Christian churches—certainly not in Montgomery.

The McDonough Street building is distinctive but restrained, certainly not ostentatious. The buff brick exterior is decorated with contrasting brown brick at the corners, and both under and above the grouped, round-headed windows. The most distinctive feature is the octagonal roof and drum that is capped by a low dome. The worship and teaching hall is entered through a vestibule that is tiled with mosaics.

Although the worship and teaching hall is octagonal, the traditional central arrangement (ark on the east wall and raised reading desk in the center, surrounded by movable seats) was never followed at Agudath Israel Synagogue. The ark and the reading desk were on a raised platform on the east wall. Fixed pews in three sections faced east. (Facing east—or more accurately, Jerusalem—during certain parts of the worship service was made a requirement by the Talmudic sages. The practice of orienting Christian churches to the east comes from the same tradition.)

Except for the stained-glass windows decorated with tablets of the law, Torah scrolls, altars, and menorahs, the worship and teaching hall has been altered considerably since 1957. The dome is completely hidden by a lowered ceiling. This alteration also hid the women's balcony and the choir balcony that was above the ark and reading desk. The ark and reading desk have also been removed. The pews are now divided into two sections rather than three.

The building is owned and used by The Ephod Church, an independent interdenominational Christian church with Full Gospel and Pentecostal associations. In ancient Jewish temple worship, when a Levite priest went into the Holy of Holies, he wore a vestment, or ephod, that displayed the names of the Twelve Tribes of Israel (Exodus 28). The Ephod Church is using this ancient vestment as a symbol of the church's worship being for all peoples.

MONTGOMERY'S first public high school developed from the private Montgomery Female College in the late 1870s. There was no public high school for boys until 1895, two years after the girls' high school had been built at the corner of High and South Lawrence streets. The boys' high school was conducted in one room of the Capitol Hill School. Unlike the girls' four-year program, the boys attended for only two years. The boys' program was eventually increased to four years and, in the first decade of the twentieth century, moved to the Hamner Hall School building, a former Episcopal school for girls built in 1860 (burned 1909).

In 1910, the city's first coeducational high school was built at the corner of South McDonough and Scott streets. It was named after writer and musician Sidney Lanier, who lived in Montgomery from 1866 to 1867, and who supported himself teaching at Prattville Academy, clerking in his grandfather's Exchange Hotel, and serving as organist at First Presbyterian Church. The first Lanier high school building is now the Baldwin Arts and Academics Magnet School. The school quickly established a reputation for academic excellence. By 1917 its serious interest in football was established and, in 1922, its outstanding band was formed by a former member of John Philip Sousa's band. The school's reputation for scholarship, football, and band were carried over to the new high school built on South Court Street.

By 1923, the McDonough Street location was overcrowded, and it had no land for expansion. In August 1928, construction began on the twenty-two-acre site on South Court Street, at that time on the southern edge of the city. The school opened its doors in September 1929.

▼

Sidney Lanier High School

1756 South Court Street

The new high school consolidated the city's central high school with the county's high school. (The county's 1922 high school building is today's Cloverdale Junior High School.) The name of the new high school may have been decided by the outcome of a 1928 football game between the city and the county high schools. The city won, and the new Montgomery consolidated high school had its name, Sidney Lanier. The new school was built by Algernon Blair, the city's foremost builder, and designed by Frederick Ausfeld, born and educated in Austria, one of Montgomery's prominent architects. His work includes the 1907 Bell Building (one of the city's first skyscrapers), the 1919 Empire Theatre, and the 1922 Jefferson Davis Hotel.

Ausfeld was noted for his technical innovations, but to ensure that the latest in educational innovations were incorporated into the design, he was assisted by consultants from Columbia University. The results cost $750,000, which earned the school the nickname "The Million Dollar School."

Early in the twentieth century, Montgomery invested more money per student in school construction than Mobile or Birmingham. By 1930, Montgomery had the highest white literacy rate of any county or city in the South. (At the same time, the city had the lowest homicide rate of any Southern city.)

Late Gothic, or Tudor, elements, while not integral to the building's construction, were applied as decorations to the school's exterior and interior. (Flowers Memorial Hall at Huntingdon College is a much more accurate historical adaptation of the late–English Gothic, or Tudor, style.) The handsome and imposing building certainly makes a powerful statement regarding the importance of public education and civic pride to its builders, and to generations of its students.

The three-story red-brick building rests on a basement of stone and brick. Its asymmetrical facade is divided by engaged buttresses decorated with stone shields, open books, and lamps of knowledge. Over the first-floor windows is a limestone entablature with a running grapevine motif. The facade is punctuated by an octagonal stair tower, and by a massive tower that serves as the main entrance. The latter is decorated with limestone owls of wisdom, and with a Gothic blind arcade at the top.

The interior is characterized by quality workmanship and fine detailing, and by space and light. Most of the original ceiling-light fixtures have been retained in the broad corridors. Except for some tile and the brass-bordered terrazzo of the foyer, floors are of narrow-width maple over concrete sub-floors. The classrooms have high ceilings and large windows.

Original innovative features included a centralized vacuum cleaner system (no longer functioning), a system of electronic bells that connected classrooms and administrative offices (also no longer functioning), refrigerated-water fountains (replaced), and a draft system that cooled the building by allowing hot air to rise through two-foot square ducts from each room to large exhaust hoods on the roof. This system is no longer operating. The building's walls are two feet thick, masonry on the exterior and plaster over metal lath on the interior, separated by a dead-air space. Only one of the original commodes remains; when weight is removed, its seat automatically rises, activating the flushing mechanism.

The foyer, auditorium, and library are handsome rooms. The foyer has hollow tile walls that resemble stone. Pilasters, bordered with red molding and decorated with shields, support shallow Gothic arches. The plaster ceiling is decorated with intertwined leaf-and-strapwork molding. The doors have hood architraves, superimposed Gothic arches, and Gothic hardware. The wide foyer opens into the auditorium.

The auditorium's decorative scheme is also Gothic. The stage's Gothic proscenium arch, the widest in the city, is a Gothic arch topped with a blind arcade. The ceiling is decorated with Gothic arches that spring from foliated corbels, octagonal Gothic tracery ventilators, and the original lighting fixtures. Additional decoration includes high wooden wainscoting and Stuart-style strapwork over the doors. The orchestra pit has been covered over. Sconces that were once on the side walls have been removed. The auditorium, which originally seated 1,900, was modified to accommodate the larger anatomy of today's students; it now seats 1,680, the second largest auditorium in the city. The old, metal Gothic ends of the rows of seats have been retained. The acoustics are excellent. Katherine Hepburn, Gertrude Lawrence, and many other great American actors performed in this auditorium.

Lanier's library, which is directly above the foyer, has retained its original oak shelving. The coffered ceiling is decorated with egg-and-dart and acanthus moldings. A stylized rose is in the center of each of the ceiling's octagonal medallions. The ceiling, once multicolored, is now painted gray.

Private donations paid for the school's original landscaping. A pine windbreak was planted behind the athletic fields, and a double row of gardenias lined the semicircular front drive. There was also a beautiful rose garden. All this succumbed to the Great Depression, as the school could not afford labor, or even the water, to maintain the landscaping.

The Depression did have one positive effect: students, having very few job opportunities, stayed in school longer. Consequently the curriculum was expanded. This included a work-study program. During World War II, the extensive shops in the basement were used twenty-four hours a day to train defense plant workers.

From its founding, Sidney Lanier High School maintained a reputation for academic excellence, based in large part on an exceptionally talented faculty who demanded scholastic vigor from the students. The school was once ranked in the top seven in the country. In 1957, it trailed only Bronx High School in New York in the number of National Merit Scholarship recipients.

Kress Building

39 Dexter Avenue

SAMUEL H. KRESS, a Pennsylvania school teacher, was an entrepreneur at heart. In 1887, when he bought his first business, a stationery store, he was following in the footsteps of Frank W. Woolworth, who just seven years earlier had invented high-volume retailing of inexpensive merchandise. Kress was not the first to follow Woolworth's example. J. G. McCrory and S. S. Kresge (now K-mart) preceded Kress. They were followed by others, among them W. T. Grant and J. J. Newberry. In 1896 Kress purchased his third store, the first in his dime-store chain. This Memphis store was followed a year later by a store in Nashville and, a year later, by one in Montgomery. The 1898 Montgomery store building was the first of four Kress buildings in Montgomery.

Dime stores were purposely located near one another to increase customer traffic. Silver (Green), Newberry, Woolworth, and Kress dime stores were located in the first block of Dexter Avenue. Not only were these stores clustered together, but Montgomery's major department stores were also at the western end of Dexter: Belks, Montgomery Fair (now Dillard's), Penneys, Pizitz, and Sears.

With the exception of a few small stores in Cloverdale, on east Madison Avenue, on High Street in Centennial Hill, and on Bell Street in the West End, Montgomery's retail trade was concentrated downtown. Sidewalks and stores were thronged with shoppers, especially on Saturdays and between Thanksgiving and Christmas. The streets were full of automobiles; after the electric streetcars were replaced by buses in 1936, there were two rows of head-in parking down the middle of Dexter Avenue and Commerce Street. It was only quiet on Sundays and on Wednesday afternoons (Montgomery's stores closed at one o'clock on Wednesdays). This thriving trade gradually died after World War II. Suburbs were built to accommodate the housing shortage caused by nearly two decades of economic depression and war, and by the rapid increase of families as servicemen were demobilized. These suburbs, with their ubiquitous automobiles, came to be served by shopping centers, and then malls, that dispersed the retail trade. The first of these shopping centers in Montgomery were Cloverland, which appeared soon after the war, and Normandale, in 1954.

Samuel Kress differed considerably from the other low-price/high-volume retail entrepreneurs. He was a public benefactor and patron of the arts. The Kress Collection eventually consisted of more than three thousand works of art. Unlike most other great collectors, Kress did not keep his collection together. He gave it to the people who had given him his wealth. Between 1930 and 1961, he donated the art works to ninety-six institutions around the country. In 1934, fifty-five Italian paintings, mostly from the fourteenth to sixteenth centuries, were displayed at Huntingdon College. Two years later, Kress gave a fourteenth-century Madonna and Child to the college. His letters indicate that he was trying to encourage the growth of the Montgomery Museum of Fine Arts.

But Kress was a patron of the arts before he began collecting in 1927. Rather than lease buildings, as most of his competitors did, he built his own. In 1900, his architectural division was established in New York. At one time he employed as many as one hundred architects and draftsmen. Kress himself approved the architectural plans. The stores, especially in the 1930s, sold inexpensive goods in spacious, well-lit, even opulent surroundings.

At first, his stores had a certain similarity: they were symmetrical buildings of pale-yellow brick trimmed in white. The store's name, Kress, was

Fluted Doric columns supporting full Doric entablature

displayed near the top of the buildings. To draw window shoppers into the stores, curved display windows led to recessed entrances. Eventually, Kress stores were designed in a variety of styles. The most elaborate, however, were designed by George E. Mackay in 1929. Montgomery's store is one of these.

In late 1927, the Victorian commercial building that had been the Kress store was extensively damaged by fire and had to be demolished. In 1929, after a rainy spring, the sides of the hole that had been dug as the basement of the new store gave way, and three adjacent buildings were damaged as their adjoining walls collapsed into the hole. Although there were four injuries, there were no fatalities.

The new store's facade, one of the most remarkable facades Mackay ever designed for Kress, is related to an event in Kress's life. In the 1920s, Kress had been knighted by the king of Italy for helping preserve ancient monuments. One of these was the Temple of Hera in southern Italy, a classical temple in the Doric style. Consequently, Mackay designed the new Montgomery store with a facade featuring two huge free-standing Doric columns flanked by *antae*, the piers formed by thickening the lateral walls. The fluted columns, with simple capitals and without bases or plinths, are historically accurate. In addition to the two columns, the terra-cotta facade features an historically accurate Doric entablature composed of architrave, metopes, triglyphs with blue accents, blue guttae on a red field, and cornice with acanthus molding. The entablature supports a parapet, displaying the KRESS logo, and is topped by an acroterion.

Originally there were two double front doors recessed behind curving display windows. Two of these curved windows were retained when the doors were altered in 1984. At that time, the awning and handsome pressed-metal marquee were removed.

The Monroe Street facade is asymmetrical so as to accommodate the loading platform and freight elevator. The facade, of yellow brick, terra-cotta, and glass, has three bays with stacked windows separated by Doric pilasters. They are surmounted by a full entablature, identical to the Dexter Avenue facade. The parapet is similar, but somewhat less elaborate. Curved windows survive at this entrance.

The main floor is one huge, long, rectangular room. Other than the floor's terrazzo squares bordered in brass, only the ceiling and the fluted pilasters are reminders of how the store looked in 1929. Unlike the facade, these pilasters are not accurate examples of classical architectural details. Their capitals are in the contemporary Art Deco style—loosely inspired by Corinthian capitals. The coffered ceiling features decorations using several classical motifs. At one time the pilasters and ceiling were painted so as to accent the detail; today all is white or beige.

Some of the ceramic and marble wainscoting remains intact, but in the 1960s, the marble water fountains were removed. The mahogany counters and cabinets, ceiling fans, and bell-shaped lighting fixtures are gone. Samuel Kress's coat of arms, and the plaster wall sconces with shell motifs that once adorned the panels between the pilasters, are also gone. (Samuel Kress's coat of arms was from a design by Albrecht Durer for the German Kress family, from whom Kress claimed descent.)

Half of the west wall was devoted to candy. It is gone, as is the large lunch room with table service that originally occupied the rear of the store. A kitchen in the basement provided pork chops, ham, fried chicken, chicken and dumplings, collards, turnips, blackeyed peas, and homemade pies and cakes. The "world's best vegetable soup" cost five cents—seven cents with fresh corn muffins. Next to the back door, on a lower level, a very small snack bar was available for black customers.

The second floor, reached by a long metal staircase and by two freight elevators, was the stockroom. Its oak floor and long pine bins are still in place. It is still lit by skylights. It is quiet now; its scurrying stockboys are gone. The basement also was originally a stock room. Over the years, it has alternated as a stock room and a bargain basement. Both basement and second floor reveal that the building is substantially built of poured concrete.

Kress has given America a greater architectural, and perhaps art, legacy that any other company in the country. Approximately a hundred stores still stand. Many now have alternative uses; some have inspired downtown renewal.

In 1980–1981, S. H. Kress and Company was liquidated. The Montgomery Kress was acquired by McCrory Stores of York, Pennsylvania—an early competitor of S. H. Kress—and was operated as a variety store before going out of business in early 1997.

Davis Theatre for the Performing Arts

251 Montgomery Street

THE CITIZENS of Montgomery have been interested in the performing arts from early in the city's history. Although a theater building was not opened until January 1830, in December 1822—only three years after Montgomery was incorporated—the Thespian Society performed Shakespeare's *Julius Caesar*. Of the twenty-three citizens who participated in the play, three later achieved distinction. Benjamin Fitzpatrick (Julius Caesar) became governor of Alabama, United States senator, and president pro tempore of the United States Senate. George W. B. Towns (Octavius Caesar) became governor of Georgia. Henry Goldthwaite (Mark Antony) became an associate justice of the Supreme Court of Alabama.

The Davis Theatre was named the Paramount when it was built in 1929. It was then the only theater in Montgomery, and one of the few in the South, that was designed for both motion pictures and live vaudeville performances. Film cowboy Tom Mix and his horse performed on the stage; Lauren Bacall tap-danced at the Paramount and stayed at the Whitley Hotel next door. At that time, Montgomery Street was full of life, with nearby hotels, and the Empire movie theater just across the street.

The architectural integrity of the south side of the 200 block of Montgomery Street is rather well preserved. Especially noteworthy is the 1906 Bell Building, one of the city's first skyscrapers; Troy State University

Montgomery's Whitley Hall, formerly a hotel; and, until demolished in 1997, the Empire Theatre. The latter is believed to have been the first theater in the country to have electrically refrigerated air conditioning. The 1919 system was designed by Frederick Ausfeld, who also designed the Bell Building and the nearby Jefferson Davis Hotel. It was at the Empire Theatre in 1938 that a teenaged Hank Williams got his first break by winning an amateur-night prize of fifteen dollars.

The Davis Theatre fits in well with the adjacent limestone-trimmed, red-brick Whitley Hall. Although the Davis Theatre's exterior is rather plain, conforming to no architectural style, it does incorporate several classical details. Its restrained, red-brick facade is decorated with limestone dentils, cornice, and Tuscan pilasters. The limestone walls, four arched windows, and ticket kiosk of the street-level front may be restored. The entrance alcove, with two blind arches and gilt-trimmed cornice, has already been restored. The west side is laid in fine Flemish bond and decorated with limestone belt courses and cornice. There was once a large lighted sign that extended from the marquee to above the red-tiled roof. Replicas of the sign and of the original marquee will eventually be restored.

Early in the century, movie palaces were often elaborate, even exotic, buildings. Their architecture and interior decorative schemes, which could evoke Moorish, Renaissance, or Oriental palaces, for example, were intended to heighten the excitement of an evening at the moving pictures. The interior of the theater has been restored. Although not so exotic as many movie palaces of its time, the Davis does have an elaborate, eclectic decorative scheme.

On each side of the lobby, four large beveled-glass mirrors with gilt frames expand the room and, at the same time, contribute to the excitement of attending the theater by making it seem crowded. Tuscan pilasters echo those on the building's facade and those in the auditorium. The gilt stenciling echoes that of the auditorium. The lobby ceiling has an octagonal medallion from which hangs a chandelier. Walls are scored and painted to give the appearance of stone.

The auditorium, reached by two broad flights of stairs, is a large rectangular room with an arched ceiling that is decorated with classical motifs and recessed, star-shaped lights. These lights were originally lit with colors that were appropriate for each evening's feature film. Each of the ceiling's shallow arches is supported by pilasters that are topped with Composite capitals. Between the pilasters on each of the side walls are five blind arches that are supported by Tuscan pilasters. Decoration within the arches is gilt stenciling on rough plaster that is painted rust red. The stenciled designs approximate the originals. In front of each arch is an elaborate ironwork chandelier. The stage's proscenium arch is surrounded by wide, twisted and stenciled molding in rust red and gilt. On both sides of the stage, free-standing fluted columns with Corinthian capitals flank gilt grills.

The theater is named for Tine and Eunice Davis, who provided the initial funding that allowed the building to be saved and restoration to go forward. Eunice Davis-McNeill has continued to support the theater. She also contributed the glass-roofed alley that is named, in Tine Davis's memory, Tine's Grande Finale.

The Davis Theatre now serves a number of Montgomery's performing-arts groups, both professional and amateur. It seats twelve hundred, and has good sight lines and a full orchestra pit. Additions at the rear of the building have significantly increased the versatility of the stage. The Troy State University System owns and operates the Davis Theatre for the Performing Arts.

E ARLY SETTLERS selected the fertile river bottoms that they knew would produce bumper crops of cotton and corn. It was not, however, until the 1830s that planters realized the black and red prairie lands south of Montgomery also made fine farm land.

John Gindrat developed a plantation, which he called Fairview, south of what is now Fairview Avenue and east of Norman Bridge Road. His house was recognized as the finest plantation house in the environs of Montgomery. An avenue of cedars led from Norman Bridge Road to the front of the house. A similar avenue, which led north from the side of the house, is now named Mastin Lane after Peter and Mary Myrick Mastin, who acquired the plantation about 1851. The cedars are now large and festooned with Spanish moss.

After Mastin's death in 1865, the plantation was divided. Dr. Brannon Hubbard, a noted surgeon and horseman, eventually acquired the land east of Mastin Lane, which was the bulk of Fairview. Unfortunately, the plantation house, long since fallen into disrepair, had to be torn down. In 1922, Dr. Hubbard and his wife, Caroline, replaced it with another mansion. A victim of expanding and contracting prairie soil, the Hubbard's house also had to be torn down.

▼

Tower House

3183 Lexington Road

The part of Fairview west of Mastin Lane was platted as a residential neighborhood and appropriately called The Cedars. Lexington Road, the neighborhood's principal street, has an outstanding collection of homes, most of which were built in the 1920s and 1930s. The streetscape is very appealing because of complementary landscaping and the scale, quality, and detail of the houses. Although many of the houses have Tudor detailing, each house is distinctive in its own right.

The most unusual house is Tower House, 3183 Lexington. Fred J. Cramton built the house for his daughter, Hazel, about 1929. Cramton, a local building contractor, had an unusual house himself at 1857 South Hull Street. As a native of Saginaw, Michigan, he was accustomed to professional baseball and football, and wanted a stadium in Montgomery. He donated land and built the stadium for cost. Cramton Bowl was one of the first lighted stadiums in the South.

Subsequently, the house was occupied by Lieutenant Colonel Frederick Irving Eglin, who was an instructor at the Air Corps Tactical School at Maxwell Field. Colonel Eglin was killed in an airplane crash in 1937. In the same year, Eglin Field, Florida, was named in his memory.

Many Montgomerians associate the house with Nora Cox, a noted piano teacher. Her most famous pupil was her own daughter, Mary Anthony Cox. After being graduated at fifteen from Margaret Booth's School for Girls, Miss Cox studied at the Paris Conservatory of Music for about ten years. She subsequently taught at Juilliard in New York.

Like all the other houses on Lexington Avenue, Tower House is eclectic. Whimsical details give the house its appeal. The facade is dominated by a two-story tower with a conical roof capped with a copper weathervane. Only close examination reveals a stepped buttress and fine brickwork of alternating headers and stretchers. What cannot be overlooked are the tower's three Carpenter Gothic–style windows with heavy, rough stone surrounds. The casement windows have leaded glass whose beveling and "jewels" create a rainbow of colors inside the house. Although the tower dominates the facade, there are other interesting details. The window lintels are heavy, rough-cut timbers. The clapboard gable on the right had an operable dovecote, and the half-timbered gable on the left has an in-fill of decorated plaster. The nogging of the half-timbered gable on the projecting porch is laid in a herringbone pattern, as is the angled walk and the porch floor.

The wide, curved front door, decorated with wrought-iron strap hinges, opens into the base of the tower, which is part of the large living room. Two tower windows and two large rectangular windows ensure that the room is filled with light. Wider at its base than top, the massive chimney has a firebox surrounded by wide slabs of black marble, which is also used for the hearth. Flanking the fireplace are two of the living room's four built-in bookcases. Gothic arches at the tops of the bookcases complement those of the door to the hall, and the wider opening to the dining room. The dining room has a wide rectangular window. Originally, an air-conditioning unit under the window protruded into the room. Enclosed in a furniture-quality cabinet, this unit, and a similar one in the living room, was four feet wide, three feet deep, and two feet high.

A Gothic-arched door opens into the kitchen, and two Gothic-arched glass doors open onto a rear screened porch. This porch has a high cathedral ceiling supported by large timbers. The porch is paved with red and buff broken tile that extends as an uncovered terrace across part of the rear of the house.

There are three bedrooms and two bathrooms on the ground floor. Most of the original fixtures of the tiled baths have survived. One bathroom has a tub recessed in a Gothic arch, and the other has a shower with a Gothic arched door. The ceilings are nine and a half feet. Flooring throughout the house is narrow-width red oak. The pine woodwork in the living and dining rooms has never been painted, but most of the woodwork throughout the rest of the house is now painted. The doors are single panel. One door on the second floor is solid cherry and, luckily, unpainted.

On the second floor there are two very large rooms and several smaller rooms, one of which is a half-bath. The tower's circular room is notable: it is opened to the conical roof that is made of tapered boards. This circular room has an unusual acoustical quality. The room's atmosphere is enhanced by the light from the one leaded-glass window. Another of the small rooms, the one in the gable with the dovecote, has a door to an even smaller room. The low, narrow door has a barred peephole. Legend has it that Nora Cox's recalcitrant piano students were threatened with confinement in this room.

The rear porch and terrace overlook a glade-like setting of trees, a flagstone-paved terrace, and brick retaining walls. Down a path paved with bricks in a herringbone pattern is a garage made of brick and rough stone to complement the house. Beyond is Mastin Lane and its cedars. To the south of the house is the drive; it and the private road west of Lexington once formed the cedar-lined drive from Norman Bridge Road to the front of Fairview plantation's mansion.

Jim Goodwyn and Lyn Frazer bought the house in 1979. They have restored it, retaining most of the original details and ensuring that the modernization is compatible with the house's architectural integrity.

Austin Hall

55 LeMay Plaza South,
Maxwell Air Force Base

THE FIRST EUROPEANS to visit the site of what is today Maxwell Air Force Base may have been Spanish soldiers under Hernando de Soto, who is believed to have been in the area in September 1540. Later in that century, the Alabama Indian village of Towassa, on the high bluffs above the Alabama River, may have been visited by another Spanish soldier, Tristan de Luna. Although he failed to found a town on the Alabama River, he did succeed in establishing St. Augustine (Florida) in 1565. In 1715, the village of Towassa was yet again visited by soldiers, this time the French, under the orders of Jean-Baptiste Le Moyne de Bienville, sometime governor of French Louisiana and founder of Mobile (1710) and New Orleans (1718). They were on their way to establish Fort Toulouse, as part of the French policy to encircle the English colonies on the Atlantic Seaboard.

The site of the base also has connections to early aviation history, for it was here that Wilbur and Orville Wright conducted a civilian flying training school from March 26 to May 28, 1910. One of the first night flights took place here. The site then reverted to cotton farming, its former use. The majority of the land was owned by Frank D. Kohn, who had leased land to the city for the free use by the Wrights, and who was to lease and eventually sell it to the federal government.

In April 1918, construction began on an aviation-repair depot to serve eight bases in the Southeast, including Taylor Field in the Pike Road community east of Montgomery. The west Montgomery base was to have been a temporary facility, like numerous World War I installations. The facility was able to repair and manufacture almost every airplane part, as well as test-fly the repaired aircraft.

After the war, the base served as a supply and storage facility. It was not until the late 1920s that permanent construction began. Still standing from this period are the one-story single-family, and two-story duplex, houses for noncommissioned officers, the hospital (now the headquarters of the Civil

236

A Sense of Place

Air Patrol), two barracks (now offices, including those for the Community College of the Air Force), and the stables (now a self-help store). The interwar period was not without significant milestones. In 1925, Maxwell Field was the hub in an experiment that resulted in expansion of airmail service (which began in 1918) by connecting the Gulf Coast with Chicago and, hence, with the East and West Coasts. In the late 1920s, 14,000 square miles were mapped by aerial photography for the Tennessee River Project, later the Tennessee Valley Authority. During a five-day period in March 1929, 281 relief missions were flown; Alabama was the state hardest hit in the Great Flood of 1929. The federal prison that opened in 1930 was then, as now, for nonviolent offenders—primarily moonshiners and bootleggers at the time. By 1931, Maxwell Field had become Montgomery's leading source of business income.

During the interwar period, there were links between the city and the base. Among these were dances, amateur theater, and a variety of sporting events. Although football and boxing were popular sports, polo seems to have been the most popular, after thirty horses were sent to the base for equitation training of the personnel. Single polo matches at Maxwell eventually attracted nearly three thousand spectators. Teams from the base, the city, and from throughout the Southeast played on the large parade ground that was on the block now occupied by the Senator Lister Hill Building, which is named in honor of the Montgomery politician who is considered the godfather of Maxwell Field. It was Hill who saved Maxwell from closure in 1925 and who secured the major construction authorizations.

The most significant event of the interwar period, however, was the relocation of the Air Corps Tactical School from Langley Field, Virginia, where it had been established in 1920. With this school, Maxwell fixed its place in American military history.

The academic and administrative building was designed by the Army Office of the Constructing Quartermaster as part of the 1927 Army Air Corps Five-Year Expansion Program. The building was completed by Samford Brothers of Montgomery in 1931 at the cost of $119,273. It was named for Lieutenant Charles B. Austin, a native of Illinois and graduate of DePauw University, because of his brilliant teaching at the school when it was located at Langley Field. Austin Hall, a two-story building above a full, half-sunk basement, was originally I-shaped. In 1934, Algernon Blair of Montgomery added the south wing for the cost of $107,627; it almost doubled the building's size.

The Spanish Colonial style was considered more appropriate for the South and Southwest. (Today, red roofs on cream or buff buildings predominate on Maxwell and provide a unifying element.) The Spanish Colonial style of Austin Hall is characterized by rough-textured stucco, a hipped roof covered with variegated barrel tile, and curved rafter tails. The three round-headed main doors with multi-light transoms, which once faced the parade ground, have limestone pilasters and architraves. One of the doors has finials above its pilasters. The original multi-light steel-frame windows have been replaced.

The most distinctive feature of the building's exterior was the two-story loggia that was added to the center of the west side after 1934. The loggia's main floor was enclosed by five heavy masonry arches, and the roof of the open gallery on the second floor was supported by paired Tuscan columns. The arches have been filled in and the open gallery has been enclosed.

Austin Hall originally housed ACTS classrooms, conference and map rooms, library, auditorium, instructors' offices, and administrative offices. Although the interior of the building has been altered numerous times, most extensively in the late 1980s, the building's historical significance is based on its being the intellectual center of the pre-war air force.

Theorists such as Muir Fairchild, Kenneth Walker, Robert Webster, and Donald Wilson developed airpower doctrine, techniques, tactics, and strategy at the Air Corps Tactical School. In 1941, Kenneth Walker and other faculty members, such as Hal George, Haywood Hansell (nicknamed "Possum" for his habit of sleeping in class when he was a student), and Lawrence Kuter, used those theories, especially the idea of high-altitude precision strategic bombing in daylight of the enemy's industrial infrastructure, to develop Air War Plan Division 1. Although their theories were known to be well ahead of the technical capabilities of aircraft of the day, this plan was the basis for the production goal of 6,834 bombers and the Combined Bomber Offensive. It has been called the air war plan that defeated Hitler.

ACTS closed in June 1941 and its faculty and students were sent to war. The school produced the Air Force's wartime leaders, as well as generals Hoyt Vandenberg, Nathan Twining, Thomas White, and Curtis LeMay—all postwar Air Force chiefs of staff.

During the war, Austin Hall served as the headquarters of the Southeast Air Corps Training Center that was responsible for all pilot, navigator, and bombardier training in the Southeast. It trained more than 100,000 aviation cadets during the war.

After the war, the building was the home of the Army Air Forces School, which became Air University in 1946. The Air War College was on the second floor. Today, Austin Hall is the headquarters building for Air University. It is responsible for the Air Force Institute of Technology (in Dayton, Ohio), all Air Force officer and noncommissioned-officer professional military education, the Reserve Officer Training Corps and Officer Training School commissioning programs, schools for Air Force chaplains and lawyers, the Community College of the Air Force, and numerous specialized resident and correspondence courses. The traditions of the Air Corps Tactical School are maintained by the Air War College, School for Advanced Airpower Studies, Air Command and Staff College, and Airpower Research Institute.

THE GILMER/THOMAS family plantation, Edgewood, dates from the early 1830s. In 1916, Jett Thomas had the plantation platted as a subdivison. In time, Thomas Avenue, with its divided roadway, became one of the city's most fashionable addresses.

Ralph and Nell Quisenberry were among the first purchasers; they bought three acres on the corner of Thomas Avenue and Woodley Road. The Quisenberrys did not build, however, until 1932–33. For their architect they selected Frank Lockwood, Montgomery's most fashionable architect for more than thirty years. Algernon Blair, a prominent regional contractor, was the builder.

Although Lockwood had had a very successful career, the future did not look particularly bright for an architect in the early Depression. He had been building very fine Georgian-Colonial, Tudor, and Mediterranean–Spanish Colonial houses for the richest families in Montgomery. In 1932, he essentially ended his career. In that year, he had only three commissions: the Steiner House at 1634 Gilmer Avenue, the Quisenberry-Bryan House, and the Federal Building. (Blair was also the contractor for the Federal Building.)

The Tudor style, one of the historical styles of the academic revival popular from about 1910 to the early 1930s, was inspired by English vernacular architecture of the fifteenth century. It is characterized by asymmetrical massing, half-timbered walls filled with brick or plaster, accentuated gables, steeply pitched roofs of slate or tile, Tudor arched doors, and irregularly placed casement windows that were often leaded. Tudor features were much less likely to be used for interiors. But the better examples had interior decorative and structural features that helped create a period atmosphere.

Quisenberry-Bryan House

3113 Thomas Avenue

The Quisenberry-Bryan House actually has the appearance of a large English Tudor house, rather than a modern house with applied decorative features. The flat tiles on the steeply pitched roof and the irregularly laid brick have the appearance of great age. In fact, the exterior brick, and that used for the interior walls of the sun room, are from Montgomery's 1852/1871 city hall, which burned in 1932.

Asymmetrical massing and variety in window size and placement add to the house's authenticity. It seems to have evolved over time. What is actually a porte cochere and access to the motorcourt and three-car garage appears to be a gateway to a courtyard. Heavy overhanging gables on the three sides of the south end of the house, and the overhanging gable on the central bay, create an almost brooding atmosphere. These half-timbered gables and the timbers of the porte cochere illustrate the integrity of design and construction. The heart-pine timbers, some of which are twelve inches square, are hand hewn. Many of the timbers are not applied over a brick wall; the brick is actual in-fill, and the pegs are actual pegs.

The main entrance is from a semicircular tile step into a vestibule with identical tile flooring. Lockwood repeated this feature, but with brick, from the sun room to the large terrace at the back of the house. The shallow-arched doorway has a wide, heavy paneled door of heart pine.

The large stair hall is raised from the entrance vestibule, and from the living room and study. The broad, gently rising staircase encircles the stair hall on three sides; the stair landing is on the fourth side. The wrought-iron balustrade and chandelier add to the period character. Several pieces of Tudor-style furniture were made for the house, including a short pew in the stair hall. The pew has a linen-fold paneled back and poppyhead ends. The floor is random-width oak.

To the right of the stair hall, and at a lower level, is the living room. The walls, like all the plaster walls in the house, are rough cast. The living room is dominated by a stone mantel that incorporates a variety of Gothic and Tudor decorative elements, including the Tudor rose. The sun room opens off the living room. Its walls and floor are brick; several burned bricks from the city hall are visible. The iron chandelier is unusual in that it incorporates a small, multiple-blade fan—an original fixture. Also adjoining the living room is the library. Its floors are random-width oak. The fireplace is surrounded with deep molding and there is no mantel shelf. Millwork throughout the house is fine; most of it is unpainted. But the vertical cypress paneling in the library is exceptional. The room, which includes built-in bookcases, has an unusual frieze: stars alternating with three vertical bars. This feature, which certainly would not have been a choice of Lockwood, as it does not contribute to the period character of the house, is believed to be the requirement of Ralph Quisenberry.

Across the stair hall from the living room is the large dining room. The floor is random-width oak, the walls rough-cast plaster, and the chandelier is iron. The breakfast room has the random-width oak flooring, fine mill work, paneled solid doors, and same iron hardware and fittings used throughout the first floor. It also has two corner cupboards, a feature Lockwood frequently used.

There are four bedrooms and a cedar-lined sleeping porch on the second floor. The house's high-pitched roofs add character to second-story walls and ceilings. Even some doors are cut at diagonal angles to accommodate the pitch of the roof. Floors are narrow-width oak. All the second floor's three bathrooms have their original fixtures. The tubs, which are fitted with showers, are set in arched alcoves. The black and white, black and cream, and green and cream ceramic-tile floors and walls are laid in three patterns. Lockwood is noted for built-in closets, drawers, and cupboards. The bathrooms have built-in cupboards and clothes hampers, unusual features for the period. The linen closet has adjustable shelving; there is a built-in ironing board; one set of three closet doors is faced with beveled full-length mirrors.

Throughout the house, steam radiators are concealed behind grilles that are incorporated in deep-set windows. The house was originally cooled by a large attic fan located in the center of the house, at the top of the stairs.

The owners have preserved the complete blueprints, catalogues for windows and bathroom fixtures, and landscaping design by C. D. Wagstaff of Bolling, Alabama. Wagstaff's plan was not closely followed, but the informal and natural landscaping complements the Tudor style of the house. The appearance of the front yard is changed, because four huge oaks that predated Edgewood plantation have recently died. Many old trees still survive in the side and back yards, as do the brick borders for the formal rose garden. The red-clay badminton court is overgrown with grass, but the large, curved barbecue area is intact.

Nell Quisenberry sold her house to Donald and Helen Bryan in 1939. Bryan was the president of the Dr. Pepper Company. Betty Lou, one of the Bryan's daughters, married Stanley, one of the Quisenberry sons. Another Bryan daughter, Emma Jean, and her husband, Chet Brown, made the house their home.

Frank M. Johnson Jr. Federal Building

15 Lee Street

POSTAL SERVICE for Montgomery began in 1820. The post office occupied a succession of buildings on Commerce and Montgomery streets. It also was housed (1860–75) on the ground floor of the Montgomery Theatre at Perry and Madison streets and, finally, across Madison Street in the 1852 city hall.

The 1884 federal courthouse, post office, and customs house on the southwest corner of Dexter Avenue and South Lawrence Street was Montgomery's first building constructed specifically for the federal government. The Richardsonian Romanesque–style building's most distinguishing feature was the corner clocktower. (The most distinguishing feature for children was the city's first elevator; they stood in line to ride it.) This building was demolished about 1958.

The economic situation of the early 1930s differed considerably from that of the boom years, when the Dexter Avenue post office had been built. A new federal building was needed, not only because the 1884 post office was inadequate for expanded federal services, but also because the construction would provide work for some of the Depression's unemployed.

In 1930, Congressman, later Senator, Lister Hill obtained funding for a new federal building. The building was designed in 1931 by Frank Lockwood, who had come south from New York in the 1880s and had moved to Montgomery by the 1890s. Although he appears to have had no formal training in architecture, the quality of his work, probably acquired on the job with George B. Post of New York, made him the most prominent Montgomery architect during the first third of the twentieth century. He was known for attention to detail, masterful manipulation of traditional design, and a fine sense of proportion. His local work includes the 1906–1912 additions to the state Capitol, Huntingdon College's 1928 Houghton Library, and many fine Tudor, Georgian-Colonial, and Mediterranian–Spanish Colonial houses. Not only did the Federal Building culminate his remarkable career, but it is probably the most handsome building in Montgomery; certainly it is the most monumental.

The supervising architect was James A. Wetmore, a prominent government architect, who would, under normal circumstances, have been the designing architect. It was unusual that a local architect served as designer. Lockwood's reputation aided in his securing that position.

Lockwood often worked with Algernon Blair, Montgomery's most prominent builder. The federal building is the result of such a collaboration. Blair established his reputation in Montgomery with the 1902 Standard Club. He became a major regional builder, and the king of the post offices, eventually building more than two hundred. He was noted for the quality of his construction and for finishing ahead of schedule. He was also known for his monumental buildings. His work in Montgomery includes city hall, Baldwin and Sidney Lanier schools, and the veterans' hospital.

In July 1932, a thousand spectators watched the Masonic service as the cornerstone was laid. Eleven months and $801,175 later, the new Federal Building was completed—ahead of schedule. It housed the post office, federal courts, Veterans' Bureau, Internal Revenue Collector, military recruiting offices, and, on the roof, a meteorological station.

The Classical Revival–style building may have been inspired by Gabriel's pair of buildings facing Paris's Place de la Concorde, which were built for Louis XV in the mid–eighteenth century. It also resembles the 1836 federal Treasury Building designed by Robert Mills, America's first trained architect.

The five-story U-shaped building is constructed of brick on a granite base. The brick is faced with limestone on the ground floor and sandstone above. The limestone on the ground floor has grooves to give the blocks a rusticated appearance. The sandstone above the ground floor is smooth. The fifth floor is hidden behind the entablature. The shallow, hipped roof is covered with red terra-cotta tiles.

The Church Street facade occupies an entire city block. The facade's central block is bracketed by end blocks, each of which has four attached fluted columns that rest on the slightly projecting ground floor. The Roman Doric columns support a modified Doric entablature and pedimented gables. The Lee Street facade is the most monumental, having a colonnade of eight free-standing fluted columns resting on the projecting ground floor. The west facade is less elaborate but still handsome, with fluted pilasters defining the seven bays.

The building's cornice and pedimented gables are decorated with modillions, rosettes, and fleurs de lis. Windows on the ground floor are set in round-headed arches. Those on the second floor are crowned with gabled pediments or with molded cornice lintels.

The two entrances on Church Street and the three on Lee Street are similar to the ground-floor windows—set in deep round-headed arches. The bronze-and-glass double doors with marble surrounds have granite pylon frames. Each door is surmounted by a stone eagle on a plinth, on which there is a Latin inscription. The eagle is backed by a decorative bronze grille. Each doorway is flanked by large bronze lanterns.

The Lee Street lobby has a high, coffered ceiling of gold-leafed plaster. The walls are sandstone, the pilasters are marble, and the floor is inlaid travertine marble edged with green marble. The 168-foot corridor on the Church Street side was for the post office, whose brass-and-bronze service windows and grillwork are intact. The post office is no longer there.

The corridors of the upper stories have terrazzo floors with green marble borders, baseboards, and thresholds. The walls have brown-marble wainscoting. Office doors are of natural wood and translucent glass. The second-floor corridor is somewhat more elaborate, having some molding above a row of dentils.

The finest room in the building is the U.S. District Courtroom on the second floor. It has an elaborate painted and gilded wooden ceiling in the style of the Italian Renaissance. Behind the wide (judge's) bench is a large stone niche that is decorated with gold stars on a blue ground. The high, round-headed windows on each side of the room are framed in stone. The wainscoting and door framing are marble. Acoustical plaster, some leather-padded doors, and a cork floor, now carpeted, are to absorb sound. The courtroom has a balcony, an unusual feature for an American courtroom.

From 1955 to 1979, this was the courtroom of Judge Frank Minis Johnson, Jr. In 1955, President Eisenhower appointed Judge Johnson, then thirty-seven years old. The judge was a native of Winston County, which, like most of north Alabama, had opposed secession. Winston County disavowed slavery and, according to legend, (unsuccessfully) seceded from Alabama when the Civil War began. It is not surprising that a man with Judge Johnson's heritage would have the courage to hand down many significant decisions relating to the civil rights movement. His decisions include striking down segregated seating in buses. This 1956 decision extended the principle of the U.S. Supreme Court's landmark 1954 *Brown v. Board of Education* decision to other areas of public life.

In 1992, the United States Congress renamed the building the Frank M. Johnson Jr. Federal Building and United States Courthouse.

FIRST UNITED METHODIST CHURCH traces its beginnings to Montgomery's first decade. For many years, church growth was extremely slow. It appears that early Montgomery preferred the profane to the sacred. The pious were outnumbered by the raw and crude in the frontier river town. Qualifications for acceptance into many churches were extremely strict, as were standards for remaining in good standing within the congregation. The Methodist Episcopal Church was one such denomination. Growth was also hampered by the relative poverty of its adherents. It was not until the great revivals of 1839 and 1845 that membership in Montgomery's struggling churches significantly expanded.

The first Methodist services were conducted by the Reverend James King of North Carolina. He stayed in the local area in the spring and summer of 1819. But it was not until late 1823, in a cooperative effort with

First United Methodist Church

2416 West Cloverdale Park

Montgomery's Architectural Heritage

245

Gothic arches, flanked by decorative pinnacles

Baptists and Presbyterians, that a meeting house was begun on what is today Lee Street. Because of scarcity of funds, this 48-by-24-foot framed building was not completed until 1825. The Union Church was used by the three denominations until 1830, when it came into the sole possession of the Methodist congregation.

Two years later, the congregation almost lost the church during an auction of the unsold lots of the Alabama Company. The church had made enemies with the local theater group, which was considerably larger and more affluent, and which intended to retaliate by buying the lot on which the church building stood. General John Scott, a native of Georgia and founder of the town of East Alabama, literally saved the church at the eleventh hour by raising the bid to five hundred dollars. But it was not until more than a month had passed that the congregation realized what had happened, when General Scott conveyed the title of the lot to the congregation as a gift from the Alabama Company. General Scott's wife was a Methodist; one of their sons was to become a Methodist minister.

The old Union Church soon proved too small. After another very difficult financial trial, a new Court Street Methodist Church building was dedicated in March 1835. This wood-frame building was approximately 60 by 45 feet and had a gallery, usually used by black members of the congregation, across the back and along two sides of the sanctuary. By 1853 this building was too small. It was moved to Holcombe Street, where it stands today as the Old Ship African Methodist Episcopal Zion Church. Although mostly veneered with brick, the old frame building's east end is still visible.

The massive new building, begun in 1853, was usable in two years but was not dedicated until 1856. The building was designed by German-born Charles C. Ordeman, surveyor and city engineer. Although thought by some to be plain and unattractive, the building was a very fine neoclassical structure of restrained elegance and sophistication. Divided stairs rose to the main-entrance portico flanked by two columns and two pilasters. The roof, hidden by a parapet, was surmounted by a low tower. Between 1871 and 1874, this structure was Victorian Gothicized. The main entrance was changed to street level. Stained glass replaced the clear glass. Eventually, the tower was replaced with a tall steeple. Many considered the renovated building to be the most beautiful in the city; with an estimated seating of two thousand, it certainly was the largest.

Early in the century, the neighborhood became increasingly more commercial and less residential. Rather than repair the badly deteriorated building, the congregation decided to move, which they did in 1931. In the same year, the old church building was razed to make way for a new federal post office and courthouse. The congregation decided to move to the prestigious suburb of Cloverdale, incorporated into Montgomery in 1927. There the church would be in the vicinity of the Methodist women's college. From 1931 to 1933, the congregation met at what is now Huntingdon College. During that time, the church's name was changed to First Methodist Church, in recognition of its being the mother church of Montgomery Methodists.

Dr. John Frazer, First Methodist's minister, wanted the new church building to be as beautiful as Idlewild Presbyterian Church in Memphis. That Gothic-style church was built under the pastorate of Dr. Frazer's brother. George Awsumb of Memphis, a specialist in Gothic architecture and designer of Idlewild Presbyterian, was retained as architect. He helped select the site for the new building on a ridge above what is now Cloverdale Park. There is some evidence that the park may have been intended to have been a lake, and the ridge may have initially been intended for the park.

Painfully aware of its history of financial difficulties, the church decided to build on a pay-as-you-go basis. Construction began on the education building in February 1932. The building was essentially complete in December 1932 when a gas explosion destroyed the work aready done, and set back construction by a year. Construction of the sanctuary began in 1935. The financial difficulties of the Great Depression probably prompted the congregation to question the decision to build in the extremely expensive Gothic style. By 1938, the sanctuary was usable—with tamped gravel floor, homemade pews, no windows in the summer, and windows covered by stretched canvas in the winter. World War II restrictions further complicated construction. First Methodist was finally dedicated in November 1947: "For light to those who seek the Way." The wait, sacrifices, and privations were certainly worthwhile, for First Methodist is one of the city's most spiritually inspiring structures.

The exterior of the complex is a delight to the eye. There are chimney pots and parapets; oriel windows, leaded casement windows, hood molding over windows; dormers and gables; "cloisters" and garth; buttresses and copper downspouts; the 112-foot tower surmounted by a cross; the lead *fleche*, or spire, probably inspired by the one that Viollet-le-Duc added to Paris's Notre Dame Cathedral in 1860; and the Italian-made Christ statue between the two doors of the main entrance to the sanctuary. All these details do not, however, confuse the eye. Rather, they are all unified by the steep, weathered slate roofs and, especially, by the rough Tennessee sandstone walls trimmed in cut Indiana limestone.

The interior is as inspiring as the exterior. There are chapels and classrooms with high, beamed roofs; a labyrinth of steps and passages; and innumerable Christian symbols, all little sermons in stone, glass, and wood.

Montgomery's Architectural Heritage

By European standards, the sanctuary is not large. (In fact, this sanctuary seats about eight hundred, considerably fewer than its Court Street predecessor.) French Gothic was obsessed with height; Beauvais Cathedral's chancel vault is 157 feet high. The English were obsessed with length; Winchester Cathedral is 556 feet long. Although First Methodist, sometimes called the Cathedral in the Pines, more closely resembles the size of an English parish church, it does capture the spirituality that was an objective of the Gothic masters. The height of the nave, the visual focus on the elevated altar with its delicately carved reredos screen, and the otherworldly light made by the stained-glass windows, contribute to this spirituality on a subconscious level.

On the conscious level is the overwhelming quantity of Christian symbols and art: Christ and the four Gospel writers in the 14-by-25-foot window over the sanctuary's main door; Old Testament symbols in the clerestory windows, and New Testament symbols in the aisle windows; the high-relief, polychrome statues of the Apostles (Matthias replacing Judas) flanking the choir; and, behind and over the altar, the reredos's polychrome statue of Christ flanked by four Apostles. First Methodist has published a ninety-two-page book to explain the Christian symbolism of the building's architecture and decorative detail.

The sanctuary consists of a chancel and nave, separated by the high chancel arch. The chancel is raised on two levels. The oak pulpit is on the left side and the stone and oak lectern on the right. The choir is divided, with its seats perpendicular to the axis of the sanctuary. The altar, two steps higher up, is backed by the reredos. High on the wall above the altar is a rose window. The sanctuary is cruciform in plan, but because the transepts are very small, the room appears to be rectangular. Flanking the nave proper are two aisles, separated from the nave by limestone columns and arches. The aisle windows are rectangular with inset trefoil tracery, and the clerestory windows are twin lancets, also with inset trefoil tracery. A decorative plaster frieze of vine and grapes is at the top of the nave wall. The fine hammerbeam roof springs from corbels. The ceiling is painted in geometric patterns. The balcony, being over the narthex, does not detract from the aesthetics of the sanctuary. It does not obscure the huge east window with its fine glass and tracery of quatrefoils, trefoils, circles, and triangles.

Throughout the church building, but especially in the sanctuary, are marble floors and stained-glass windows. The marble (green, red, pink, and white) is from Belgium, Arkansas, Tennessee, Alabama, Georgia, and Italy. The grisaille, painted, and stained glass is from Germany, England, France, Italy, Slovakia, and the United States. Golden oak is used throughout the sanctuary.

Gothic cathedrals and churches were erected to the Glory of God, but also as symbols of civic pride. The artistic beauty of Gothic structures was an offering to God. They also employed art to teach the faith. First United Methodist Church has maintained this tradition.

THE LAND on which Maxwell Air Force Base is built once comprised the cotton plantations of the McGillivray, Ashley, Edwards, Reese, and Kohn families. Descendants of slaves who had worked the antebellum plantations sharecropped the same land. By 1900, they had built Douglasville, a community of about a hundred households, with its own church, school, general store, and cemetery. Located along Washington Ferry Road (now Maxwell Boulevard) and the area of Chennault Circle, the black community coexisted with the base from 1918 until 1930. By 1931, it had been obliterated to make room for the rapidly expanding Maxwell Field—especially for officers' housing. Even the cemetery was relocated. Only the community school was retained, for use as the post-elementary school. Before it was razed in 1987, it served as the kindergarten for Maxwell Air Force Base.

Between 1932 and 1935, ninety-nine officers' quarters were built. Funding initially came from the Army's 1927 five-year expansion program, and later from the Emergency Relief and Construction Act. The project cost approximately one million dollars. Following city planning and landscap-

Senior Officers' Quarters

322 Center Drive
Maxwell Air Force Base

ing concepts of Frederick Law Olmsted, Jr., and George B. Ford, family housing was separated from the administrative and industrial areas of the base. To create a park-like setting, the houses were set on large lots along curving streets. Maxwell's senior officers' quarters surround three large parks (in the 1970s, one-story housing units were built in one of these parks), and the two streets that do not have parks are adjacent to a deep, wooded ravine and a golf course.

The ninety-nine houses follow nine designs. There are five designs for three-bedroom houses originally designated for lieutenants and captains, and three designs for four-bedroom houses for majors and colonels. Curry House, which is the commander's house, has five bedrooms and a unique exterior and interior. Although the houses were originally designated for all officer ranks, they now house colonels and general officers.

The houses, designed by architects of the Army Office of the Constructing Quartermaster, were described as being in a French Provincial style. This was an attempt to use a style with historical connection to the base's location; the same style was used at Barksdale Field, Louisiana. Similiar floorplans were used elsewhere, but in Georgian-Colonial, Tudor, and Mediterranean–Spanish Colonial styles—all attempting historic continuity. The officers' club and bachelor officers' quarters are also built in the pseudo–French Provincial style, but the base's administrative, industrial, and earlier permanent housing units were built in a pseudo–Spanish Colonial style.

All the houses are built on three-foot concrete foundations. They are of wood frame construction with plastered interior walls and hollow-tile exterior walls. The exterior is covered in textured concrete stucco, the corners are delineated with concrete quoins, and the steep, hipped roofs are covered with flat tiles. Most roofs have dormers. A variety of window treatments include double-hung sash and casement windows. The first floor's principal rooms have French windows with wrought-iron railings. There are three entrance designs: a small central one-story portico with square wood columns that support an extremely handsome balustrade; decorative wrought-iron supports capped by a small copper roof; and a small enclosed porch trimmed in limestone and capped with a copper roof.

Most houses have a living room with fireplace, dining room, breakfast room, kitchen, and maid's room and bath. The ceilings are nine feet, and the floors are narrow-width oak. Interior trim is stock molding, and the hardware is simple. At the side or rear of most of the houses there was a first-floor open porch and a second-floor screened sleeping porch. These are now enclosed.

The houses are imposing-looking, but they are not particularly livable by today's standards. The rooms are small, and few of the floorplans allow for traffic circulation. However, by military housing standards that preceded and followed the Army's 1926 Housing Program, Maxwell's officers' quarters were, and are, luxurious.

Representative of these houses is 322 Center Drive. The first residents of this house, like its neighbors, were faculty and senior students of the Air Corps Tactical School. This school taught strategy, tactics, and techniques of airpower deployment to flying officers. Although concerned with attack, pursuit, and observation aviation, ACTS emphasis came to be dominated by advocates of bombardment.

The quarters at 322 Center Drive was the residence of Claire and Nellie Chennault and their eight children. Chennault entered the Army as a lieutenant of infantry in 1917 and became a pilot in 1919. He was graduated from the ACTS at Langley Field, Virginia, in 1931. He then joined the ACTS faculty and moved to Maxwell with the school in the summer of 1931.

The Chennaults first lived six miles west of Maxwell in the 1856 Stone-Young mansion on Old Selma Road. (Although extensively altered in 1939, it is still the finest antebellum plantation house in the environs of Montgomery.) Legend has it that Chennault flew his P-12C under the Highway 31 bridge, flew home for lunch, and even allowed a son to fly the plane—solo. When the Chennaults lived at 322 Center Drive from 1935 to 1937, they were noted for their untidy housekeeping, the antics of their children, and the numerous junk cars in the yard.

Chennault's unconventional behavior was not confined to his private life. He was opposed to the strategic bombing theories that were coming to dominate the school. Rather, he believed in the importance of fighters, air superiority, and an air-defense warning net (this was before radar had been developed). Chennault's abrasive personality, life-style, and especially his airpower theories, led to his retirement in 1937, in his permanent rank of captain. That same year he went to China, at the invitation of Madame Chiang Kai-shek, and organized and trained for the Chinese air forces. In seven months in 1942, his Flying Tigers shot down 299 Japanese aircraft, and lost only 32 aircraft and 19 pilots. Although Chennault returned to U.S. service in 1942, he maintained a strong connection with China, specifically with the Nationalist Chinese, even after World War II.

The architectural and landscaping plans begun in the late 1920s have established a high standard for Maxwell. Red-roofed, cream or buff buildings predominate. The park-like landscaping has never been better, thanks to the maturation of trees, thoughtful planting, outstanding maintenance, and the absence of offensive signs and utility poles. Maxwell is probably the country's most aesthetically unified Air Force base.

▼

Fort Dixie (Armory Learning Arts Center)

1018 Madison Avenue

ABOUT 1936, a new National Guard armory was completed in Montgomery. The old Montgomery Grays' armory, on the third floor of the 1852/1871 city hall, burned in 1932. Although the fire destroyed $50,000 worth of equipment, it did not destroy the unit's ammunition. Captain John Schneider and Lieutenant C. J. Hillard were able to remove 20,000 rounds of ammunition before the fire reached the third floor. Lanier High School ROTC cadets, who were to have drilled in the hall that evening, were pressed into service to control the crowds.

City hall was rebuilt, with the federal government paying most of the construction cost through the Works Progress Administration. Federal funding was the result of political pressure from Mayor William A. Gunter, Jr., Governor Bibb Graves, and Senator Hugo L. Black, who served as associate justice of the U.S. Supreme Court after 1937. (Although their local power base was composed of strange bedfellows, these were New Deal Democrats in the twenty-year period preceding World War II, in which Alabama was considered one of the most progressive states in the Deep South.) The neo-Georgian building, designed by Frank Lockwood and built by Algernon Blair, was dedicated in September 1937.

Funding for the new armory was secured in the same time. The Armory was completed in 1936–37 and named for Senator Dixie Bibb Graves, the first woman to represent Alabama in the United States Senate.

The militia system, which required white males from 18 to 45 years of age to muster for training four to eight days a year, was established for the Mississippi Territory in 1807. Although this system was not particularly effective in a territory so thinly populated, and with such a high proportion of its population composed of slaves, it did provide troops for the Creek Indian wars of the early nineteenth century. In the 1820s and 1830s, the state was divided into four military districts, and men were required to muster in the spring and fall. These musters were little more than social and political gatherings. After the Upper Creeks were removed following the treaty of 1832, the militia began to atrophy; by 1859, it only existed on paper. There were also independent companies, but these were essentially social clubs.

Alabama did not rely on the militia system to mobilize troops for the Confederacy. Volunteer companies were formed instead. Of a white male population of about 270,000, approximately 100,000 fought in Confederate gray and 2,700 in Union blue. Many of the latter fought in the First Alabama Cavalry, U.S.A., recruited in the hill country of northwest Alabama. Also fighting for the Union were perhaps as many as 10,000 blacks; they were recruited in the Tennessee Valley during Union occupation.

The militia system was reorganized in 1877 with the formation of the Alabama State Troops. By 1896, there were 2,500 voluntary members. In 1897, the volunteer militia became the Alabama National Guard.

Because of increasing civil unrest, especially in large industrial cities, and because of the debacle of the Spanish American War, National Guard troops came under increasing federal control. Alabama's guardsmen acquitted themselves well in the Mexican border troubles of 1916 and in World War I. From late September to early November 1918, the 167th Infantry, 42nd (Rainbow) Division was involved in the Meuse-Argonne offensive, which, until 1944, was the greatest battle that American troops had ever participated in.

After World War I, the National Guard was reorganized, and it participated in maintaining public order during strikes and riots, and in helping during natural disasters. The Guard was hampered by lack of facilities, however. The Works Progress Administration aided the Armory Commission of Alabama, established in 1935, in constructing armories throughout the state. German aggression accelerated training. After Alabama guardsmen were federalized in 1940–41, a Home Guard was formed for internal security. In the early 1950s, additional armories were built so that each county in Alabama would have one unit and one armory. Today, there are some 22,000 citizen-soldiers and more than 220 units in Alabama.

Fort Dixie was constructed by the Armory Commission of Alabama. The federal government provided approximately $65,000, and the state and city $6,000. The city provided the land, formerly Gunter Park, adjacent to the streetcar barns. Earle G. Lutz, Jr., of Montgomery was the architect of the Streamline Moderne–style building. Lutz also designed other armories under the WPA Armory Commission of Alabama program.

Art Deco and Streamline Moderne were the fashionable styles of the 1920s and 1930s. Because Art Deco and the similar Zizgag Moderne used expensive materials for decorative purposes, the styles were only infrequently used during the Great Depression. Streamline Moderne, although self-consciously modernistic, used ornamentation sparingly. It prevailed over Art Deco about 1930, reached its peak at the New York and San Francisco fairs of 1939, and essentially ended with World War II. An historical style, such as the neo-Georgian style used on Montgomery's new city hall, would have been too expensive for an armory during the Depression. Art Deco, besides being too expensive, was not popular for public buildings and would have been inappropriate for a utilitarian building. Bauhaus, or the International Style, was not used extensively in the United States until after World War II.

Other than strictly utilitarian, Streamline Moderne was the only choice. It offered style without excessive expense, and a style that represented the modern machine age. Before it was an architectural style, Streamline Moderne was used for ships, trains, automobiles, and airplanes. The style is characterized by aerodynamic features symbolizing the future. To help achieve this effect, it used flat roofs, horizontal lines, windows grouped in bands, curves, metal strips, glass brick, and a smooth surface.

The north facade of the armory exhibits many of these characteristics. Streamlining is evident in rounded corners of molded brick for window shouldering and for corners. The horizontal effect of the frieze is carried across the three octagonal windows by a metal grill, which was originally painted black. Although the north and west elevations are streamlined, the building conveys an impression of massiveness, solidity, and permanence. The facade is dominated by the central door (originally walnut) defined by four large recessed arches, which are now emphasized by being painted in variations of gray. The theme is carried through with metal and glass just above the door. The brick exterior has always been painted. The building is given a military appearance by the projecting corner towers on the center block and, especially, by the simulated arrow slots in the center block.

The interior of the armory was almost strictly utilitarian, except for the former stage's molded brick pilasters and architrave, and the flanking decorative brick arches in the large, high-roofed assembly and drill hall. The front of the building and the basement had administrative offices, supply rooms, and arms vaults. The one-story west wing was for supply.

Originally, Fort Dixie housed three units: the headquarters of the 31st Infantry Division; headquarters of 3rd Batallion, 106th Quartermaster Regiment; and the 167th Infantry, which occupied most of the building. Maintaining the historical link, the 167th's letterhead included the slogan, "Montgomery Greys, organized January 10, 1860."

The armory is an excellent example of alternative use of an historic building. It has been converted into a learning-arts center owned and maintained by the Montgomery Parks and Recreation Division. Remodeling of the original armory, the new gymnastics center with projecting corner towers, and even the handrailings and benches in front of the building, are compatible with the original building's Streamline Moderne style. The center, supported in part by the Arts Council of Montgomery, provides professional instruction in the visual arts, drama, music, gymnastics, and dance.

HAROLD PURCELL, youngest son of an Irish coal-mining family in Pennsylvania, joined the Passionist congregation at the age of fifteen. Passionists were often sent to serve in isolated environments that were hostile to Roman Catholicism. In 1904, at twenty-three, he was ordained a priest. In the 1920s and 1930s, Father Purcell became an influential voice of American Roman Catholic opinion. He believed in not just professing the faith, but also in living it by being socially responsible. He was particularly interested in alleviating the plight of black Americans. As early as 1933, Father Purcell had a master plan for a city whose role would be to pioneer nondiscrimination in health services, education, and social services. The following year, he asked his superior for permission to

St. Jude's Roman Catholic Church

2048 West Fairview Avenue

Montgomery's Architectural Heritage

go to Alabama with the intention of building a city "for the religious, charitable, educational, and industrial advancement of the Negro people."

In May 1934, during the height of the Great Depression, Father Purcell arrived in Montgomery. He died October 22, 1952, having spent the last eighteen years of his life building the City of St. Jude.

In 1935, more than forty acres were bought in southwest Montgomery, just south of a very large black neighborhood. The city that Father Purcell began to build was in sharp contrast to the black neighborhood, which had no water mains or sewers. He recognized the connection between environment and human dignity, individual worth, and self-esteem. The first building was, appropriately, the church itself. It was built from 1937 to 1938. Its basement provided classrooms and, for a short time, living accommodations for the nuns. From the very beginning, the church building was associated with worship, teaching, and service.

Like all City of St. Jude buildings that were constructed in Father Purcell's lifetime, the church was in the Italian Romanesque style. Perhaps Father Purcell, who was himself very interested in architecture and its impact on the public, associated Romanesque with a down-to-earth Christianity, in contrast to the otherworldly Christianity associated with the Gothic style. Or perhaps it was Father Purcell's practical side. Brick, which is generally used with Romanesque architecture, is less expensive than stone, which is generally used with Gothic. Furthermore, as he insisted on using black craftsmen and laborers as much as possible, he would be able to find the necessary skills in the local community. Even the construction supervisor was black. Electricians and plumbers were not, however, because union rules prohibited black membership.

The red-brick building with limestone embellishments is raised on a full basement. It is quite impressive at the end of an avenue of pines. The facade is dominated by a 105-foot bell tower that is surmounted by a cobalt-blue tile roof and a metal cross. Each side of the open bell chamber has three arches supported by limestone columns. The tower is decorated with a large Cararra-marble sculptural group of the crucifixion, executed by Palladio Pallidini.

Broad stairs lead to a terrace that may symbolize what early Christian narthexes did—God and the church reaching out to embrace the world. On either side of the main entrance are arcades with round-headed arches and barrel vaulted ceilings. In the tower's base, a Romanesque gabled archway, supported by two simple limestone columns, forms the central entrance. Its semicircular tympanum is a bas relief of Christ with outstretched arms, and the inscription, "Come Unto Me All Ye That Labor And Are Burdened."

Shallow corbeling supports the cornice. The roof is made of cobalt-blue glazed clay tiles. Blue is associated with the Virgin Mary, whom Father Purcell has selected as his special patroness.

The church is cruciform with shallow transepts. The nave, which has a balcony over the vestibule, is long and wide. The floor is marble and oak. The walls are paneled from floor to ceiling. The flat plastered ceiling is supported by large horizontal beams on which the Ten Commandments are presented. The large round-headed, stained-glass windows of the nave are also used for religious instruction. The seven sacraments, with explanatory texts below, are presented in the windows on the left. Similarly, windows on the right present the Apostles' Creed with explanatory texts. Between the windows are paintings of the stations of the cross in carved frames. Inscriptions are evident on altars, lecterns, and lintels.

The transepts contain altars and niches with carved, polychromatic statues, including St. Jude (the apostle also called Thaddeus and Judas, son or brother of James), patron saint of difficult or hopeless causes. The chancel is flanked by narrow, round-headed clerestory windows in groups of three. The high altar has a magnificently carved reredos and hood. The ceiling of the chancel is decorated with a carved wheel-within-a-wheel, representing the Holy Trinity. The sanctuary lamp is decorated by silver angels made by Giuseppi Moretti, the sculptor of Birmingham's Vulcan.

William Callahan of New York was the architect of St. Jude's church. Stained glass is by Edward J. Byrne Studios of Pennsylvania, and interior furnishings are by Frank Fennick and Company of New Jersey.

The City of St. Jude came to include a school, social center, residential and administrative buildings, a gym, and a hospital—all set in landscaped grounds. St. Jude's was the most comprehensive institution for blacks in the South.

The hospital was perhaps the most significant for its pioneering role in nondiscriminatory health care. It was partially funded by the Hill-Burton Hospital Survey and Construction Act of 1946; Senator Lister Hill was present at the hospital's dedication in 1951. Because Alabama law prohibited blacks from using white medical facilities, the hospital, which had an integrated staff and served all regardless of race, creed, or ability to pay, was vital until the mid-1960s. St. Jude's was the first hospital in the city to have a school of practical nursing, the first in the county to give public prenatal care, and the first in the state to have a drug and alcohol treatment center. The hospital was leased in 1975, and closed ten years later. In 1992, it was renovated and became St. Jude's Apartments, serving low-income, elderly residents of the West Side.

The City of St. Jude continues, as it has for more than sixty years, serving in the spirit of Christian charity.

Archives and History Building

624 Washington Street

ALABAMA'S department of Archives and History is the legacy of Dr. Thomas Owen, a lawyer by training, but, by avocation, one who loved the history of his native state. In 1901, he convinced the state to found a Department of Archives and History. Alabama's archives claims to be the oldest fully supported state archives in the country. Dr. Owen was the archives' first director, serving until his death in 1920. His first facility was the cloakroom of the Senate.

Alabama's fine Archives and History Building, however, is the legacy of the remarkable Marie Bankhead Owen, director of the Department of Archives and History from 1920 until 1955. Before succeeding her husband, she declined an offer to work for the Hearst newspapers in New York for $10,000 a year, a princely sum in those days. Rather, she was destined to serve her state, not only as state archivist and builder of the Archives and History Building, but as author of eight volumes of Alabama history and three novels. (She also survived raising her exuberant niece, Tallulah Bankhead, who became the flamboyant mezzo-basso-voiced Broadway actress and Hollywood starlet.)

By the mid-1930s, the archives had outgrown their space in the Capitol, but the state could not afford a new facility. Mrs. Owen convinced Governor Bibb Graves to seek federal funds for such a project. There are several versions of how federal funds were made available to help construct an archives building. According to Tallulah Bankhead, Governor Graves was unsuccessful with Works Progress Administration director Harry Hopkins, who did not "have enough money to construct a building for every little old lady down in Alabama." After being informed, however, that Mrs. Owen's brothers were Senator John Bankhead, Jr., ranking member of the Senate Appropriations Committee, and Congressman William Bankhead, speaker of the House of Representatives, funding quickly materialized for the construction of an Alabama World War Memorial. The Archives and History

258

A Sense of Place

Building was dedicated to the memory of Alabamians who served in World War I. In 1985, the building was rededicated to Alabama veterans of all wars.

The new building for Alabama's Department of Archives and History was part of a larger plan to create a dignified state government complex. In 1889, Governor Seay had engaged Olmsted Brothers of Boston, probably the leading landscape architects in the country, to devise a plan for the Capitol, which, at the time, had no landscaping. Unlike the usual approach of building in the most practical location and without regard for how the streetscape would appear, J. F. Dawson of Olmsted Brothers had vision and a developed aesthetic sense. His plan focused on the existing Capitol grounds and the immediately surrounding area. The Archives and History Building was part of the evolving Olmsted Capitol Complex plan. Its main entrance is on the north-south axis of the Capitol.

Work on the central block began in 1937 and was completed in 1940. The flanking east wing, built to the plans of the original architect, was not built until the 1970s. A flanking west wing has yet to be built. Consequently, the building is asymmetrical, and the terrace is too large for the existing building.

William Warren of the Birmingham architectural firm of Warren, Knight, and Davis designed the building in what he referred to as the Greek Revival style, so that it would harmonize with the Greek Revival style of the Capitol. Warren's design could more accurately be referred to as the "national style." This style, first based on the architecture of the Roman republic, was promoted by Thomas Jefferson, who believed it to be appropriate for the American Republic. Subsequently, classical-Greek and imperial-Roman styles were incorporated. This national style has been used extensively in monumental public buildings.

The archives building's north facade is dominated by the entrance portico, with six two-story fluted columns capped with Ionic capitals. The proportions of the portico are exceptionally fine. The intention of Mrs. Owen, often called the Tiger Lady because of her indomitable will, has not yet been realized in regard to completing the pediment over over the portico's colonnade. The wall within the pediment is temporary, built of hollow tile so as to be easily removed for installation of a sculptural group in the Greek fashion. Mrs. Owen wanted a sculptural group of Indians depicting the early history of what is now Alabama. Indians, especially their pottery, were Mrs. Owen's special interest; she was known to catch schoolchildren in the halls and send them to examine the pottery.

The door of the north entrance has scroll brackets that support a cornice. The door jambs are battered, slightly wider at the bottom than the top—again in the Greek style. This entrance had a pair of ten-foot-high bronze doors. These slid into pockets on either side of the smaller swinging bronze-and-glass doors set in a bronze frame that is decorated with a Greek

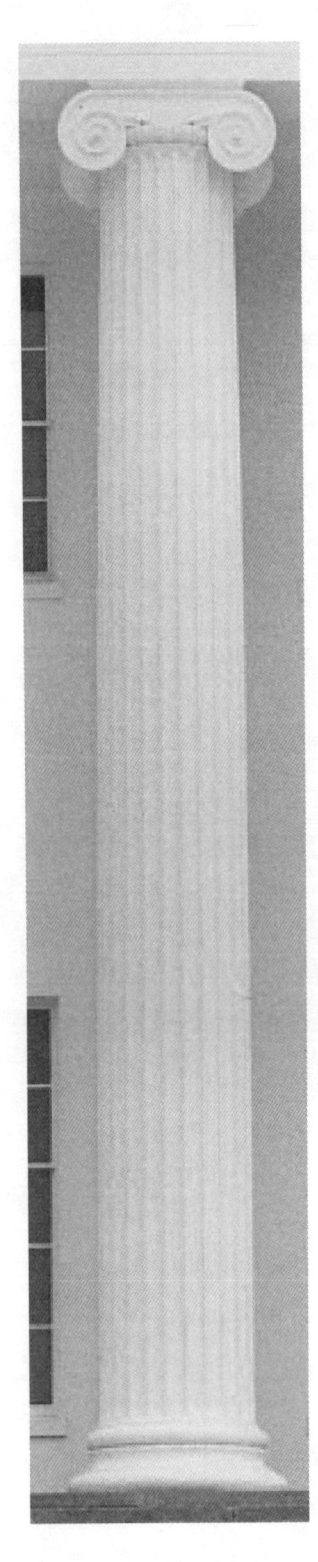

Fluted column with Ionic capital

fret motif. Each of the large bronze doors has four bas relief panels. The eight panels, designed by Nathan Glick, a native of Birmingham, depict events in Alabama history, from the October 1540 meeting of De Soto and Chief Tuscaloosa, to the May 1919 welcoming ceremonies for the returning World War I heroes. These doors have been removed from their pockets and are temporarily on exhibit in the Milo B. Howard, Jr., auditorium.

The south, or Adams Street, facade, is less elaborate than the north facade. Its portico does not have a pediment. There are, however, six fluted columns with Ionic capitals. The three bronze doors and two flanking windows under the portico have bronze transom grills identical to those above the door on the north portico. The three doors and two windows are surmounted by five ornamental panels that present the coats of arms of the five countries that have exercised authority over Alabama: Spain, France, England, the Confederacy, and the United States.

The projecting east wing has four columns on the north and south elevations and eight on the east elevation. These match the columns and capitals of the main block. The wing, which appears to be two stories over a basement, actually contains nine levels of bookstacks.

The entire main block of the building—walls, columns and pilasters, window and door surrounds, cornices and decorative details—is of monolithic construction in poured concrete. The original building is, therefore, one mass of masonry, having been made of concrete poured into forms.

The Adams Street doors open into Alabama's World War Memorial. The walls with simple pilasters and restrained panels are of Alabama marble. The floor is of darker Tennessee marble. The caisson-paneled ceiling is decorated with gilded stars. The room is dominated with a larger-than-life-size bronze statue that commemorates Alabama's sons who lost their lives from 1898 to 1902 in the Spanish-American War, the Philippine Insurrection, and the China Expedition.

The building's main entrance opens into a grand foyer with Alabama-marble walls, Tennessee-marble floor, and a caisson-paneled ceiling decorated with gilded Greek rosettes. The foyer is dominated by two monolithic Doric columns of Alabama marble. Pilasters and the two columns support a Doric cornice, also of Alabama marble. Two marble staircases rise from the foyer. The lobby of the second floor is almost as elaborate as the foyer of the main floor. Its two monolithic columns are in the Ionic style. The walls, also of marble, have pilasters and sunken panels. Two alcoves have marble benches and matching veined-marble panels.

Although grand in its concept and execution, the building is utilitarian. Much of the state's archives are housed in the building. The building also displays artifacts related to Alabama history. The building is open to the public.

Grove Court Apartments

559 South Court Street

HOUSING CONSTRUCTION was drastically curtailed during the Great Depression and World War II. The resulting housing shortage was compounded by the demobilization of more than ten million servicemen at the end of the war. To help alleviate the housing shortage, the Federal Housing Agency provided government-insured 90-percent mortgages. FHA policies almost ensured that private builders could not lose, if they built to FHA specifications. Many builders used the least expensive tracts of land, and built houses of FHA-minimum room size, specifications, and materials. While numerous builders got rich without having to take the risks associated with traditional entrepreneurs, the cities were disrupted by an explosion of automobile suburbs, and many new homeowners got poorly designed, poorly built houses.

Grove Court Apartments were built with an FHA-secured load. Four single-family houses were demolished and replaced by an apartment complex with fifty-four one-bedroom units and twenty-seven two-bedroom units—on a site measuring 211 by 287 feet, including off-street parking. But what is amazing about the Grove Court Apartments is the quality of design and construction that was possible under the FHA specifications. Clyde C. Pearson and Farrow L. Tittle, the architects, were mentioned in the 1947 *Progressive Architecture* awards for design of an apartment complex.

Grove Court Apartments consist of five three-story blocks connected by covered walkways on all three levels. The blocks are set in landscaped grounds that separate most apartments from South Court Street, a major thoroughfare. Although slightly more than a quarter of the apartments are along Grove Street, it is not a through street. To provide for a garden-like setting, the parking area is consolidated and accessible from an alley at the rear of the complex. While this arrangement is aesthetically pleasing (as opposed to a complex sited in the middle of a parking lot—the current practice), distance from parking to the apartments is increased, and privacy is somewhat decreased. Access to each unit is from exterior staircases and galleries; there are no internal staircases or common hallways.

On the top floor in the connecting block is a laundry with automatic washers and dryers. Originally, there were attendants for this facility. There is also a covered play area for children.

By pre-war standards, the apartments are small: the two-bedroom units have approximately twelve-by-seventeen-foot living rooms, eight-by-thirteen-foot dining rooms, and ten-by-twelve-foot bedrooms. Each apartment has an individual six-by-eight-foot storage room in the basement. By post-war standards, Grove Court apartments were considered luxurious and were first occupied by doctors, lawyers, and businessmen.

The construction, by Bear Brothers of Montgomery, is also remarkable. The complex has maintained the best fire rating in the city. The buildings are constructed of hollow tile faced with brick or plaster; floors and staircases are of concrete; all electrical wiring is in metal conduits; window and door frames are steel. The floors are covered with asphalt tile, except in the bathrooms, which have black and white tile floors and white tile wainscoting. Wood was used only for doors and kitchen cabinets. Except for individual gas heaters in each room, the apartments are electric.

Although there is excellent cross ventilation, and masonry walls provide some relief from the heat, there was no air conditioning when the apartments were built. Only half of the apartments are shielded on the south; but the summer sun is minimized by the east-west alignment of the blocks. The flat roof and the eight-and-a-half-foot ceilings are not well designed for the climate. Because the solid construction prevents retrofitting for central air conditioning, window units are now used.

The apartments are characterized by the horizontal look achieved by flat roofs, belt courses above and below the strip windows, corner windows, long galleries, and balconies with solid balustrades (not functional for the climate). Although there is a horizontal emphasis, the buildings are boxy, because there are no curves. The complex was originally gray brick and white concrete trimmed in green. The window frames were cream and the doors were burgundy. The interior of the galleries was green. The interiors of the apartments were all white.

The architectural style of Grove Court Apartments is remarkable for Montgomery; it is reminiscent of German architecture of the late 1920s. The apartments were the city's first big construction project after the war, and there had been a revolution in design since the late 1920s, when the last significant building occurred in Montgomery.

Modernism was late in coming to the United States, where architectural historicism prevailed over modernism until the mid-1930s. The conflicting styles in architecture were merely part of a larger conflict between the traditional establishment and the modern world. Essentially, the United States stayed aloof from modernism until the mid-1930s. But modernism had begun in Europe in the late nineteenth century. What became known as the International Style is attributable to the Swiss-French architect, Le Corbusier, and two Germans, Walter Gropius and Mies van der Rohe. The latter two were associated with Bauhaus, the German design school founded in 1919; Bauhaus is now almost synonymous with the International Style. The style rejected classical forms, proportion, decorum, and, especially, decoration. It advocated functionalism, social responsibility, and an industrial aesthetic. Craftsmanship was replaced by technology, mass production, prefabrication, and standardization. Stone and wood were replaced by metal, glass, and reinforced concrete. Monumentality and permanence were replaced by simplicity, vulnerability, and the disposable.

Both Hitler and Stalin despised the new style and embraced the safety of historicism, but for differing reasons. Ironically, Hitler can be credited with making the style international by closing Bauhaus in 1933; this spurred the advocates of Bauhaus to emigrate. The style had been connected with socialism, which was concerned with social engineering (something that most architecture is concerned with), uniformity, and providing good design at affordable cost to the working classes. Suddenly, the style became acceptable in the United States based on the logic that if Hitler was trying to repress the style, it must be good. It came to represent freedom from oppression, and the style for the new age.

In the late 1930s, Gropius became head of the architecture department at Harvard and van der Rohe became head of what became Illinois Institute of Technology. Their influence on American architecture was revolutionary. And, as the United States was no longer a cultural backwater after World War II, the style became international.

One aspect of the International Style is that good design, theoretically, should not vary from place to place. Good design is good design anywhere and everywhere. Good design is determined by its being functional. (Ironically, the Grove Court Apartments' eight-and-a-half-foot ceilings and flat roofs were not functional in Montgomery, before air-conditioning.)

The International Style dominated architecture until the advent of the Post-Modern Style. Its tenets, such as "buildings are machines for living and working" and "less is more," appealed to business, especially large corporations. So did the industrial aesthetic, the uniformity, the impersonality of the design, and of course the lower cost relative to traditional building. It did not, however, appeal to the public as a style for residences. People apparently rejected the idea of the intelligentsia and cultural elite deciding which design best met their sociological needs, and imposing it from above.

The U.S. government had resisted modernism and held to historicism. Ironically, the government, through the FHA, dictated design and construction standards for private residences. In effect, the government was dictating an approved living standard.

There are very few International Style houses in Montgomery. In 1947, Allen Northington, an architect, designed and built one for his own residence at 3202 South Hull Street. (Northington later relocated to Florence, Alabama.) The Bartlett House at 836 Park Avenue was designed by Stevens and Wilkinson of Atlanta, and built in 1948.

Abraham Brothers have owned and operated Grove Court Apartments since 1950.

IN 1949, construction began on the State Coliseum, located adjacent to old Kilby Prison northeast of Montgomery. But this coliseum, with its state-of-the-art engineering, was not Montgomery's first exhibition facility and fairground to attract national attention.

As early as the 1820s, Montgomery had a racetrack; the jockey club was organized in 1828. Before the Civil War, several racetracks served the city. From 1857, the privately owned Carter Course, just north of the city, was one of the finest racetracks in the country. It had a two-story ladies' stand and a two-story public stand, plus seven large stables each surrounded by a covered horse walk. Horses arrived from throughout the country by steamboat or railroad, as a wharf and the city's railroad station were close by.

The fairgrounds were adjacent to the racetrack. By the mid-1850s, the 30-acre complex featured an enclosed amphitheater seating 10,000 and an "Industrial Palace" with 14,500 square feet of exhibition space. The fairground was one of the finest in the South. Montgomery's fairgrounds first hosted the Alabama State Agricultural Society Fair in 1855. Some fifty committees judged Alabama manufactures, as well as livestock and horticultural entries. Alabama's fair, like similar fairs throughout antebellum America, was intended to foster agricultural improvements. They also provided public entertainment and opportunities for socializing. At six annual fairs before the Civil War, large crowds from throughout Alabama and southwestern Georgia enjoyed brass bands and military companies accompanying visiting dignitaries, plowing contests, the midway, and even stylized jousting tournaments. After the Civil War, behavior so degenerated at the annual fairs that ladies and children stopped attending. Eventually the city government banned the state fair, and it moved to Birmingham.

In 1945, the legislature established the Agricultural Center Board and began funding a state agricultural center. The State Coliseum, renamed Garrett Coliseum in 1963 after W. W. Garrett, who was the first chairman of the Agricultural Center Board, was conceived as the largest, and the centerpiece, of nine state coliseums. The objective was to support the state's agricultural economy.

Garrett Coliseum

1500 Federal Drive

Photo by Lissa Monroe.

Montgomery's Architectural Heritage

Construction of the coliseum in Montgomery began in 1949 using a revolutionary design of the local firm of Sherlock, Smith, and Adams. Betty Robison, the first woman graduate from Auburn University with a degree in architecture, designed the building. It was the building's design, rather than agricultural exhibitions, that attracted national and even international attention. Although the building's shell was completed in 1951 and exhibitions were mounted in austere conditions, the building was not completed until 1953. The coliseum contains 2,000 tons of steel and 15,000 cubic yards of concrete, and the coliseum and related facilities on the site cost $5 million. The building, whose footprint in a perfect circle with a 340-foot diameter, resembles a turtle from ground level. Twenty-two huge steel-reinforced A-frames support the concrete slab roof, which is three inches thick at its center and five inches thick at its edges. This design, unique at the time, accommodated a 60-by-130-foot arena, then the largest enclosed arena in the United States. Every one of the 8,526 permanent seats rising on concrete tiers had unrestricted sightlines. This too was an engineering feat, as the building had the highest percentage of clear-vision seats of any enclosed facility in the world. The arena's floor was originally dirt with a wooden covering. In that configuration, the arena could accommodate 3,000 couples for dances. In 1985, the dirt floor was replaced with concrete; a clay and sand mixture is used when events call for a dirt surface.

In 1954, the South Alabama State Fair (renamed the Alabama National Fair in 1997 as exhibitors previously featured at the state fair in Birmingham moved to Montgomery) was established at the State Coliseum in northeast Montgomery.

The Alabama National Fair, sponsored by the Kiwanis Club of Montgomery, attracts more than 200,000 people each year to the coliseum and adjacent exhibition halls on the 118-acre site. The annual fair's attractions do not differ appreciably from those of the city's antebellum fairs. Garrett Coliseum is also used for circuses, equestrian events, rodeos, ice shows, the Junior League Rummage Sale, truck pulls, and mystic balls.

Photo by Lissa Monroe.

INDEX

A. H. Howland and Associates 112–113, 114
A. O. Clapp House 212
Abraham Brothers 264
African Methodist Episcopal Church 107
Agricultural and Mechanical College 61
Agudath Israel Synagogue 220, 222
Air Corps Tactical School 237, 238, 250–251
Air University 238
Akron Plan 140
Alabama (town) 36
Alabama Artists Gallery 87
Alabama Bureau of Publicity and Information 62
Alabama Company 36, 246
Alabama Historical Commission 51, 71
Alabama Parent Teacher Assn. 182
Alabama River 36
Alabama State Council on the Arts 87
Alabama State Employees Assn. 147
Alabama State University 109, 215
Alabama World War Memorial 259–260
Alexander, Nathan 182
Allen, Bishop Richard 108
Allen, Richard 107
Allen, Wade 66
American Builder's Companion 23
American Institution of Architects 178
American Soc. of Arts and Crafts 190
Anderson, Pelham J. 99, 109
apse 40
arch: Gothic 76, 107, 110, 195, 197, 198, 201, 246; ogee 41; Romanesque 255; round-head 131, 143, 151; segmented 131; Syrian 152
Architecture: traditions of: Southern 25; vernacular 22
Archives and History Bldg. 26, 258–260
Armory Learning Arts Center 254. *See also* Fort Dixie
Arnold, Herman Frank 96
Arnold's Southern Band 96
Arrington, Samuel Lewis 123
Art Deco style 228, 253–254
Arts and Crafts movement 190, 212
Arts Council of Montgomery 254
Ashley, William 38
Ausfeld, Frederick 39, 186, 224, 231
Ausfeld, Walter 39
Austin, Charles B. 237
Austin Hall 237–238
Awsumb, George 247

Bailey, Walter Thomas 108, 206
Baker, John 182
Balch and Bingham, L.L.P. 29

Baldwin Arts and Academics Magnet School 131, 223
Baldwin, Buddy Willie 104
Baldwin, Captain William O., Jr. 105
Baldwin, Dr. William Owen 104
Baldwin High School 200, 242
Baldwin, Marion Augustus 105
Baldwin, Mary Jane Martin 104
Bank of St. Mary's (Georgia) 28
Bankhead, Tallulah 258
baptismal font 42, 72, 77, 200, 203
Baptist Church (1854) 57
Barganier, Jim and Jane 22
Barnes, Elly Rufus 33
Barnes, Justus McDuffie 33, 100
Barnes School for Boys 33
Bartlett House 264
basilica plan 73
Bauhaus 254, 263
Baylinson, David 201
Bear Brothers 262
Beauties of Modern Architecture 47, 52
Beauvoir Club 46, 48
Beaux Arts style 54, 167, 171, 172
Belcher Agency 106
Bell Building 46, 186–188, 224, 230
Bell, Mr. and Mrs. Hardie 172
Bell, Newton J. 186
Bellingrath Hall 200
Belser House 189, 190–192
Benjamin, Asher 23
Bernhardt, Sarah 97
Bibb, Sophie 21
Bibb, Thomas 36
Bibb, William Crawford 26
Billingslea, Caroline. *See* Lomax, Mrs. Tennent
Bird (Pickett servant) 33
Black, Hugo L. 252
Blair, Algernon 39, 200, 224, 237, 239, 242, 252
Bolton, Alma Baldwin 105
Booth, Edwin 96, 97
Booth, John Wilkes 96
brackets 24, 26, 30, 32
Bragg, Braxton 32
Brantley, Wilkerson & Bryan, P.C. 86
Brewer, Maude 80
brickwork: polychromatic 131; pressed 131, 143
brickworks 37, 43
Brittan House 88–94
Brittan, Ora 88
Brittan, Patrick Henry 88
Bronson, Andy 93
Brown, Chet and Emma Jean Bryan 241
Brunelleschi, Filippo 178

Bryan, Donald, Helen, Betty Lou 241
Bryant's Minstrels 96
Buckner, Mary Stay 142
Bull, Ole 97
bungalow style 212
Burr, Aaron 24
Business Council of Alabama 49
Button, Stephen Decatur 46, 52, 56, 85, 184

Caffey, Abraham Calvin 215
California-bungalow style 189
Callahan, William 257
Calloway, Willis 26
Cantey, Lucy Rice Naftel 172
Capital City Insurance Company 79
capitals: Composite 184; Corinthian 57; Doric 228; Gothic 200; Ionic 49, 206, 260; Romanesque 204; Scamozzi 185, 219; Tower of the Winds Corinthian 47, 53
Capitol, Alabama 24, 30, 32, 46, 52–55, 57, 62, 85, 242, 258, 259
Capitol Heights 189, 211–212
Capitol Heights Development Company 189, 211
Carnegie, Andrew 166
Carnegie Building 65, 166–168
Carpenter Gothic style 116
Carr, Thomas 74
Carter, T. Weatherly 172, 183, 184, 194
Cassimus, Alex 145
Cassimus, Alexander M., Sr. 145
Cassimus House 146–147
Cassimus, Speridon, 145–146, 147
cathedrals, architecture of 247–248
Catoma Street Church of Christ 98–100
Catoma Street synagogue 33
Cavalier District 24
Cedar Grove 32
Cedars, The 233
Centennial Hill 105, 163–164, 180–181, 208, 227
Central Bank of Alabama 46
Central Bank of Alabama Bldg. 85–87
Chalon, Father Gabriel 72
Chappell House 36–37
Chappell, James 37
Chateauesque style 172
Chennault, Claire and Nellie 251
Chesterfields 183
Chestnut, Mary Boykin 25
Chicago Columbian Exposition 167
Childs, Enoch 130
Chilton, Lavinia Bradford 130
Church of Christ 33, 100
Church of the Ascension bldg. 198–201

Church of the Good Shepherd 77
Church of the Holy Comforter 115–117
Cillie, Jean 131
City Federation of Women and Youth Clubs 65
City Hall, Montgomery 87, 95, 97, 200, 240, 252
City of St. Jude 255–257
City Water Works 112–114
Civil Rights Act of 1875 97
civil rights struggle 55, 65, 97, 109, 180, 196, 206–207, 209–210, 244, 255–257
Civil War 59, 69–70
Classical Revival style 243
Classical style 47
Clay, Clement C. 31, 142
closets 89, 190, 191, 213, 241
Cloverdale 193, 217, 227, 247
Colonial Revival style 50, 70, 183
columnettes 32, 35, 63, 79
columns: Corinthian, 56; Doric 36, 228; fluted 47, 57, 184, 228, 260; Ionic 49, 260; Roman Doric 69, 70, 243
Community House 65. *See also* Jackson House
Composite capital 184
Confederate Powder Magazine 38–39
Confederate States of America 24–25, 27, 54, 55, 57, 58, 60, 63, 70
Confederation, The 88
Congregational Church 65
Connor, Catherine Harrison 202
Connor, Martin 202
Corinthian capital 57
Cottage Hill 101, 120
Court Square 28
Court Street Methodist Church 44, 214, 246–247, 248
Cox, Mary Anthony 234
Cox, Nora 234
Craftsman style 189–192, 212
Craik, Jennie Baldwin 105
Cram, Daniel 95
Cram, Ralph Adams 199, 200
Cramton Bowl 234
Cramton, Fred J. 234
Cramton, Hazel 234
Creek Indians: War of 1836 31, 52
cupola 194
Curbow and Clapp Marble Company 138
Curtis, Joe 33

Daily Messenger 86, 88
Davenport-Harrison Shotgun 164
Davidson House 160
Davis, Jefferson 24–26, 27, 32, 55, 57, 70, 96
Davis, Mrs. Jefferson 24–26
Davis Theatre for the Performing Arts 230–232
Davis, Tine and Eunice 231–232
Day Street Babtist Church 196–197
de Soto, Hernando 72, 236, 260
Department of Commerce Building 168
Depression, Great 199, 225, 239, 242, 247, 253–254, 256, 261
desegregation 65
Dexter, Andrew 21, 28, 34, 40, 42, 52, 142
Dexter Avenue King Memorial Baptist Church 109–111, 210
Dexter Avenue King Memorial Baptist Church Parsonage 208–210
Dexter Avenue United Methodist Church 131, 138–140
Dickerson, John 69
dime stores 226–227
"Dixie" 96
Dixie Boys Club 71
Doric column 36, 44, 228
Doric entablature 228
Dorsette, Dr. Cornelius 105, 182
Dorsette, Sarah Hale 105
Douglass, Frederick 216
Douglasville 249
Dowdell, Mrs. Annie S. 82
Dowe House 83, 101–103
Dowe, John 102
Dowe, Mary 102
Dowe, Michael 102
Dudley, Henry 75

Early English style 200
East Alabama 21, 28, 37
Eastlake style 119
ecclesiological architectural movement 75
Ecole des Beaux-Arts 167
Ecunchate 36
Edgewood 21–23, 239, 241
Edward J. Byrne Studios 257
Eglin, Lt. Col. Frederick Irving 234
elevator 186, 188
Elks Lodge 59
Emmett, Daniel 96
Empire Theatre 224, 230
English Tudor–Gothic style 193–194
entablature: Doric 228
Ephod Church, The 222. *See also* Agudath Israel Synagogue
Exchange Bank 61
Exchange Hotel 24, 27, 42, 158, 175

fairs 265–266
Fairview (Avenue and plantation) 233
Faith Crusades Fellowship Ministries 119
Falconer House 34–35
Falconer, John 34
Farley, Alice Dowe 102
Farley House 160
Farley, James 102
Federal Building 33, 40, 239, 242
Federal Housing Agency 261, 264
Federal Road 37
Federal style 22, 25
Figh and Williams contractors 123
Figh, George 30, 33, 86, 99
Figh, Jane McCain 30
Figh, John Poston 29, 30–32, 40, 43, 86
Figh-Pickett House 30
Fine, Geddie and Associates 86
Fire-eaters 42
fires: 1865 59; 1927 59; 1995 65
First Alabama Bank building 200
First Baptist Church 30, 57, 108, 178–179
First Baptist Church, Colored (Ripley Street) 205–207
First Congregational Christian Church building 180
First National Bank 61, 175
First Presbyterian Church 25, 30, 40–42
First United Methodist Church 40, 178, 214, 245–249
First White House of the Confederacy 24–26, 90, 93
Fitzpatrick, Governor Benjamin 104
Fleming's Restaurant 97
Flowers Memorial Hall 224
Foley, Emily Ligon 183
Folmar, Emory 154–155
Folsom, Jim 184
Ford, George B. 249
Forest Farm 32
Forrest, Edwin 96, 97
Fort Dixie 252–254
Frank Fennick and Company 257
Frank M. Johnson Jr. Federal Bldg. 242
Franklin Academy 130
Frazer, Lyn 235
Frazer, Rev. John 247
Frazier Lanier Company 155
Freedmen's Bureau 162, 180
Freeman, Fleming 25, 90
French Provincial style 250
Frost, Jim and Carole 68

Gabriel, Ange-Jacques 243
Garden District 198, 217

Gardiner, Elizabeth 80
Garrett Coliseum 265
Garrett, W.W. 265
Gassenheimer, Bettie 175
Gassenheimer, Simon 175
Gay, Charles Linn 159–160, 161
Gay House 160–161
Gay, Ida Belle Smith 159, 161
Gay, John 49
Gay-Teague Hotel 49, 132
Georgian style 45, 217, 252
Gerald, Camilla 82
Gerald, Perley S. 82
Gerald-Bethea Mansion 74
Gerald-Dowdell House 82–84, 128
Gilmer, Caroline Thomas 21
Gilmer, George 21
Gilmer, James J. 43
Gilmer, Peachy Ridgeway 21
Gindrat, John 28, 233
Glick, Nathan 260
Goodwyn, Jim 235
Gorgas, General William Crawford 83
Gorren, Mary 57
Gothic arch 40
Gothic Revival 40, 75, 109, 116
Gothic style 172, 179, 193–194, 196–197, 199–201, 224–225, 246, 256
Governor Jones House 135, 136–137
Governor Shorter House 69–71
Governor's Mansion 70, 136, 171, 183–185
Grace Episcopal Church 116
Graham family 49
Graham, William 42
Grand Central Terminal 167
Grand Theatre 97
Grant, Edward Hutton 135
Grant, Emma Jerusha McIntosh 135
Graves, Bibb 252, 258
Graves, Dixie Bibb 252
great room 190, 191
Great Western Railway of Alabama Freight Depot 157–158
Greek Revival style 22–23, 37, 43, 45, 47, 49, 56, 63, 64, 67, 109, 119, 184, 259
Green, Charles Sumner 212
Green, Henry Mather 212
Greil, Jacob 69
Griffin, William and Nettie Jones 137
Grove Court Apartments 261–263
Gunter, William A., Jr. 252

Haardt, John 175
Hale, Anne 105
Hale, James 104–105

Hall, Knox 184
hammerbeam roof 194, 200, 248
Hamner Hall 102, 120, 223
Hanrick, Edward 72, 101, 120
Hanrick Plat 101
Harris, Laura May Tyson 126
Harris, Samuel Smith 32
Harrison, Edmond 24, 25
Harrison, Maria 165
Haskell, Slaughter, Young & Gallion, LLC 71
Hawkins, Benjamin 36
Heflin, Howell 74
Helms-Roark Inc. 129
Henderson, Robert and Ida 118
Hendrix, Mr. 92
Henley, Hoyt 144
Henry, H. W. 141–142
Henry, John Hazard 141–142
Henry, Martha Falconer 142
Highland Avenue School 169–170
Highland Home College 33
Highland Park Improvement Co. 79
Hill, Lister 237, 242, 257
Hillard, Henry 60
Hillard's Legion 60
Hole in the Wall, Jr. 95
Holloway, Elliott & Moxley, LLP 150
Holmes, Nicholas H. 54
Holt, Barachias 52
Hood, J. B. 32
Horseshoe House. See Stay House
House of the Mayors 60–62
Hoxey, Asa 34
Hubbard, Dr. Brannon and Caroline 233
Hugger Brothers 33, 160
Hugger, Robert and Emile 160
Hunt, Richard Morris 153, 167, 172
Huntingdon College 22, 193, 195, 201, 227, 242, 247

Imperials 182
Indian mounds 36
International Style 254, 263–264
Ionic capital 260
Italian Romanesque style 202, 256
Italianate style 28, 46, 56, 60, 61, 63, 69, 136

Jackson, Eleanor Clark Noyes 63
Jackson House 63–65
Jackson, Jefferson Franklin 63
Jackson, Mahalia 108
James, Walter and Allen 97
Janney's Foundry 53, 58
Jean & Co. 131
Jefferson Davis Hotel 27, 186, 224

Jefferson, Thomas 47
Jerre (Pickett servant) 33
Jim Wilson and Associates 155
John Jefferson Flowers Memorial Hall 193–195
Johns, Vernon 208–209
Johnson, Frank Minis, Jr. 244
Jones, Col. Samuel Goode 115
Jones, Georgena Caroline Bird 135
Jones, Harry 39
Jones, Richard 174
Jones, Thomas Goode 135–136, 137
Jones, Walter Burgwyn 137
Jordan, Margo and Jess 150
Jordan, Myers, and Locklar 81
Jordan, Richard 81
Joseph, Edwin 79
Joseph, Elizabeth Smith 79
Joseph Hirsch and Associates 222
Jourdan mansion 74
Jubilee CityFest 155
Jubilee Community Center 117
Junior League 35, 71
Junius Bragg Smith Theatre 117

Kahl Montgomery 98–100, 220. See also Temple Beth Or
Keller, Helen 126
Kennedy, Absalom (the elder) 148
Kennedy, Absalom (the younger) 149
Kennedy, Ann McQueen 148
Kennedy, Eunice Estelle Thrash 149
Kennedy, Joseph 148–149
Kennedy, Mary Irvin 149
Kennedy-Sims House 149–150
Kilby, Thomas 216
King, C. A. 213
King, Coretta Scott 209
King, Horace 54
King, Rev. Martin Luther, Jr. 55, 108, 109, 111, 209–210, 216
Klein and Son Jewelers 86
Klein, Leo 86
Knox Hall 44, 46–48, 57, 62, 85
Knox, William 25, 46, 85
Kohn, Albert 165
Kohn, Frank D. 236
Kress Building 228–230
Kress, Samuel H. 226, 227–228

Lafayette, Marquis de 32
Lafever, Minard 47, 52
Lahey, James 91
Landmarks Foundation 47, 59, 62, 71, 90, 137, 155
Lanier, Sidney 42, 223
Larry E. Speaks and Associates 103

Lasseter, Frank S. 211, 212
LeGrand Building 87
Lewis, C. D. 212
Lewis House 212–213
Lewis, Sallie 33
Ligon, Aileen Means 184
Ligon House. *See* Governor's Mansion
Ligon, Robert 183
Line Creek 82
Lobman, Nathan 132
Lockwood, Frank 54, 117, 168, 178, 217, 219, 239, 241, 242, 252
Loeb family 62
Loeb, James 103
Lomax, Carrie Lizzie 43
Lomax Fire Company 128
Lomax House 30, 43–45
Lomax, Mrs. Tennent 43
Lomax, Tennent 43, 128
Lomax, Tennent, Jr. 43
Long & Parish, P.C. 137
Long, LuAn 137
Lost architectural treasures: Baptist Church (1854) 57; Empire Theatre 230–231; Gerald-Bethea mansion 74; Jourdan mansion 74; Montgomery County Courthouse (1854/1894) 61; Moses Building 61; Pollard mansion 57; Winter-Freeman house 28, 56
Louisville & Nashville Railroad 152, 157
Ludlow, Richard R. 118
Ludlow, Willard R. 118
Lutz, Earle G., Jr. 253

M. P. Wilcox House 212
Mackay, George E. 227–228
Mackenzie, Roderick 55
Maner Building 87
Maner, Sally Tyson 126
Manly, Basil 57
Manly, Sarah 57
Manning, Dr. 36
Martin, Mrs. Thomas W. 67
Masonic Hall 72
Mastin, Peter and Mary Myrick 233
Mathews, George 25
Matthews, Father Theobold 72
Maxwell Air Force Base 37; history of 236–237, 249; Senior Officers' Quarters 249–251
Maxwell, Cecile Baldwin 105
McAlpine Tankersley Architecture 173
McBryde, Andrew 66
McBryde, Ann Allen 66
McBryde-Screws-Tyson House 66–68, 102

McCrory Stores 229
McGrath, R. W. 138
McGregor, Pat and Milton 219
McKee and Associates 144
McKee, Walter T., Jr. 144
McKenzie, Alexander 40
McKim, Charles Follen 54, 167
McKim, Mead, and White 168
McKinley, William 216
Mediterranean–Spanish Colonial style 217–218, 250
Memory, Glenda and Von 126
Memory & Gilliland, L.L.C. 126
Miers, Benjamin Travis 39
militia system 252–253
Mills, Alfonso 120, 122
Mills House 120–122
Mills, John Proctor 120
Mills, Robert 243
Mission style, furniture 190, 213
Mitchell, Maggie 96
Modernism 263–264
Montgomery and West Point Railroad 95
Montgomery Area Chamber of Commerce 132, 175
Montgomery Area United Way 62
Montgomery Baptist Institute 206
Montgomery bus boycott 109
Montgomery County Appraisal Department 168
Montgomery County Courthouse 30, 61, 67
Montgomery County Historical Soc. 33
Montgomery federal courthouse 200
Montgomery Female College 130, 223
Montgomery Gas and Electric Co. 61
Montgomery Housing Authority 36
Montgomery Library Association 166
Montgomery Ministerial Association 39
Montgomery Museum of Fine Arts 227
Montgomery Parks and Recreation Division 254
Montgomery post office 95, 242–44
Montgomery State Power and Electric Company 113
Montgomery Theatre 55, 59, 95–97, 242
Montgomery Visitor Center 155
Montgomery Water Works and Sanitary Sewer Board 58, 59
Montgomery's Little Theatre 117
Mordecai, Abram 36, 98, 220
Moretti, Giuseppi 257
Moses, Alfred 60
Moses, Alfred Huger 174–175
Moses Brothers 60–61, 61
Moses Brothers Banking and Realty Company 174
Moses Building 174
Moses Building (1888) 61
Moses, Jeanette Nathan 174–175
Moses, Mordecai 74
Moses, Mordecai Lyon 60–61
Moses-Haardt House 174–176
Mount Zion AME Zion Church building 215
movie palaces 231
Murphy and Company 59
Murphy, Edgar Gardner 39, 78
Murphy, Edwin Gardner 166
Murphy family 57
Murphy House 44, 56–59
Murphy, John H. 56
Murphy, Susan (Mrs. John) 56

National Guard, history of 252–253
national style 259
neoclassical architecture 52
New Philadelphia 21, 28, 34, 36, 52
Newell, William 150
Nicrosi House 160
Norman style 200
Norrman, George 178
North Alabama Land and Immigration Company 61
Northington, Allen 263–264
Norton, Charles W. 88, 90
Norwood, Joseph 61
Noyes, Mary 63

Oakwood Cemetery 57
O'Brien, Frank 55, 96
O'Connell House 160
ogee arch 40
Old Alabama Town 89, 93, 153
Old Ship African Methodist Episcopal Zion Church 214–216, 246
Olmsted Brothers 212, 259
Olmsted, Frederick Law 211
Olmsted, Frederick Law, Jr. 195, 249
Opp Cottage 83
Ordeman, Charles C. 246
Ordeman-Shaw House 89, 93, 153
Orphan Asylum 63
Owen, Berry 49
Owen, Marie Bankhead 258, 259
Owen, Thomas 258
Oxford Movement 75

Palladini, Palladio 256
Paramount. *See* Davis Theatre for the Performing Arts
Parish, J. Edward 137

Parker, Edward B., II 45
Parks and Recreations Division 254
Parks, Bishop Henry Blanton 108
Parks, Rosa 108
Paterson Court 39
Patterson, Dr. Samuel 130
Peabody, George 166
Pearson, Clyde C. 261
Pellicer, Father Anthony Dominic 72
Pendant brackets 26, 28
Pepperman, Jacob Edward 118
Pepperman, Mary Ellen 118
Pepperman-Ludlow House 118–119
Perry, Francis M. 118
Perry, Isabella 118
Pickett, Albert James 31–32; *History of Alabama* 32
Pickett, Sarah Smith Harris 32
"Pickle Palace." *See* Whitfield House
Pierson, Joseph W. 116
pilaster 184
Pinckard, Col. James S. 211
pinnacle 246
Planters' Hotel 36
Pollard, Charles 56, 95
Pollard, Emily Virginia Scott (Mrs. Charles) 56
porte cochere 160, 173, 185, 212, 218, 240
Portier, Bishop Michael 72
Post, George B. 242
post office 95, 186, 242–244, 247
Powder Magazine Park 36
Powell, James 48
Powell-Reese House 128
Practical House Carpenter 23
Pratt, Daniel 52
Prattville Academy 42
Preferred Life Insurance Company 44
pressed brick 131, 143
public buildings, architecture of 259
Purcell, Harold 255–256

Queen Anne style 60, 61, 119, 120, 149, 160
Quisenberry, Ralph and Nell 239, 241
Quisenberry-Bryan House 239–241

racetracks 265
Randolph, B. F. 95
Rayfield, Wallace A. 196
Red Mass 74
Reese, Warren Stone 112, 128
Reid-O'Donahue Advertising 48
Renaissance Revival style 53, 178
Renaissance style 172

reredos 77, 200–201, 202, 248, 257
Reynolds, Ethel 172
Reynolds, Gibson 172
Richardson, Henry Hobson 153, 169
Richardsonian Romanesque style 131, 138, 153, 169, 178, 206
Riverfront Center 156, 158
Riverside Heights 36, 39
Roark, Randy 129
Roark, Ray 129
Robert Frank McAlpine Architecture, Inc. 173
Roberts, Charles 96
Roberts, T. K. 138
Robinson, Mary Jane 34
Robinson, Seth 34
Robison, Betty 265
Rococo Revival style 58
Roman Doric column 69, 70, 182, 243
Roman, Sigmund 46
Romanesque capital 204
Romanesque Revival style 72, 75
Rushton, Stakely, Johnston, and Garrett, P. A. 134

Sabel, Hattie 172, 183
Sabel, Jeanette 172
Sabel, Marx 171
Sabel, Moses 171, 172, 183
Sabel, Samuel and Jeanette 171, 172
Sabel-Cantey House 171–173
Samford Brothers 237
saw-work 35, 64, 67, 82, 101
Sawyer, Philip 168
Sayre Street School 138
Sayre, William 25, 42
Scamozzi capital 166, 185, 219
Scheuer, Herbert and Esther 23
Schmidt, Peter 55, 96
schools. *See* Baldwin Arts and Academics Magnet School; Barnes School for Boys; Highland Avenue School; Highland Home College; Prattville Academy; Sayre St. School; Sidney Lanier High School; St. Mary of Loretto High School; Strata Academy.
Scott, John 21, 28, 36, 246
Scott, Rev. John Jackson 115
Scott Street Firehouse 128–129
Scott Street Grocery 84
Screws, William Wallace 63, 66, 112
Seay, Thomas 259
Second Colored Baptist Church 109
Seibels-Ball-Lanier House 184
Self, Rev. and Mrs. Larry T. 192
Selma-to-Montgomery March 55
Sheridan, Richard Brinsley 95

Sherlock, Smith and Adams 265
shoo-fly 35
Shorter, John Gill 43, 69
Shorter, Mary Jane Battle 69
Shorter, Reuben Clark, Jr. 43
shotgun house 163–164
Sidney Lanier High School 131, 186, 200, 223–225, 242, 252
Sims, J. Marion 42, 142
Simson, Robert T. 82
skyscraper 61, 174, 186, 188
slavery 31, 32, 54, 56, 75, 95, 104, 109, 128, 162, 163, 164, 180, 214, 215, 244, 249, 252
Sloan, Samuel 28, 56, 90, 91, 99, 184
Smith, Annie 100
Smith, Benjamin 178, 183, 194
Smith, Benjamin Bosworth 153
Smith, Bowman, Thagard, Crook, and Culpepper 29
Smith, Chauncey, Jr. 80
Smith, Edna Terry 79
Smith, F. Patterson 194
Smith, Jane E. 79
Smith, Pickett Chauncey 79
Smith-Joseph-Stratton House 79–81
Southern League 88
Southern Telegraph Company 27
SouthTrust Bank 155
Spanish Colonial style 72, 237, 250
St. Andrew the Apostle Roman Catholic Church 202–204
St. John's AME Church 108
St. John's Chapel Church 107
St. John's Episcopal Church 39, 57, 59, 75–78, 115, 166
St. Jude's Roman Catholic Church 256–257
St. Margaret's Hospital 74, 184
St. Mary of Loretto High School 74
St. Peter's Boys School 165
St. Peter's Roman Catholic Church 72–74, 165
Stakely, Charles 178
Standard Club 200, 242
Starr, Anna Stay 142
State Bank 60
State Board of Education 71
State Fair Association 61
Stay, Ernest W. 142
Stay, Hazard 142
Stay House 142–144
Steam Engine Company No. 2 128
Steele, George 44
Steele's Army Corps 96
Steiner House 239
Steiner-Lobman Building 132–134

Steiner, Louis 132
Sterne, Agee & Leach, Inc. 176
Stevens and Wilkinson, architects 264
Stewart, John 99, 184
Stickley, Gustav 190
Stone-Young mansion 251
Strata Academy 33
Stratton, Judge Asa Evans 80
Streamline Moderne style 253–254
Street car 169, 189, 193, 198, 211, 227
Streetscape 29
Stringfellow, Rev. Horace 115
Stuckey's Office Products 106
Sullivan, Louis 186
Sunday School movement 140
synagogues, history and architecture of 221–222
Syrian arch 152

Tandy, Sadie Hale 105
Tandy, Vertner Woodrow 105
Teague Building 132–134
Teague, Eugenia Isabelle Jackson 49
Teague Hardware Company 132, 133
Teague House 44, 49–51
Teague, William Martin 49, 132
Teague-Gay Hotel 132
Temple Beth Or 98, 201, 220
Ten Times One is Ten Club 65
Thiess, Benjamin 66
Thomas House 160
Thomas, Jett 21
Thomas, John Gregory 22
Thomas, William 194
Thorington, Jack 60
Thorington, Mary Lord Parker 60
Thorington, Sallie Gindrat Winter 94
Tiller/Rosa Associates 106
Timon, Bishop 72
Tittle, Farrow L. 261
Toombs, Robert 32
Touro, Judah 98
Tower House 234–235
Tower of the Winds Corinthian capitals 47, 50, 53
trompe l'oeil 41, 54
Troy State University 230, 232
Tudor style 193–194, 224, 239–240
Tulane Building 181–182
Tulane, Victor Hugo 180–181, 182
Tulane, Willie 181, 182
Tulane-Simmons House 182
Turner, Wilson and Sawyer 35
Tuscaloosa, Chief 260
Tuskegee Normal and Industrial Institute 108, 196, 206

Tyson, Anne Arrington 125
Tyson, Archibald 26
Tyson, Archibald Pitt 123
Tyson, Ellen Nicholson Arrington 123, 126
Tyson, John Caius 67
Tyson-Maner House 123–126

Union Church 40, 178, 214–215, 246
Union Station 152–155, 157
United Daughters of the Confederacy 21
Universalist Church 115
University Club 71
University of Alabama 83, 86

Vance, Robert B. 32
Vernacular style 63
Veterans' Hospital 242
Vickers, James 158
Vickers plantation 211
Victorian Gothic style 105, 109
Victorian Romanesque style 73
Victorian style 67, 74, 123, 142, 145–146
Vulcan 257

Wagner, Effingham 118
Wagstaff, C. D. 241
Walker, Leroy Pope 27, 32
Wallace, George 108
Wallace, Jim and Mary 122
Walleck, James 96
Waller, Daniel and Emma 96
Walter, Thomas Ustie 178
Ware Family 49
Warren, H. Langford 194
Warren, William 259
Washington, Booker T. 108, 182, 206, 216
Water Works Board 114
Watkins, William 109
Watkins, Zachariah T. 21
Watts, E. S., Sr. 61
Watts, Elizabeth Winter 93
Watts, Thomas 61
Watts, Thomas Hill 63, 69, 184
Watts, Virginia Norwood 61
Webb and Crumpton, law firm of 137
Webbers 97
Weil, Mrs. Roman 48
West End 38, 78, 227, 257
Westcott and Ronneberg, engineers 186
Wetmore, James A. 242
Whaley, Richard S. 189, 212
White House Association of Alabama 26
White, Stanford 167

Whitfield House 217–219
Whitfield, L. B., Sr. 217
Whiting, John 60
Whitley Hall 230
Whitman, George 25
Williams, Brother Thorp 107
Williams, James M. 175
Williams, Mary Baldwin 105
Wills, Frank 57, 75
Wilmer, Bishop Richard Hooker 78
Wilson, General James 49, 59
Wilson, Thomas 214
Wilson's Raiders 21, 59
windows: casement 174, 194, 247; double-hung 25; fanlight 143; four-over-four 162, 180; four-over-six 58; French 65, 171, 174, 249; Gothic 41, 76, 115, 195, 197, 198, 201, 245; nine-over-nine 21, 25; one-over-one 121, 123, 142; oriel 194, 247; sidelights 22, 47, 102; six-over-one 211; six-over-six 48, 65, 67, 97, 101; stained glass 42, 54, 62, 74, 201, 222; transom 22, 47, 102; two-over-two 34, 118, 133, 135
Winter Building 27–29
Winter, John Gano 91
Winter, John Gindrat 91
Winter, Joseph 25
Winter, Joseph Samuel Prince 28, 56, 90, 115
Winter, Lucy (Mrs. James Lahey) 91
Winter, Mary Elizabeth Gindrat 28, 56, 90
Winter Place 90–94, 102
Winter, Sallie Gindrat 91
Woman's College of Alabama. *See* Huntingdon College
Woods, Gen. Charles 78
Works Progress Administration 252, 253, 258
Worthington, J. B. 131, 138
Wright Grocery 183
Wright, Wilbur and Orville 236

Yancey, Kate (Mrs. John T. Simpson) 88
Yancey, William Lowndes 42, 57, 88
York and Sawyer, architectural firm 168
York, Edward Palmer 168
Young Men's Christian Association 166–167
Young Women's Christian Organization 34

Zigzag Moderne style 253